A Garden of
Eden in Hell

MELISSA MÜLLER is an author and journalist living in Munich.
Her collaboration with Traudl Junge was translated into more
than twenty languages and became an international bestseller.
She is also the author of *Anne Frank: The Biography*.

REINHARD PIECHOCKI is the author of a number of works
of cultural history and has been a close friend of
Alice Herz-Sommer's for many years.

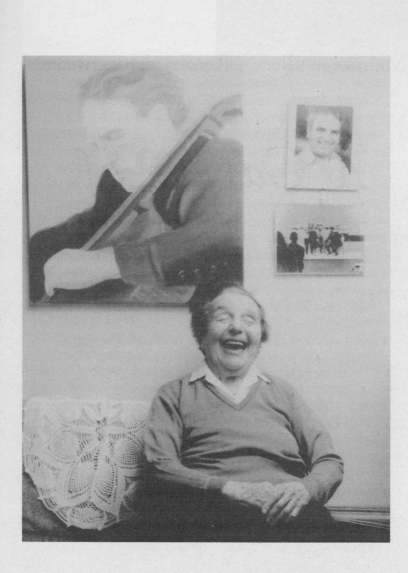

Melissa Müller · Reinhard Piechocki

A Garden of
Eden in Hell

The Life of Alice Herz-Sommer

Translated by Giles MacDonogh

PAN BOOKS

First published 2007 by Macmillan

First published in paperback 2008 by Pan Books
an imprint of Pan Macmillan Ltd
Pan Macmillan, 20 New Wharf Road, London N1 9RR
Basingstoke and Oxford
Associated companies throughout the world
www.panmacmillan.com

ISBN 978-0-330-45159-8

1 3 5 7 9 8 6 4 2

A CIP catalogue record for this book is available from
the British Library.

Typeset by SetSystems Ltd, Saffron Walden, Essex
Printed and bound in Great Britain by
Mackays of Chatham plc, Chatham, Kent

In memory of Raphael Sommer

CONTENTS

Foreword *by Alice Herz-Sommer*, ix
'The Story of a Miracle' *by Raphael Sommer*, xiii

1. Twins, 1

2. Roots, 20

3. World War, 39

4. Music, 56

5. Marriage, 78

6. Occupation, 101

7. Theresienstadt, 123

8. Happiness, 143

9. The Gates of Hell, 161

10. Inferno, 190

11. After the Inferno, 208

12. Liberation, 228

13. Homecoming, 245

14. Prague, 261

15. Zena, 288

16. Jerusalem, 305

Epilogue 'Music takes us to paradise', 321
Notes, 327
Acknowledgements, 333

FOREWORD

by Alice Herz-Sommer

'Practise the Chopin Études, they will save you.'

LIFE GAVE ME the talent to play the piano and to inspire happiness in people through music; and I am just as grateful that it gave me a love of music. Music makes us humans rich. It is the revelation of the divine. It takes us to paradise.

Since my childhood music has been my real home. It provided me with security when I had to confront my first inner torments and through it I found support, when death robbed me of my loved ones. Its meditative power provided me with the determination to cope first with the fascist and then the communist dictatorships that declared me and others like me subhuman.

When, in the early summer of 1942, my seventy-two-year-old mother was issued with a deportation order and I had to go with her to the assembly point and say goodbye to her for the last time, I was out of my mind. How was it possible to tear an old lady away from her world with nothing more than a rucksack on her back and send her to a concentration camp? Even to this day I can clearly hear the inner voice that spoke to me: 'Practise the Chopin Études, they will save you.'

Although Chopin's Études are among the most difficult pieces ever written for the repertoire, I began to learn them immediately. They were my refuge but they made huge demands on my discipline and strength of will, which I had not experienced before. In my despair I had chosen an ambitious project, but they provided me with hours of freedom in a world which was collapsing about me.

Every day for a year, I knuckled down to this seemingly insuperable task and mastered all twenty-four of them before I myself, my husband and our then six-year-old son were also deported to Theresienstadt. There I gave more than a hundred concerts for my fellow prisoners, and at more than twenty of them I played the Études.

Music gave heart to many of the prisoners, if only temporarily. In retrospect I am certain that it was music that strengthened my innate optimism and saved my life and that of my son. It was our food; and it protected us from hate and literally nourished our souls. There in the darkest corners of the world it removed our fears and reminded us of the beauty around us. Music supported me as I turned my back on my home town of Prague for the last time and had to think of learning new languages, and I am thankful for it too, at my great age, when I spend many hours alone. It hardly matters where I am: I am not prone to loneliness. Although I no longer travel any more, through music I can see the world.

Music has been a great friend to me. Even today I receive visits almost every day. Many friends come regularly and every Saturday afternoon I receive a call from Zdenka Fantlová, who was in Theresienstadt at the same time as I was. And every Sunday afternoon at around five the cellist Anita Lasker-Walfisch pays a call; she only survived Auschwitz because she played in a girls' orchestra for Josef Mengele and the SS. Above all I thank music for the privilege, even today, at the age of 103, for the ability to speak to and laugh with people all over the world. That makes me happy.

A few years ago the love of music brought me into contact with Reinhard Piechocki, himself a great music-lover. He rang me from his home on the island of Rügen and asked me a question no one had asked me since my liberation from Theresienstadt: where had I found the strength and inspiration to perform Frédéric Chopin's uncommonly difficult 24 Études in the concentration camp? I told him that playing them was – albeit transitory – liberation. He visited me in London soon afterwards and it was the beginning of a wonderful friendship. We became close, we laughed together, and since then we talk almost daily on the telephone. We don't just talk about music; we talk about God, philosophy and the world.

When he suggested writing a book about my life, I immediately said no thank you. My life has been marked by its highs and lows like other people but to have a life that is longer than most people's is, I feel, both a test and a gift. Becoming old is a difficult business but in my heart I am happier today than I was when I was young. Young people expect great things from life. As an old person one is very often aware, however, of what is worthwhile, and what one can do without. 'Humour is the path to good sense. It helps you understand the nonsense of the past with a smile on your face, and that liberates you,' wrote my brother-in-law, the philosopher Felix Weltsch, about the humour of his close friend Franz Kafka. 'It is an antibiotic against hatred.' I agree with Weltsch and Kafka that humour is always self-critical. When Kafka was with us children he, too, was like a boisterous child and told fabulous stories.

Reinhard Piechocki finally managed to convince me to agree to this book, because it was to be a book about the power of music and love, a book about a person for whom others were more important than she was to herself. As it came together two other people played important roles: Reinhard's wife Katrin Eigenfeld and Melissa Müller. I found an affinity with Katrin, who in the past few years has fed entire drafts of chapters into her computer, not only because of her modesty but also for the courage with which she fought the consequences of Stalinism in East Germany. The author Melissa Müller, who co-wrote this book with Reinhard, inspired me from the first because of her feeling for language and her clever and intuitive way of asking questions.

People are often breathlessly pursuing their next goal in life without looking around them. They become attached to material things, and – to quote Felix Weltsch once again – are incapable of circumspection or far sightedness, because they lack the necessary material detachment. Detachment from possessions also creates detachment in oneself, and teaches us the modesty that makes it a pleasure for us humans to live and work together. In my opinion people take themselves too seriously as a rule. Culture and politics both suffer from this, so does humanity. Modesty brings happiness. Is that not so? Whoever is ready to understand this should absorb the greatness and dignity of a work by Beethoven or Bach. I have never learned to give up hope.

London, February 2007

'The Story of a Miracle'

by Raphael Sommer

THIS IS A TRUE STORY. I can swear to that because I lived it myself. Even in the darkest days of the twentieth century miracles occurred. In the middle of hell, my mother created a Garden of Eden for me. She built a strong wall around me out of love and gave me such security that I could not find anything extraordinary in our lives, and in retrospect I can say with good conscience that my childhood was wonderfully happy. How my mother managed it I cannot say. She says it was the obvious thing to do. For me it remains a miracle.

My mother has a gift which, I believe, is given above all to Jewish and central and eastern European women. Without any self-pity they make their own requirements secondary to those of their families. I lived under the protecting veil of my mother and so cannot describe the darker side of our lives in the concentration camp. I was a child and I understood events as they seemed to me; I naturally believed everything my mother told me. Not once did she allow me to see the humiliations and insults she had to suffer. With inner strength and inexhaustible reserves of love she concentrated on just that: me, her beloved son and the creation of a joyful and 'normal' environment around me that had little to do with the reality in which we lived. With her attentive care my mother managed to shift the terror away from my gaze and provide me with the most valuable of gifts – a happy childhood. That this was possible behind the wire of a National Socialist concentration camp must, in all truth, be called a miracle.

In Theresienstadt I shared a bunk with my mother. I was so close to her that I never actually felt frightened. During the day, when my mother had to work in the factory, I played in the kindergarten. I was so little aware that our lives were in any way unnatural that I also have no recollection of our concern when my father, together with 3,000 other men, was sent away and never returned.

A single trauma lodged itself like a splinter in my heart and is still there, and to this day the scar is not fully healed: my mother was forced to work. I screamed, I dropped my guard and my fever raged. My mother and I clung to one another and we went from one building to the next to find someone who was prepared to look after me. The nagging uncertainty that took hold of me on that day I shall never forget. Children's worries are abiding worries and, although I got my courage back after my mother had told me that she was only going to be transferred from the factory to the laundry, my childish trust was temporarily shaken. For all that my early childhood, which for all those close to me seemed to be horror and nightmare, seemed to me happy and utterly normal. For this I thank my mother – she performed miracles.

Raphael Sommer died in 2001. He wrote this account a few years before his death.

ONE

Twins

'One happy, one sad . . .'

FRANTA CAME OUT of his employer's office with a delivery note in his hand. A consignment of pharmaceutical scales had to be taken to the station that afternoon and put on a train for Vienna. On the way to the stables the servant paused to listen to the music coming from the drawing room of the flat in the courtyard. As she so often did after lunch, the heavily pregnant Sofie Herz was playing the piano. Longing and mourning were intermingled in her playing.

Franta sat on a bench in the courtyard and looked up to the windows above. For nearly thirty years he had been employed by Herz Brothers. How many thousand times had he loaded the carriage since then, how often had he harnessed the horses and taken the consignment over the Moldau to the station? It was a part of his routine on that grey Prague morning in November 1903, like any other.

Sofie Herz was a precise interpreter of Bach. The little preludes and two-part inventions were among her favourites. In the last weeks of her confinement, however, she had often played Chopin, his poetic nocturnes and above all his sad waltzes. The melancholy melody reminded Franta of his master's marriage in 1886. The factory director Friedrich Herz was thirty-four then, almost twice the age of his bride, Sofie. There had been not a hint of that exuberance that is meant to be a part of traditional Jewish wedding ceremonies.

For nights on end the young woman had bemoaned her lot: barred from marrying the man to whom she had given her heart. She had developed a romantic infatuation for a student of her own age in her home town of Iglau (Jihlava) in Southern Moravia, who shared her love of music and literature. Finally Sofie bowed to her parents' will. Ignatz and Fanny Schulz were prominent merchants in Iglau and had worked to provide themselves and their children with a modest income. This would chiefly benefit Sophie's two brothers. For the pretty, refined daughter they had been prepared to pay for four years of *Volksschule* (infant school), three of *Bürgerschule* (secondary school) and piano lessons, but since her fourteenth birthday she had been obliged to help in the business. Now a good match needed to be found for her. According to the Ashkenazi tradition a *schadchen* or marriage broker had to be entrusted with the business of finding the right man. Means and possessions, social class and position, knowledge and wisdom; these were believed to be the basis of a reasonable marriage among *schejnen leit* (the right sort of people), the wealthy. She should not be starved of affection either. It was taken as read that love would blossom soon after the wedding. 'Look at those miserable people who apparently wed for love; they are fickle and their marriages frequently end up in divorce. That is the proof.' Thus her mother sought to console her daughter.

The broker found his man 150 kilometres away from Iglau. Friedrich Herz lived in Prague, he was a well-built, good-looking man who was known to be aware of his responsibilities, decent and warm-hearted, and one who had accumulated a modest wealth through his own industry. He was one of the most important producers of precision scales in the Habsburg Empire, from devices for goldsmiths and pharmacists to industrial scales to carry heavy weights. The only thing that the 'director' – as those around him respectfully addressed him – lacked now to complete his happiness was a family. He was pleased with Sofie Schulz.

The young lady's contrariness was clear from the start –
together with her indifference to the Jewish tradition in which
she had grown up. At their wedding Sofie would not listen to the
badchen, the entertainer that the bridegroom and wedding guests
praised and laughed with until everyone was crying their eyes
out, or the *Kletzmermusik*. She was deaf to the proceedings and
let them pass her by, as Franta now recalled. She maintained a
proud and upright posture as she was solemnly enthroned in her
second chair and covered with a veil. Her delicate fingers clutched
the bridal stool while a cousin declaimed the rights and duties
of a married woman. She looked lovely in her white lace, coldly
lovely.

All eyes were on Sofie as she was led forward by her retinue
under her *chupe* – a canopy of shining gold brocade – and handed
over to her future husband. There followed the first blessing of the
rabbi and the first sip of wine: 'With this ring you are sanctified
by the religion of Moses and Israel', Friedrich said as he placed
the ring on her hand. She scarcely looked at her husband. Even the
next seven blessings left her unaffected. The wedding guests waited
in vain for the tears which would give some indication of Sofie's
emotions – all part and parcel of ancient tradition.

Another sip of wine, then the groom crushed the glass chalice
underfoot to cries of '*matzeltow*' from the guests. Splinters bring
you luck, supposedly, even when the custom recalls the expulsion
of the Jews and should symbolize the smashing of their joy through
banishment. Sofie took the smashing of the glass to signify destruction of her happiness.

Franta was stirred by his employer's wife's playing. He
respected Sofie. She was a no-nonsense woman, so they said, who
spoke her mind. She was always appreciative of Franta and had a
kind word for him, perhaps because he was kind to her children,
perhaps because he was the only one who recognized that behind
her apparently tough facade, she was responsive to beauty. There
might even have been a tacit understanding between the two of
them that Franta could relax for a few minutes after his midday

break and sit down on the bench in the courtyard to listen to Sofie's playing before getting back to his job.

All of a sudden there was a smell of burning. 'Fire! Fire!', shouted Franta.

Franta's cry shattered Sofie's concentration. She was expecting her fourth child any day. She lurched towards the window from the piano. Flames were shooting out of one of the factory buildings. Workers were rushing in all directions and gathering before the burning workshop. No one dared go in.

Friedrich Herz got up from his short siesta on the sofa when he heard cries for help. His days were as regular as clockwork. He worked from six o'clock in the morning to six o'clock at night, six days a week. At midday he interrupted his work for exactly one hour. At this point he walked up the few steps from his office on the ground floor to his flat on the first floor where the table was laid and his family were already sitting round it waiting for him. He had remained a modest, unpretentious man, despite his rise from a meagre apprentice ironmonger to a successful businessman with several dozen employees.

Little was known about his origins. Friedrich's father came from the small Bohemian village of Rischkau about fifty kilometres north of Prague and was a member of its Orthodox Jewish community. Thanks to the 'new liberality' permitted to the Jews after 1848, he and his family left the ghetto for the outskirts of Prague in the hope of finding work. We can only speculate on how he managed to feed his wife and seven children. We know for certain that he found apprenticeships for two of his sons – Friedrich and Karl – in an ironmonger's shop. Friedrich was just twelve, and had six years of schooling under his belt.

Friedrich's success would have been unimaginable had it not been for the reforms of Emperor Joseph II. Joseph's mother, the Empress Maria Theresa, shortly after her accession in 1740, had made the Jews the scapegoat for Austria's poor performance in the war against Prussia. She decreed that 'from this moment onwards no more Jews will be tolerated in the kingdom of Bohemia', and the Jews had to leave Prague and settle in ghettos. They were excluded from higher education and barred from many branches of the professions. For the forty years of her regency, the Empress strictly adhered to her anti-Jewish policies.

Joseph II introduced the century of Jewish emancipation – albeit not entirely altruistically. The Jews represented a tenth of the total population, and he appreciated their potential and decided that they were to be culturally and economically integrated into society once more in order to be 'more useful'[1] to themselves and his empire. Influenced by the European Enlightenment he issued his so-called Patent of Tolerance in 1781, first in Bohemia and Prague in particular: the city where it is said there were more Torah Rolls than in Jerusalem itself. It stipulated that 'rich Jews' could lease land without interference from the guilds and they could turn their hand to trade and industry. Schools were to be established where Jews would be taught in German, for the emperor wanted to 'Germanize' the elite in order to bind them politically, administratively and economically as tightly as possible to Vienna. The new Jewish upper class played a decisive part in the economic development that raised Prague from a small, provincial city to a tri-racial metropolis. By 1825, out of 550 merchants and traders 240 were of Jewish origin. Thirteen out of a total of fifty factories were in Jewish hands.

When the Jews received equal rights in 1867 their prospects once more decisively improved. Friedrich Herz had just turned fifteen and he exploited the new possibilities to the full. In the 1870s, together with his brother Karl and with the help of a private loan he created the firm Gebrüder Herz and built it up to become one of the biggest of its sort in the Empire. Karl died young, before Friedrich's marriage.

'Fire!'

A horrified Friedrich Herz had leapt up and was on his way downstairs when he realized that his trousers were falling down. With the passing years he had begun to put on weight and with time he had started to ask his tailor to cut his trousers a little more liberally to accommodate the increase. He now wore braces to hold them up. He told many different versions of exactly what transpired that day, and each one made his children laugh – even years later.

Outside the cries for help grew louder and louder, while from inside Friedrich Herz roared in ever-growing despair: 'My braces! Gentlemen, where are my braces?'

'Fire!'

'My braces!'

'Fire!'

'My braces!'

The outraged mother and three children ran all over the flat looking for the braces, until one of them finally noticed them, fastened to their father's trousers. In his excitement he had merely forgotten to pull them up over his shoulders.

At last Friedrich stumbled down the stairs and without a moment's hesitation, he ran into the burning workshop, identified a leaking gas tap as the cause of the blaze, turned off the gas pipe and thereby prevented the flames from consuming his life's work. Together with Franta and the rest of his workers, he succeeded in putting out the fire.

*

A WEEK LATER, on 26 November 1903, Sofie went into labour. Friedrich placed great hopes on the birth of his fourth child, for although he was running his business with great success, he was concerned because he had not yet decided who would succeed him.

Georg, the eldest son, was already fifteen and causing him concern. The child had been born with a club foot. At the beginning his mother had kept his disability a secret, as dumb, lame, blind or mutilated children were generally perceived as proof of parental guilt.[2] As an open-minded assimilated woman Sofie rejected the superstitions and rituals from the Schtetls of their past. Despite that, she was gripped by feelings of guilt when she saw her crippled child for the first time. Was it not a punishment for her frigid behaviour towards her husband? Had she not threatened to throw herself out of the window shortly before the birth? She took Georg to the best Prague specialists but none of them could help. When he was twelve and no longer growing much she consulted a celebrated Würzburg orthopaedist, from whom she was expecting a miracle. She spent nearly a year in Würzburg with her son, and during that time he was operated on several times. In the meantime the household in Prague was looked after by Sofie's mother Fanny, who selflessly cared for Georg's sister Irma and her son-in-law. Unfortunately, Georg was not wholly cured. His father found the boy's unstable character worse than his shuffling gait; above all he disliked his frivolity. Repeatedly, there were serious arguments with his parents that persisted into adulthood.

Irma, was born three years later, but there was no question of a girl taking over the running of the business. The third child, Paul, was nine years younger than Irma, and his father's favourite, but his impetuous character and his tendency to daydream led Friedrich Herz to doubt that the lad would ever be capable of taking over the company. Maybe the fourth child would be another boy? And maybe he would be called to take over the company when the time came?

That afternoon, to the annoyance of the midwife, Friedrich Herz stuck his head through the double doors to Sofie's bedroom again and again. It had been dark for some time, and Friedrich was pacing up and down uneasily in the flat. Finally the news of a successful birth was announced in the early evening.

'A boy?', cried Friedrich Herz, in an entreating tone.

He slumped when he heard the answer: 'No, not a boy!'

With disappointment he said: 'A girl . . .'

The midwife again said: 'No'.

Not a boy and not a girl? Before he could come to his senses the midwife's voice hit him like a slap in the face: 'Two girls!'

*

ALICE HERZ WAS born into Habsburg Austria a few minutes before her twin sister Marianne on 26 November 1903. As Marianne weighed only 1.9 kilos it was feared that she would not live long. Alice was 2.5 kilos, appreciably heavier. She looked altogether healthier and more robust, although later on she would grow much more slowly than her sister. Her mother was full of love for the weaker child and called her Mizzerl or Mizzi, and naturally gave her more attention and care. In spite of this, Mizzi remained all her life the anxious one; a pessimist who in her life always saw the dark side of things first. Alice, on the other hand, developed into a courageous person who was sure of herself. Very soon her mother would be heard to say 'We don't need to worry about Alice; she will go her own way.'

Although the girls not only thought differently and looked different, Sofie dressed them both in the same clothes. Their bright red bonnets could be seen from far off: the Herz twins are coming! Beside her twin sister Alice was less striking. Alice said that Marianne was as pretty as a picture: she had tender white skin, expressive dark eyes, a sweet little mouth and fabulous pretty black hair. Her mother often picked up her favourite child and hugged and kissed her, while Alice, who was more capable of dealing with life, looked on with her winning smile.

The room shared by the twins lay immediately next to their parents' bedroom. One night when the girls were five, a violent storm broke the silence. Snatches of lightning illuminated the nursery with an uncanny, flickering light. Distorted shadows burst like monsters across the walls, disappearing and reappearing all at once. Mizzi crept under her blankets. On the other hand, although nervous, Alice was none the less fascinated and watched the spectacle from the window. The pauses between lightning and thunder grew ever shorter until finally the deafening crashes were right over their heads. Screaming, Mizzi took refuge in her parents' bedroom and threw herself, quivering, into her mother's arms. In the meantime, Alice had also been seized with fear and ran in after her. Sofie Herz was, however, wholly preoccupied with Mizzi and it was her father who finally calmed Alice down by giving her a hug. Although it was a comfort to feel his protection, the fact that her mother seemed to have forgotten about her hurt terribly.

Alice heard few words of praise from her mother. Sofie reproached her children when they failed to do their schoolwork neatly or did something silly, but she found it hard to utter a phrase of encouragement. After the thunderstorm, Alice became a remarkable creature of habit for one so young. Night after night with great pride and astonishing meticulousness she polished the family shoes: eight pairs in all – the parents, her brothers and sisters and even those of the Czech maid, Marie. And as if the five-year-old had not made enough of an effort, every morning she got up shortly after six and crept out to run a few doors down to the baker to pick up the family's order for bread and rolls. This was actually the maid's job, whose duties began at first light when she raked the oven and got the hot water ready for the family's morning wash. Alice, however, refused to countenance giving up her role as bread-runner. Her father praised her efficiency, but her mother continued to lavish all her attention on Mizzi, despite the fact that, even taking her age into consideration, she never lifted a finger in the house.

Mizzi enchanted even the strangest of people. Or so it appeared to Alice – who was generally standing unnoticed next to her at the time. Aged six, the twins were out walking with their older sister Irma on Letna Hill in the Belvedere Garden, part of the nearby Crown Prince Rudolf Park, when an old friend of the family came up. Alice already had an idea what was going to happen. Enraptured with little Marianne the woman cried out: 'My God, this child is lovely!' This time, however, Alice was ready to quip: 'But I am cleverer!'

Soon Alice found a new way to win her mother's love. Every two weeks Sophie and her daughters were busy for four whole days doing the family laundry. The air in the large kitchen would be filled with steam and the smell of soapy water. Little Alice literally fell over herself to show her mother what an industrious washerwoman she was. She sorted out the bed linen and the articles of clothing; dark clothes had to be separated from light ones; silk from cotton. She helped to brush the clothes as they soaked and to rinse them. And she went up to the roof with Marie, where the clean clothes were hung out to dry. Alice could not be discouraged from pinning a few articles of clothing to the washing line. To do this she stood on her tiptoes on a wooden stool – risking life and limb in the process.

As there was no tap in the kitchen, bucket upon bucket of water had to be brought in from the hall. One day Alice's grandmother Fanny was coming down the stairs from her flat on the second floor when she ran into the little girl. Alice's face was bright red from the exertion of dragging a bucket filled to the brim with water across the hall to the kitchen. Fanny was a quiet, reserved woman who preferred to avoid conflict. This time, however, she lost her temper and gave her daughter a talking to: 'Have you not noticed that you are turning your child into Cinderella? Can you not see that every child needs the same amount of attention and love?'

'You are a fine one to talk,' her daughter exploded, 'you who arranged my marriage, you speak of love?!'

Alice could not see what the bucket had to do with love, but uncertain as to whether she had been responsible for the fight between her mother and grandmother, she began quietly to sob. A word that she had never heard before seemed to play a role in the battle: *mischpoche*. In the war of words between the two women a few words of Yiddish had surfaced, possibly because they had become over-excited, perhaps to spare the children. The foreign-sounding words, the outraged tone and her feelings of guilt puzzled Alice.

Finally Sofie turned to her weeping child and gave her an affectionate cuddle:

'Alice, it is not your fault that we are having a row. I love you as much as I love Mizzi; only you are strong, I am proud of you.

You will make your own way in life. Mizzi is weaker, and she is going to have a tougher job of it than you.' And she stroked Alice's hair. The child felt better than she had done for a long time.

Her grandmother's final words kept going through her head: 'You don't have to love your mother', she had told her daughter, 'but you owe her *derech-erez. Derech-erez.*' Then her grandmother left and went off in the direction of the Belvedere Gardens and sat down on her favourite bench. She was usually to be found there, come rain or shine, when she was not at home.

In an agitated frame of mind, Alice told her sister what had happened. 'Do you know what *derech-erez* means?'

Mizzi shook her head.

'And what does *mischpoche* mean?'

She shook her head again.

So the two girls decided to ask their grandmother and ran off to find her. The park was only a few hundred metres from home but the twins were completely out of breath by the time they reached the bench.

'Grandmother,' Alice panted, 'tell us what *mischpoche* means?'

Her grandmother smiled: '*Mischpoche* means family and that is all of us together who belong to the family. Our family is daddy, mummy, grandmother, grandfather and the children.'

'And *derech-erez*?'

'That means respect.'

'Respect?' Their grandmother saw the question in Alice and Marianne's eyes.

'Respecting your parents means honouring them, acknowledging them.' After a pause Fanny added, 'Those are Yiddish words. Yiddish is my mother tongue and your mother's mother tongue. Yiddish is the mother tongue of most Jews in our country.'

'Jews?' asked Alice.

Then, for the first time Fanny Schulz told her grandchildren of the Jewish people and the diaspora. The girls listened to her spellbound, as if it were a fairy tale.

Although the family celebrated Passover every year, their mother had never so much as alluded to the Jews, let alone allowed a Yiddish word to pass her lips. When Alice later used the word *meschugge* which she had picked up from other children, her mother gave her a firm dressing down: 'Don't use it again.' Sofie tried stubbornly to prevent anything that recalled her Jewish origins from reaching the children. For her, Judaism was a belief she had rejected. She felt she had good reasons. One was the Ashkenazi tradition which had been her misfortune and which had caused her unhappy marriage. Another was her conviction that the worrying and frequent outbreaks of anti-Semitism in the multiracial Habsburg Empire were chiefly directed against Orthodox Jews, taking their cue from perceived Jewish traditions. Even in the early twentieth century it was widely believed in Bohemia and Moravia that the Jews 'needed Christian blood at Eastertide, and therefore slaughtered little children and virgins.'

In the last years of the nineteenth century, a considerable number of Prague Jews, above all from the working class, had begun to align themselves with the Czech majority and plumped for the Czech language before the German in their choice of schools and universities. According to figures published in 1900, 14,576 Jews described themselves as Czech-speaking, as opposed to 11,599 German-speakers.[3]

Sofie, however, identified with liberal-thinking Germany – like most educated Prague Jews. To be assimilated into the German-speaking cultural circle of the city was for her – much more than for her husband – not just a measure of security, it satisfied a deep, inner need. Her access to higher education had been blocked, but she saw herself as part of a world steeped in culture. She instilled in her children a respect for German high culture, a culture that was open to the world. They were to become artistically minded, cosmopolitan Germans, without bearing the stigma of Judaism. It was therefore from their grandmother that Alice and Mizzi first learned that there were not just Germans and Czechs in Prague, but that there was a third group of people: Jews. Only a few months later they would become painfully aware of what it meant to be a Jew.

*

IN THE PART of the city where Friedrich Herz had settled generally nobody would have asked about origin or religion. Only in 1884 were the former villages of Bubna – where the Herz factory was to be found – and Holešovice incorporated into the former walled city as its seventh district. Bubna on the left bank of the Moldau was rapidly industrialized, but even twenty years later it still had a villagey feel about it.

Alice and Marianne played with many children in the Belvedere Gardens or in the streets and courtyards closest to their home. They played with their skipping ropes or catch, hide-and-seek and hopscotch. Playing with Czech, German or Jewish children made not a jot of difference to them.

The twin girls grew up bilingual. In the family they naturally spoke German but with many of their friends and with their father's workers they spoke Czech. The nationality problem, however, had become increasingly acute in the Bohemian city. The majority of people were Czech. The German minority accounted for just ten per cent of the population, and was mostly made up of civil servants and the garrison, as well as a part of the old Bohemian nobility, scientists and intellectuals and some German Bohemians from the Sudetenland. From a political point of view, the Jews reinforced the Germans and were considered anathema to the Czechs for that reason. More and more German-speakers from Prague were tending towards nationalism and anti-Semitism and spurned the Jews. The children had yet to see evidence of this. Not yet, but adolescent Germans and Czechs were already trading cobbles and vile insults.

One day the twins were playing with two friends when suddenly a group of young Czechs from the area appeared in the park and as quick as a flash surrounded the girls. The lads had evidently learned that the industrialist Friedrich Herz was a Jew and began to sing a mocking song '*Smaradlawe židy – smaradlawe židy*', they kept chanting: 'you stink like Jews', while at the same time they pushed 'their prisoners' around until they fell over and began to cry. The Czechs retired in triumph and the humiliated children ran home with grazed knees. When they got in Alice and Marianne ran to their mother: 'Mother, why did they hurt us? Are we different?'

The otherwise so brave and quick-witted Sofie was lost for words.

'You stink like Jews, you stink like Jews.'

Alice and Marianne had to come to terms with the event by themselves, and it took a long time.

*

THE PARENTAL HOME was at 23 Bělsky Street. The main street in the Seventh District was named after the Mayor of Prague Václav Bělsky. For the children the building concealed a large number of secrets and surprises. It took years for them to discover every nook and cranny. Friedrich Herz had acquired the estate at the bottom of hilly Belvedere Gardens shortly before his marriage and had it constructed like an urban version of a courtyard farm. It consisted of four large buildings. Towards the street there was a two-storey dwelling, a roomy, but from the outside by no means majestic building with an unprepossessing, plain facade which failed to conform to the historical or neoclassical schools of architecture current in central Prague at the time. Next to the porter's flat on the ground floor there were the director's and secretary's offices. Up a few steps on the mezzanine, you reached the family's eight-room flat, together with a smaller one which was rented out. Three of the four units on the floor above were rented out. In the fourth lived Grandmother Fanny and her maid. With the rent from the flats Friedrich paid off the mortgage on the house.

The flats were flanked by two forty-metre-long workshops.

In the right-hand building the precision scales were made: letter-scales, pharmaceutical scales, scales for use in grocer's shops; in the left-hand building they put together scales for heavy industry.

The stable at the far end of the courtyard, opposite the flats, completed the quadrangle. It exercised a great pull on the children. They were particularly keen to watch Franta when he was looking after the horses. One day the servant pressed a carrot into the hands of both girls. The sturdy dray horses whinnied loudly and stretched their necks out anxiously towards the children. Mizzi was too frightened to feed the horses and hid behind a pillar. Alice on the other hand, pushed her carrot towards the mare Bianka. It was love at first sight. From that moment onwards she visited her favourite horse daily, and Bianka always thanked her with a joyful neigh.

Franta was particularly fond of Alice's brother Paul and let him mount the horses and ride around the courtyard. No matter how broad in the beam and powerful the horses looked, they were placid and good-hearted.

One evening Franta told the girls: 'The moment has come: today you can both have a ride!'

'Hurrah,' came Alice's spontaneous reaction, 'Can I ride Bianka?'

For her part Mizzi wasn't having anything to do with the horses and when Franta tried to talk her round she fled to the furthest recesses of the stables and disappeared behind some bales of straw.

Alice allowed Franta to lift her on to the horse. She looked tiny on its broad back and while she held on tightly to Bianka's mane, she was happy and laughed her infectious Alice-laugh.

Sofie did not get any closer to her husband over the years. She found it hard to respect him despite the fact he was a reliable, devoted and uncommonly hard-working man whose neighbours admired his friendly character and whose employees were unstintingly loyal and long-serving. He was not as well-educated as Sofie was, he never picked up a book and only rarely could he be talked into attending the performance of an opera. Sofie did not like putting up with his antiquated thinking and his deep-rooted thrift. Although he was ready to invest money in the education of his two sons, he showed little understanding of the fact that his three daughters needed to be helped too.

Sofie was also particularly unwilling to receive Friedrich's family. One of his sisters visited regularly and every time Sofie's hackles rose over the comments that came bubbling out of her mouth. When she enquired whether her brother was getting enough to eat, Sofie showed her the door.

When Friedrich Herz left the factory after his long working day, he was thinking of having a good supper, of a little chat with his family, of rounding off the day peacefully and going to bed around eight. While the midday meal was a rush, he could take his time over his dinner. He would therefore often go to the delicatessen across the road after work for some air-dried sausage or some Swiss Emmental or other, more mundane, provisions. Shortly before six every evening the children had to take their seats at the dining table with clean hands and combed hair and wait for their father. Precisely at that point, however, when her husband was hoping to relax, Sofie, as Friedrich realized, was hatching a reason to prevent this.

One day, in the summer of 1910 or thereabouts, Friedrich was supposed to bring home two jars of spicy gherkins for the evening meal. Since the advent of the deafeningly noisy tram had made the crossing of the road perilous, he took his life into his hands each time he went to the shop. On this occasion, he did not run into a tram, but a three-wheeled vehicle bearing the word 'taxi'. Although Friedrich Herz had already read a newspaper article announcing the arrival of motorized vehicles in Prague, it was the first time in his life that he had seen a rattling, stinking automobile roaring towards him. He was lost for words: thirty kilometres an hour seemed madly fast to him.

The taxi had disappeared from view leaving Friedrich standing aghast in front of the delicatessen. How much faster the smaller deliveries could be brought to the station with one of those wonderful machines! Enraptured by his brush with the taxi, and quite contrary to his usual frugal habits, he bought a bottle of expensive cognac for himself and a juicy ham for the family. He was almost leaving the shop when he noticed the jars of gherkins, which were the principal reason why he had gone there in the first place. He turned on his heels and returned to the counter.

When he entered the dining room it was twelve minutes past six. The five children were sitting as quiet as mice around the table, and Sofie looked her husband up and down. Friedrich took no notice of the menace in her voice. He placed the two jars on the table and put down the ham next to them while he announced: 'Children, imagine: your father has just seen his first ever taxi!'

'That is no reason to keep us waiting,' said Sofie sharply.

Friedrich ignored the accusation and carried on speaking cheerfully, 'In celebration of this day everyone may eat as much ham as they like.'

'Friedrich! Yet again, these are not the right gherkins.'

'There are no wrong gherkins,' her husband growled.

'I like the wrong gherkins, I should like to eat three wrong gherkins,' prattled Mizzi.

Alice, too, took her father's side: 'I think the wrong gherkins look very pretty.'

In the meantime Georg and Paul had carved the ham and were praising it to the skies. 'This cooked ham is fit for a king', said Georg, who was now twenty-one. 'And the wrong gherkins are also a knockout,' Paul chipped in.

But Sofie would not let matters rest there. 'Is it really too much to ask you to bring home the right gherkins?'

She had finally begun to rile Friedrich and he raised his voice: 'After a long working day can I not eat my dinner in peace?' But it was not Sofie's way to let someone else have the last word. 'Besides, you pinch every penny, as if we were poor people, but when I plead with you to pay for a special orthopaedic treatment for Alice so that she might begin to grow properly, you refuse to give me the money.' Friedrich refused to let it ruin his composure: 'Indeed, I said that I didn't think it a bad thing that Alice remain small. And I will abide by that.' And to cap it all he argued that there had to be small women too, so that little men would have a chance to find wives.

Now Paul joined in the argument: 'Why does Alice have to marry a little man? What happens when a bigger man comes along?' And Mizzi topped this with some childish wisdom: 'Little women with big men can have just as many children as big women with little men!' Their mother was not in a joking mood: 'Paul and Mizzi – off to bed!'

Friedrich left the dining room without another word.

The children lived through scenes like this one often, but why tempers became so frayed they were at a loss to say. 'Why don't you just take him in your arms and give him a kiss? That would make everything right,' said Alice, at least managing to get her mother to smile again.

However, as she grew older Sofie became more taciturn and increasingly kept her distance from her husband. There was certainly no question of divorce. With time Friedrich found a means to make the icy atmosphere bearable, but the family have drawn a veil over this, for decency's sake. When his youngest children – Paul, Alice and Marianne – were old enough to enjoy excursions to the country, their father ordered a coach early every Sunday morning and together they drove to a funfair. The children loved these trips more than anything. Paul and Alice were allowed to sit next to the coachman and occasionally to take the reins. Mizzi sat in the carriage with her father. While the children roamed around the fair, Friedrich would order a beer and a brace of bratwurst. Although the waitress was much younger than Friedrich she was attracted to the good-looking and friendly fifty-five-year-old. He was quite an imposing figure and he looked exceptionally dandy in his Sunday coat.

The children did not bother much about the warm-hearted way their father greeted the waitress or the fact that she came over to chat with him whenever she had a free moment, or that once he gave her a particularly generous tip or that on greeting or parting their hands were in contact for decidedly too long. They did, however, notice that every Sunday evening after dinner their father went out again, but they never asked where he was going. Sofie, on the other hand, knew soon enough where her husband was heading, but instead of getting angry, she was relieved.

TWO

Roots

'There is still the Seder night to come'

FROM THEIR EARLIEST CHILDHOOD, Alice and Mizzi were greatly attached to their grandmother. She looked distinguished, aristocratic even, in her black mourning clothes and floor-length dress and her blouse buttoned right up to the top. She wore a borderless bonnet which was fastened under her chin and laced-up boots. Despite that she was not a bit strict with the twins; not a bit of it. And she was charmingly idolized by them both: 'Why don't you marry the emperor?' Mizzi asked her once. 'You are really so lovely?'

Almost every day, generally at around half past three in the afternoon, the two girls walked up one flight of stairs to their grandmother's flat. You reached the living room through the kitchen with its window onto the stairs. This was also the route to the small en-suite bedroom. It was a typical *Bassena* dwelling, with a lavatory and a sink in the corridor. It was simple, but it bore the noble stamp of their grandmother. As Alice remembers her, the old lady sat in a leather armchair surrounded by books, with her sewing or an open book in her lap and a smile on her face to greet the children. There were books on the desk, a delicate Biedermeier secretaire of carefully polished cherry wood, and books piled up on a side table. There were more books in the bookshelf, which seemed to conceal an endless number of secrets. She had brought it, together with the rest of her furniture, from Iglau after the death of her husband, in what appeared to have been the early nineties, when she moved in with her son-in-law.

As the girls became older, they were able to appreciate the books she had. In the top three shelves in the bookcase their grandmother kept the German classics: Goethe, Schiller, and above all Lessing, whom she particularly enjoyed. On the bottom shelf there was a row of reference books next to several volumes on European history and a few cookbooks. The children were especially drawn to the second shelf with its books in Yiddish printed in a compellingly strange alphabet.

Before the First World War more than eleven million people in central and eastern Europe spoke Yiddish. Yiddish had also been the everyday language of Ignatz and Fanny Schulz in Iglau, even if she had officially cited her mother tongue as German.

After the incident when the girls were first told of their Jewish roots, Mizzi and Alice (Mizzi more than Alice) used to enjoy it when their grandmother picked up a knitting needle or a pencil and drew the Hebrew letters from right to left, first in the air and then later on a piece of paper. The girls finally began to recognize simple Jewish words and even to write them, but it was even better when their grandmother read to them or told them stories.

Fanny Schulz had a more enlightened attitude to her fellow man than her daughter Sofie. It was also unusual for someone of her age and time to be so interested in politics. Fanny 'believed' in the imperial Habsburg house; that was the source of security. She read two newspapers each day and was happy to discuss politics with her son-in-law, and it turned out that these talks often took place in Yiddish. Friedrich Herz got on with his mother-in-law who was only slightly older than him and because their characters were compatible.

Sofie Herz had little interest in politics. Her passion and her hunger for education were for classical music and books. She read a great deal, above all novels and short stories. Education was not a status symbol for her, no social embellishment, but a means to achieve inner freedom; and finally a replacement for religion. However, she thought it right and proper that the twins should be educated by their grandmother as she believed that a general education and linguistic ability were essential. Sophie rarely left the house; in justification, the business of running a family of eight took up a huge amount of time. Friedrich Herz would not hear of taking on a second maid. Production costs for the scales were high, and the margins relatively low. Sofie therefore knuckled down, for a spotless flat was clearly important to her. The floors had to be perfectly polished and the laundry had to be as white as snow.

*

FRIDAY WAS A special day for Alice and Mizzi, and they looked forward to it all week. There was no sign of anything special taking place in their parents' flat, but upstairs, however, their grandmother and her maid were preparing for the Sabbath.

As the maid was also called Fanny, the twins jokingly referred to them as 'Little Fanny' and 'Big Fanny'. Social status required them to bestow the epithet 'Little Fanny' on the maid, although she was quite big and fat. Every Friday she was busy all morning cleaning the flat. She did the dusting first, taking out every book and picking up every porcelain figure, then she scrubbed the floor before cleaning the cooker and the dishes; then she polished the silver and changed the towels. 'Big Fanny' took charge of the meal. She kneaded the dough for the Sabbath bread and plaited it. When this was done she took a bath – an elaborate business in which 'Little Fanny' had to lend a hand. Finally, she put a white table cloth on the table and placed new candles in the Sabbath candelabra.

In the afternoon there was a smell of bread on the stairs which was an indication to the children that it was nearly time to knock on their grandmother's door. On Friday she always opened it herself. Her black clothes looked lovelier than ever, for they were made of velvet.

Neither Alice nor Mizzi understood the real meaning of the Sabbath celebrations at this juncture. For them the ritual was exciting, while their grandmother always put them in the mood by telling them one of 'the old stories'. Fanny Schulz led both girls solemnly past a table laid in celebration to her armchair and sat down. At her feet there were two large cushions and Alice and Mizzi sat on these.

'Please grandmother, an Iglau story, a new Iglau story,' cried Mizzi.

'Yes, an Iglau story,' Alice joined in the chorus, 'the Iglau stories are the best.'

Their grandmother seemed to possess an inexhaustible repertoire of Iglau stories. Most of them began in the grandparents' shop, which not only sold food and other things, but was also the place where the most recent tales and rumours in the town and its seventy-five outlying villages were exchanged. Around German-Speaking Iglau customs were more intensely observed than in the Czech areas and all year round traditional celebrations took place, where the people wore their regional costumes, sang traditional songs and danced traditional dances. They liked to go to the theatre or attend concerts and the programme was astonishingly varied. As a garrison town, Iglau had its own military band, which played not only marches but also some of the best classical compositions.

The story of the little boy who marched beside the military band in his nightshirt was one Alice remembered all her life. She listened reverently as her grandmother recalled the year – 1863. Two streets away from the Schulzes' grocery the Mahlers had been living for three years. Bernhard, the father, was really a baker, but he preferred tinkering around with his schnapps distillery, which he called his 'factory', even if only he and one worker were employed in it. He later received a licence to sell wine, beer and schnapps and opened a pub in a room of his house.

Bernhard was not like other people and he was considered unapproachable by outsiders. His sudden bursts of fury were generally directed at his wife and, in the town, people pitied her.

Marie Mahler had a limp and was suffering from heart disease but because of her gentleness and patience she never opposed her husband. Their children had nothing to smile about either. In the distiller's house no one sang or played an instrument, but it did not prevent the little boy's mother noticing that music appeared to electrify her son: the light-hearted songs of apprentices; or the melancholy tunes of homesick soldiers; or wine-soaked tavern songs. On his third birthday his mother managed to give him a child's accordion, and from that day on he played with it non-stop.

One day when the lad was having his midday nap, the military band was marching through the town. As it neared the Mahler household the music became louder and the little boy leaped from his bed, grabbed his accordion and ran out into the street in his bare feet and nightshirt and toddled along behind the band. With a bright red face – or so the legend goes – he tried to keep in step but every few paces he found he couldn't keep up. Amused by the sight of the little boy, more and more people of Iglau joined the procession.

The band marched through the town to the parade ground. It was only there that the boy realized that both the place and the people were all strange to him. One person teased him: 'Little Gustav, if you can play the march back to us from memory on your accordion we will take you back to your home.' The lad did not need to be told twice. He took courage and began to march and play at the same time with the people marching behind him. He played the music almost faultlessly. 'It was almost impossible to believe,' concluded their grandmother, 'the little boy could repeat almost any melody he heard.'

'March music on an accordion!' Mizzi was impressed. 'Come on Alice, let's play *Gustavchen* (Little Gustav).' She ran to the kitchen and came back with a table spoon and a saucepan. 'Soldiers go to war and must play march music, soldiers go to war and must play march music.' Mizzi sang and marched around the room.

Although she was spontaneous by nature, Alice remained sitting pensively on her cushion. 'Grandmother,' she whispered, 'what became of Little Gustav?'

'Little Gustav became Gustav Mahler, one of the most important conductors and composers of our time. At ten he gave his first concert in the town theatre in Iglau. But your mother could have told that story much better. She was only seven years younger than Gustav and knew him well. She still has a high opinion of him. She saw him conduct a few years ago in Prague, when he performed his first symphony at the German Theatre. She even went to Vienna once in order to hear him conduct the first performance of his second symphony.' Their grandmother said: 'So now come to the table.'

Fanny Schulz lit the two Sabbath candles, then took one of the plaited loaves and broke off a bit for herself and two more pieces for her granddaughters. Then she mumbled what were for the children a few unintelligible but pleasantly familiar sounding words.

'And when I can play back any melody from memory on the piano,' asked Alice with her mouth full, 'will I also be a musician?'

'When you can do that,' her grandmother said gently, 'then you will most certainly be a musician.'

*

THAT NIGHT, AS calm had long since returned to the houschold, Alice lay awake in bed talking to herself. For a while now, she had been going to the piano to find notes that when played together sounded pleasantly harmonious. She had found some joyful, bright sounding chords and some sad and dark ones; but she had never tried to play a march.

'I wonder if a military band were to come past the house, I could play the march?' she muttered. 'What nonsense. It is already far too late, where should . . . but it doesn't have to be a march, I could play a song.'

She sat up and tried to play her favourite song on the side of the bed: 'Were I a little bird, and also had two wings, I'd fly to you . . .' It was as if she could hear the melody. 'Because it cannot be, because it cannot be, I will stay right here.' As soon as she had finished her song she leaped in raptures from her bed.

'Now I am going to try!'

The floorboards creaked softly as Alice crept past her parents' bedroom in the direction of the drawing room. She quietly closed the door behind her and sat down at the piano. Moonlight lit up the keyboard. Her father always turned the gaslamps off when he made his nightly tour of the flat. The children were not allowed to touch them.

Alice carefully pressed the keys: 'Were I a little bird . . .'

It sounded lovely.

On her second attempt she improvised a second part with her left hand, then she played the two parts together. She went back to bed in ecstasy: 'I am going to be a musician,' she promised herself. 'Yes, that is what I am going to be, so long as I am called Alice Herz!' Then she fell happily asleep.

Early the next morning (her stamina was then one of her fortes), after she had returned from the baker's, Alice sat down at the piano and repeated the night-time exercise. The first and second parts harmonized even better, and her mother came rushing out of the kitchen.

'Splendid Alice, really splendid,' she said and patted her daughter on the head. 'And can you imagine this, last night I heard this song so clearly in my dream that I was woken by it.' Alice smiled. 'Now come quickly', her mother commanded in an unusually tender voice: 'Little Mizzi is ready and waiting. School is about to start.'

For a few months Alice and Marianne, now seven years old, had been attending the first class of the German-speaking girls' elementary school. They went to the *Altstädter Volks- und Bürgerschule* (Old Town National and Citizens' School). Every day Alice and Mizzi had an approximately thirty-five-minute walk to school. This meant walking from Bělsky Street down to the Moldau, over the Franz-Joseph Bridge, the suspension bridge which had been opened in 1868, and along Elisabeth Street.

To cross the bridge they had to pay the toll, a *Kreuzer* for each child. For this reason every morning both children had to go into the office and ask their father for two coins, for he alone had access to the housekeeping. Friedrich Herz had already been working for more than an hour and sometimes his affairs led him to the furthest corners of the factory and he didn't want to be disturbed in what he was doing. Either Alice or Mizzi had to remind him that without the money they could not go to school. Each one had their own way of doing this: Mizzi was flirtatious, Alice stubborn. It often made them late and they had to run to the bridge. The bridge-keeper was waiting for them: 'Here they come – the red bonnets,' he joked, even sometimes when they weren't wearing their red caps.

That afternoon Alice could not be taken away from the piano. She kept trying out new songs and variations. When she thought of a second part-line, she would sing it first, and then she played it out on the piano.

Before dinner she gave her first little concert. The audience was composed of Mizzi, Paul, Irma and their mother, a friendly neighbour and even Friedrich Herz father – who had, at his wife's request, left the office early. Alice did her best with three children's songs.

The guests praised her to the skies, and for the first time Alice experienced what it was like to be the centre of attention. When the applause died down, Mizzi wanted to perform her own show: 'I can sing the songs too.'

Her mother suggested: 'Why don't you do it together.'

Alice and Mizzi stood together at the window in the evening light and gave their rendition of 'Were I a little bird . . .'

After a few bars Alice began to improvize the second part. The twins sang a duet, one a soprano, the other an alto. Their mother could hardly believe how musical her little ones were.

Irma was as moved by the performance as her mother. For

many years the nineteen-year-old had been having lessons with the Czech piano teacher Václav Štěpán and she was an experienced player. 'I am going to start immediately giving you lessons every Thursday afternoon if you promise to practise the piano for an hour after the housework.' That was her offer to the twins.

Alice and Mizzi were diligent schoolchildren, and their mother set much store by good marks. Alice showed promise in the first four years of her elementary school; she liked local history, geography and history and had an appetite for books. In secondary school she discovered an affinity with the romantics, and Adalbert Stifter remained her favourite writer even after decades of exploring the literature of other countries. On the downside she never fathomed the mystery of arithmetic.

'Is that what we want to do?'

Alice responded to Irma's rhetorical question with a jubilant cry. Mizzi's 'yes' was more muted.

There were five days to their first lesson. The girls were to use the time to practise a song, literally to feel the keys, which they really liked. At the same time they were to seek out the accompanying melody with their left hands.

Every day after lunch Alice ran to the piano. Mizzi practised before dinner. After a few lessons it was already apparent that Alice was showing far more enthusiasm than her twin sister. Irma was more than satisfied with Alice's performance, but she was critical of Mizzi, and in this the elder sister's teaching abilities left something to be desired. She showed herself as impatient and short-tempered and after only a few weeks there was an explosion. Mizzi came away from her lesson in tears.

'She rapped me twice across the knuckles', she told her sister between sobs.

'Why did she do that?' Alice wanted to know.

'Because she was angry about the mistakes I made in the C minor scale. First she shouted at me, saying I had to start again at the beginning, and when I made a mistake again, she shouted at me even louder. Her angry face made me really nervous and I then played really badly yet again, so she hit me across the fingers with the pointer so hard that I could not play any more.'

'And then?' Alice asked incredulously.

'Then I shouted back at her: "If you hit me again I won't come to your lessons any more." ' Mizzi's voice became ever more agitated when she recounted the tragic story.

'What happened then?'

'Then Irma answered back: "Who is it who wants to learn the piano, me or you? Who is too lazy to practise, me or you? Who is not concentrating, me or you?" '

'What happened then?'

'I ran away. And I am not going back. She can shout at whoever she likes, but not at me,' Mizzi pouted.

Neither Alice nor her mother could console Mizzi. From that moment onwards she shunned the piano. She read a lot instead and soon discovered a talent for the stage. She performed and recited all through her childhood and youth with great energy and passion.

Alice, on the other hand, could not get enough of the piano. She became used to practising for two hours every day and very soon that had doubled to four. The joy of music, the recognition she received from her family, her first performance before the class – Alice had found her voice. After only a year and a half she had made such technical progress that she could perform with her brother Paul, who was esteemed a highly talented violinist for his age.

*

IN HER CIRCLE, Irma was known as 'the lovely Herz'. The growing twins were keen to know who was paying her attention and who interested her. It was not just for her pretty face that men sought her company: the eldest Herz sister was a fascinating and impetuous personality who knew full well how to use her talents. She could be 'very funny, witty even' her later husband affirmed. 'When she is in the mood, she is fun to be with, and even more so, she is a gripping *raconteuse*.'[1]

Felix Weltsch was twenty-five years old and had studied law – 'that rather vague bread-and-butter subject for young men who took an interest in everything' – at the then 'imperial and royal' Karl Ferdinand University and he had already started working in the National and University Library when he met Irma. They were members of the same tennis club in the Crown Prince Rudolf Park.

From occasional encounters on the court or in the clubhouse there soon came regular meetings. They played tennis together, sometimes mixed doubles too – as Alice recalls – against Felix Weltsch's close friend Franz Kafka. They then promenaded through the park, along the banks of the Moldau or through the old city. Naturally Felix took his beloved home afterwards and said goodbye to her at the door. At some stage Irma asked Felix up to the flat in order to introduce him to her parents, but she must have cleared it with her mother first.

As well as his work, Weltsch immersed himself in philosophy and in 1911 acquired a second doctorate. He came from a family of cultured Prague merchants whose good name was known in the Herz household. Felix's father Heinrich was the second generation of proprietors of the cloth merchants Salomon Weltsch & Söhne. Trading in the finest materials was done more for love than profit. They lived frugally.

Sofie Herz was well aware of how much Felix Weltsch's considered style, analytical mind and logical expression influenced her moody and often angry eldest daughter. Young love and mutual admiration did their bit; when Felix heard Irma play the piano he was clearly smitten. He was not, however, simply seduced by her charm. 'Her piano playing was actually great,'[2] wrote Felix Weltsch, who had particularly cultured parents and played the violin himself. His old friend Max Brod later happily remembered the 'infinite joy' of their piano and violin duets. 'It often makes you more blissfully happy to visit a friend than to go to a concert given by a great virtuoso, who, like a keen music-lover has mastered the violin and who, with a quick nod towards the piano, invites to take your place and make the sun radiate from powerfully beautiful melodies, like us two magicians.'[3]

All Irma's brothers and sisters got on with Felix, even Georg and Paul. Georg's aimless enjoyment of life conflicted with Weltsch's ambitions. Georg, and in later years Paul, attempted to fit in with their father's business, but the all too fixed routine did not suit either man. They took their pleasures at night, and with constantly changing people.

The closest relationship developed between the rising philosopher and Alice, however; he prized her enthusiasm and curiosity as much as he did her more valuable qualities, such as talent and stamina.

When Irma was invited to Weltsch's parental home in the Gemsengässchen in the old city, she often took her little sisters with her. Decades later Alice voiced her adoration for Luise and Heinrich Weltsch, for their warmth and hospitality and, not least, for their love of music. When Alice later started going to concerts every evening, she regularly met them both standing at the back. That was exceptional for older people: Friedrich and Sophie Herz would not have gone for health reasons: she suffered from thrombosis and he had heart problems. They never went to concerts and only occasionally bought tickets to the opera.

Over the years Felix Weltsch became one of the most influential people in Alice's life and the friendship between the two lasted over fifty-four years until his death. Scarcely anyone had as much call on her thinking, whether they were talking about the problems of everyday life or fundamental philosophical issues. It was probably through him – at first as a more or less attentive spectator and later as a more active debater – that she experienced at first hand the search for a new 'Jewish identity'.

Felix Weltsch was a convinced Zionist and in the course of the years he encouraged discussions in the Herz family which had been taboo until then. 'How do individuals react to their Jewishness, above all to their consciousness of being a Jew?' Felix Weltsch asked and identified three separate groups:[4] the first group who reacted negatively through flight – 'He recognizes that he is Jewish, sees it as a misfortune and runs away.' Then there is the hysterical reaction: compensation – 'He looks to distinguish himself, and frantically at that, somehow to make up for being a Jew ... In short, they behave hysterically, seeking to hide or make good for something which makes him feel defamed or inferior.' And finally there is the creative reaction – Zionism: 'He sees his Jewishness as a task, as an incentive to deeds and performance ... The whole race should be creative.'

In enlightened families like the Herzes they maintained only occasional observations of things that had been *de rigueur* in the old days. As Max Brod expressed it: 'The only thing that finally remains for the Prague Jews is *Seder* night [at the start of Pass-over].'[5] Kafka expressed himself in a similar way in his 'Letter to His Father': 'As far as I can see it is nothing, just a joke, and not even a joke. You went to the synagogue four times a year, where you were at least closer to the indifferent than those who take it seriously and patiently perform their prayers as a formality ... that was the synagogue. At home it was even poorer and limited to the first *Seder* night, which was more and more like a farce with fits of giggles, admittedly under the influence of the growing children.'[6]

As a rule Friedrich Herz went to the synagogue once a year: on the Day of Atonement – Yom Kippur. Passover, the most intimate Jewish festival, was close to his heart and had to be properly celebrated in the family. On the other hand he allowed a modest Christmas celebration. Sofie Herz baked a stollen and Alice and Mizzi went to Midnight Mass with the maid. There was, however, never a Christmas tree in the flat.

The whole family played their part in the preparations for Passover. Sofie started out days before, cleaning up according to the traditional rules. Three days before Passover everything that was *chametz* (leavened) had to be thrown out 'if you want to completely follow the orders of the wise men' – as is ordained in the *Pesach-Haggadah*. Alice worked with her mother. Her grandmother took on the job of cleaning the vessels and dipped every pot, plate, glass and spoon in boiling hot water. From that moment onwards until *Seder* night the tableware could not come into contact with anything leavened.

The twins helped prepare the food for the Seder. Every year, while they did this, their grandmother explained to the children once again what the dishes symbolized. The roast bones recalled the sacrifice of the Passover lamb on the evening of the Flight out of Egypt; the hard-boiled egg symbolized mourning for the destruction of the Temple in Jerusalem; the bitter herbs – their grandmother generally interpreted this as horseradish – recalled the sufferings of the Jews in Egypt; the green herbs – generally parsley – represented the green leaves that the Hebrews used to sprinkle the blood of the Passover lamb on their doors. And they were termed the first fruits of the Promised Land.

The twins had to mix so much cinnamon into the mash of apples, figs and nuts that it looked like the clay that the Israelites prepared when they were slaves to the Egyptians; then a bowl had to be filled with salty water to represent the sweat and tears that the slaves had shed in their captivity. In the middle of the *Seder* dish the three matzos had to be laid, the unleavened wheat-cakes, a remembrance of the last days before the Flight out of Egypt when the necessity for speed meant there was no time to bake sourdough loaves.

On *Seder* night Friedrich Herz's house was open to his friends and the poor. All went silent when the master of the house pronounced the dedicatory prayer, drank from the first beaker of wine and finally broke a matzo. He shared out half of it with the guests then together they lifted high the *Seder* dish: 'This is the bread that our forefathers ate in Egypt. Whosoever hungers, let him come and eat. Whosoever is in need, let him come and celebrate Passover with us! This year we are here – next year in Eretz Israel! This year we are slaves – next year we are free men!'

Now it was the task of the youngest person at table to bring in the *Pesach-Haggadah* and pose the question which the eldest would recognize – to read the text – the story of the flight out of Egypt. Alice and Mizzi read together: 'Why is this night different to other nights?' and then hand the book over to their father. 'We were slaves to the Pharaoh in Egypt,' began Friedrich Herz, 'but the eternal one, our God, led us away from there with his powerful hand and outstretched arm.' The paper smelled old and venerable.

The *Seder* night ended with a number of songs. Their father's full baritone sounded like a cantor. After the feast was over it was another year before anything happened in the household to recall the fact the parents were of Jewish descent.

*

ALTHOUGH FELIX WELTSCH was rather a restrained man, he had a quiet, dry wit and Irma could do wonderfully convincing imitations for the twins that perfectly evoked his voice and speech. The twins were encouraged by their talented sister and by Felix's father, who was seen by his family as the master of the ad lib rhyme, to make up funny rhymes, too.

Throughout 1912 Felix Weltsch used to turn up with Franz Kafka. The two men had noticed one another during religious instruction classes at the Altstadt Gymnasium but they had failed to become friends. They had a friend in common in Max Brod who in the end brought the two together when they were students. That was in around 1902. The friendship was slow to develop. After 1906 their relationship became deeper but it was only in 1912 that Kafka allowed the eighteen-month-younger Felix Weltsch to address him with the familiar pronoun 'Du'. When Max Brod proved his disloyalty to Kafka's notion of male friendship by planning to wed – he married in February 1913 – Kafka and Weltsch formed what the former termed 'a sort of brotherhood of bachelors'.[7]

The insurance clerk Franz Kafka was beginning to publish his work. As far as Irma was concerned, his habit of constantly excusing himself prompted her to mock him, although she was more considerate with him than with others. Kafka was constantly apologizing: for lateness (he was always the last), for his presence, for his absence, for his reserve, or for participating in the discussion. You had the impression that he was excusing his very existence. The 'apology-rigmarole', the twins called it among themselves, was one of the best of Irma's cabaret-worthy acts. Kafka was tall and thin and from a distance could be mistaken for Felix Weltsch. When the twins saw him coming they called out to Irma: 'It isn't Felix but Franz, all over the place as ever but somehow getting here in one piece.'

However, Kafka was never all over the place when he went swimming in the Moldau with Alice, Felix and Irma on hot summers' days. They would go to the communal bath at the Charles Bridge or to the Civil Swimming School near the Kettensteg a little farther downstream. Kafka was a determined swimmer, struggling upstream not just for pleasure but to toughen himself up.

Unusually for a girl of that time, Alice was fond of swimming and even at the age of five she and Mizzi had swum unaccompanied. Alice had a hard job persuading her sister to swim across the Moldau to win her proficiency badge. Mizzi was frightened, even though the instructor was alongside her in his boat.

From Irma's stories the girls learned about the two other authors who enjoyed 'intimate bonds of friendship'[8] with Kafka and Weltsch: Max Brod, then the best known of them, and Oskar Baum. It was Brod who would later call that generation of German-speaking Jewish avant-garde writers the 'Prague Circle'. They would all be granted posthumous fame by their most illustrious member – Franz Kafka, who in fact participated least. For a long time Alice and Mizzi Herz dubbed the four 'Irma's four writers'.

Very short as a result of a childhood disease, Brod had a pronounced stoop, but was both incredibly charming and an incorrigible ladies' man, with a penchant for rather tall women. Irma did wickedly funny impersonations of his exaggerated courtship routine. Alice and Mizzi wanted to know how they should greet him when he knocked at the door. Their response didn't take long: 'Here comes our Max. He is the smallest, but as a charmer, he's much the smartest.' Brod, however, never went to the Herz family home, and only met the girls in 1915, by which time Irma had married Felix Weltsch and they had moved to the Kirchengasse, around the corner from Irma's parental home.

The twins also met Oskar Baum at the Kirchengasse. Irma had told them that Baum had had the use of only one eye since his early childhood, and that at the age of eleven he had been in a fight with some Czech schoolboys and had been totally blind ever since. At the Vienna School for the Blind, Baum received a diploma for his piano and organ playing, which impressed Alice as much as her sister's account of his cheerful, lively nature and well-balanced character. Kafka told the Herz girls that 'Oskar Baum lost his sight as a German, something that he never was and which he never recognized. Perhaps this is a sad metaphor for the so-called German Jews of Prague.'[9] At the beginning they didn't dare write comic verses about him, but then Mizzi had an idea: 'When he comes then we will simply say – "Blind is the chap, but sees full well, and knows to probe, and miss the trap."'

In the summer the Herz family went, together with maid and nanny, to the sleepy little village of Klanovice, half an hour by train from the centre of Prague, where Friedrich Herz rented the upper floor of the same farmhouse every year. He did not allow himself holidays and took the train to Prague every day. One day Franz Kafka and Felix Weltsch were announced. As the maid had the day off Kafka sprang into action and together with the two girls explored the area around the village. It is one of Alice's abiding memories. They were about eight at the time, and Alice took his right hand and Mizzi his left. Kafka walked quickly: like swimming, it was another form of exercise he had prescribed himself. For the sake of the children he slowed down, but not much. After they had gone a little way, which seemed horribly far to Alice and Mizzi, they rested on a bench and Kafka perched on a smooth milestone opposite. He began to tell the children stories about strange beasts which made the two girls roar with laughter, much to the writer's delight.

*

'COME ON CHILDREN, it's time to play.' By the time Alice was ten, it was a rare day when she and brother Paul, then not quite thirteen, did not rehearse together. Encouraged by their mother they performed their new pieces before bedtime. Sofie Herz liked this evening ritual. After the family dinner Friedrich retired to bed, while she herself sat on a bench by the stove and soaked up the heat from the pleasantly warm tiles while she encouraged them to make a start on one of her favourite pieces. Then she allowed herself to be surprised by what her little musicians had learned. They always had something new to show her.

Word soon got round the neighbourhood that in the evening almost every night there was music to be heard at the Herzes. Lots of dog-walkers stopped for a few minutes in front of the house to listen, and a few friendly neighbours were happy to be asked in – not just because of the refreshing originality with which the music was played, but also because of the way that the children discussed the music which enchanted their grown-up audience, as in their remarkable interpretation of Robert Schumann's *Träumerei*.

Alice had been able to play the popular piece faultlessly for weeks and with so much feeling that one day Paul decided to take the score with him to his violin teacher. Paul wanted to practise the piece with him, but his teacher objected: 'That is really not on, Paul. In the first place Schumann wrote *Träumerei* for the piano, and secondly it is an expression of deep love. Not loving your neighbour or the love between children! *Träumerei* is an expression of longing, or the love between a man and a woman.' Paul was agog.

The teacher carried on teaching: 'Only an adult who has known this love is in a position to close his eyes and to plunge himself into the recesses of his memory and bring the piece to life. You are simply too young to do that.'

Paul replied: 'Oh, Herr Professor, do I really have to spell it out?! For weeks now I do little more than sit in the window and wait for Adelheid. She lives opposite us. From the early hours my only thought is of Adelheid; in the evening before I go to bed, I only think of Adelheid; and when my sister plays *Träumerei* on the piano my heart is filled with Adelheid. Whenever I see her, my heart loses a beat.'

'If that is the case,' said the teacher with a smile, 'we shall practise the piece.'

'I have already been doing that for several days,' said Paul and to the astonishment of the teacher he played the melody clearly and full of expression. That evening the house concert opened with a violin solo: *Träumerei*. Their mother and the neighbours clapped with delight, even if they were perplexed that Paul had kept his eyes closed from first to last. He certainly looked rather strange.

Now Alice followed with her piano interpretation and earned herself just as much praise, but when Alice and Paul tried to play *Träumerei* together tempers began to fray. After a few bars Alice stopped playing. 'Paul, you are not keeping time. You are sometimes too fast, sometimes too slow; can you explain?'

'It isn't wrong, it is love. Only someone who knows love can play the piece properly,' said Paul triumphantly. 'And you are far too little to do that.'

'Schumann may well have been in love when he wrote *Träumerei*,' Alice retorted, 'but he had not lost his wits, and he wrote the piece in four-four time. So, let's heed Robert Schumann and not Paul Herz.' Then turning to her mother, she said: 'Mother, is Paul actually allowed to play this piece if it makes him so crazy?'

THREE

World War

'Duty comes first...'

It was baking hot in the sun and Alice and Mizzi were playing at hopping from one shadow to the next. Together with their friend Helene Weiskopf they were looking for a path using the dark splodges cast by the trees and bushes on the lawns and gravel. Every time they stepped on the light they were given penalty points. Later Irma was going to take the girls to the Civil Swimming School on the Kleinseiten bank of the Moldau. It was 29 July 1914.

Like every other Wednesday, Frau Weiskopf had fetched the twins to take them off for a walk in Belvedere Park. Helene Weiskopf's bank clerk father was a third cousin of Friedrich Herz and the Weiskopfs were the only relatives that Sofie really liked. She welcomed the fact that the children of both families had become close friends. During their childhood, the twins and Helene were inseparable, and Paul got on well with Franz Carl, who was the same age as him. Franz Carl later called himself F.C. Weiskopf, joined the Communist Party and achieved some fame as a writer.

The girls were sitting on the grass deciding which of them was going to talk Frau Weiskopf into buying them an ice cream when the Herz family maid, Marie, came running up desperately short of breath and gesticulating wildly.

'Alice and Mizzi, you must come back to the house at once,

We are at war!' The night before Austria-Hungary had declared war on Serbia – that morning it was front-page news.

War was a rather strange-sounding word for something from the distant past that girls of not quite eleven knew only from school. Didn't they say that the war of 1870–71 had settled the relationships between the European powers once and for all? Hadn't their father spoken gleefully of the progress of nations and friendly cooperation between scientists from all over the world? Despite that, Alice and Mizzi understood immediately what the normally level-headed Marie meant. Without a word, they leaped up, deserted Helene and her mother and ran home with their maid.

Their parents and elder siblings were standing in the kitchen talking when the 'little ones' came though the door. Their presence was noted, but they were expected to go to their room and make themselves scarce. Alice fled to the piano – the family were well used to that. Each new declaration of war was taken on board, Germany on Russia, Germany on France, Great Britain on Germany, and Austria-Hungary on Russia, though – for the time being at least – it all seemed a long way away. Friedrich, as far as Alice could tell, showed little of the widespread euphoria for war that was in the air at the end of July and beginning of August 1914. He was ultimately a thoughtful man and not easily roused. He did, however, align himself with those who voiced the general certainty of victory – the industrious propagandists, the famous writers and popular thinkers; and like most of the Germans who lived in Bohemia and Moravia he agreed that Austria and Germany were in the right and that war was unavoidable. The outcome would be the creation of a new member state of the Habsburg Empire.

The German-speaking Jews were happy to subscribe to the appeals printed in liberal papers, such as the *Prager Tageblatt*, which made it 'a duty above all else' to fight for the Dual Monarchy.[1] Between 300,000 and 400,000 Jewish men – 25,000 of them as officers – served in the Austro-Hungarian Army, most of them volunteers. They were devoted patriots, ready to lay down their lives for a country in which they were at best tolerated. Behind their readiness to fight was concealed not just their longing to be recognized as equal partners in the nation but also fear: fear of anti-Semitic Russia, fear of pogroms, fear of trials for ritual murder and fear of dispossession.

No one doubted that the war would be won within a few months, but a few weeks after it began the advance had already slowed down. The newspapers announced a 'strategic withdrawal' of German and Austrian troops. The Chief of the General Staff of the Austro-Hungarian Royal Army, Conrad von Hötzendorf, knew from before the official declaration of war that victory was by no means certain and each day of the war cost the lives of, on average, six thousand soldiers. Then in September came the news of the fall of Lemberg (Lvov), one of the largest cities in the Empire, to the Russians.

Sofie Herz heeded the official request to all women and was hard at work knitting socks for the Habsburg soldiers. Alice and Mizzi did their bit too; but so far the war did not affect the two girls for the simple reason that no one in their immediate family had been called up. Physical disabilities excused their brother Georg from military service. Paul was just fourteen years old and their father over sixty. As far as the children could see, even 'Irma's four writers' continued their lives as of old.

Irma's marriage to Felix Weltsch, on 30 August 1914, however, had far-reaching effects on Alice.

*

FOR THE FIRST months of their marriage the Weltsches lived in the parental home. Then they moved into a small flat just round the corner at 4, Kirchengasse, which ran directly up to Belvedere Gardens. The block of flats belonged to the Herzes, Friedrich having acquired it as a nest-egg for the family.

Friedrich was more than happy with his daughter's choice of husband, but the bridegroom's friends saw a bumpy road ahead. Kafka felt that the lovers' relationship was from the very outset

'a systematic battle for unhappiness' and that his friend had fallen
for unfathomable Irma with his eyes wide open from all that Felix
had told him. You have to desire the impossible, was Weltsch's
defence.

Kafka was in no way objective in his remarks, something which
became clear soon after Weltsch became engaged: 'My last close
unmarried or unbetrothed friend [Felix Weltsch] has become
engaged; I knew this would happen three years ago (you didn't
need to be particularly brilliant to see it), but they have only made
it official these last two weeks. This means I shall lose a friend up
to a point, because a married man is not the same. Whatever
people say to him will be silently or loudly transmitted to his wife;
and there is no woman who does not present a distorted picture of
everything in this altered state.'[2] We know from his diaries that
Kafka himself certainly intended to marry in the foreseeable future,
but he used the wedding as a pretext to loosen what had hitherto
been a very tight bond of friendship. 'But besides the fact that I
naturally wish him well, there is also an advantage for me, for now
at least. We had formed . . . a sort of brotherhood of bachelors
that was, from my point of view, completely deadly most of the
time. Now it has been dissolved, now I am free . . .'

The 'Prague Circle' still met in coffee houses and bars during
the week and on Sundays they took it in turn to visit one another
in their flats. At first these at-homes followed a roster, but after
a while, they were usually at the Weltsches, much to Alice's joy.
After her marriage Irma was very much preoccupied with looking
after her younger sister and regularly invited her to the Sunday
gatherings.

Kafka, however, visited his married friends increasingly rarely
and one Sunday they waited for him in vain. He had said he was
coming and was anything but unreliable, never wanting to offend
anyone. 'He will come late and will immediately make more
excuses,' the others said. But Kafka did not come. Instead Irma
received a card two days later on which he made a very formal
excuse. He said he was so deep in thought that he had taken a

wrong turning in the street and then lost his way and wandered around for hours without being able to find the street again. The friends laughed about it for days, because Kafka knew the area well. They were convinced that no one else would have got lost under these circumstances. Irma added another set piece to her repertoire of impersonations.

*

IN 1915 IRMA, who was contributing to the household as a piano teacher as well as teaching Alice, took her sister to her own mentor Václav Štěpán for the first time. He had studied at Marguérite Long's world famous school in Paris. Although he was only in his mid-twenties he was already appreciated as a chamber musician and coupled with this, his writings on modern Czech composers had made a name for him as a musicologist. Years later he told Alice about Madame Long and her piano school and what she felt were the most important qualities of a musician: 'transparency, accuracy and simplicity'. A more fitting description of Alice's later style is hardly possible.

Alice liked Václav Štěpán immediately. Štěpán had lost an eye in an early campaign and he spent the rest of the war as an invalid in Prague. The twelve year old found the black eye-patch he wore made him look dashing. Alice played him a Beethoven sonata with unusual technical perfection for one of her years.

'Alice that is very respectable, very, very respectable.' Štěpán was astonished. 'How long have you been practising it?'

'That is not easy to say,' said Alice in fluent Czech, 'I practise every day.'

'When do you practise?'

'Every afternoon, mostly from two to six.'

'Do you not have any friends then, someone to play with?'

'Yes, of course, my twin sister Mizzi, and Daisy and Helene. We do something together every weekend.'

'And during the week?'

'I play the piano,'

'An hour or two would be quite enough to make progress with your talent.'

'But it gives me so much pleasure,' Alice enthused. 'There is nothing lovelier than learning a new piece.'

For the next ten years, Štěpán saw Alice once a month and became her most important teacher.

Making music with her brother Paul was an additional spur. They had expanded their repertoire and were now at a loss to find new pieces for piano and violin. When Paul brought home a Czech schoolmate, an excellent cellist, for the specific purpose of practising a trio-sonata, Alice was over the moon. The three of them were so happy playing together that by the end of 1915 they were an official concert trio.

In those days Prague schools rounded off their working weeks with music. Pupils sang songs and in some places there were little concerts. Prague was more like a village than a city and the news of a promising new trio rapidly became known in Prague. Alice and her two accompanists were swamped with invitations. Nearly every Friday they performed before a new class.

After a concert at the Altstadt Bürgerschule a girl came up to Alice and introduced herself as Trude Hutter. She was about a year or two younger than Alice and her grandfather was headmaster of the school. Alice found her strikingly different, just as she found almost all girls more striking than herself.

'You really play wonderfully,' said Trude. Then she told Alice about a trip to Berlin and an unforgettable concert she had seen. 'We heard the Mendelssohn Octet,' she gushed. Since then she had acquired the piano part, a transcription for four hands.

'Shall we play it together?' Trude asked.

Alice immediately invited Trude to come to her house the next day, and the two of them practised for hours. It was the beginning of a lifelong friendship. 'When Trude entered the room the sun came out', Alice said later. From then on the friends practised together as often as they could and in the course of the year they played, among other things, pieces from the great Beethoven,

Mozart and Haydn symphonies; but their favourite piece remained the Mendelssohn Octet.

*

IN THE KIRCHENGASSE Alice and Mizzi made another close friend, Daisy Klemperer, one of Irma's piano pupils. Daisy's father was a coal merchant and the family was very wealthy. Their smart villa stood in the middle of a large garden, tended by many gardeners, and Alice found it far more splendidly furnished than her parents' flat. Daisy's kindness and easy-going nature stood in stark contrast to her lavish circle. On Sundays she often invited Alice home and she enjoyed playing Daisy's piano.

In the autumn of 1916 Alice and Mizzi left the Altstadt Bürgerschule and transferred to Daisy's class at the girls' Lyceum. Alice's friend had told such wonderful stories about the elite school at Ferdinand Strasse in the old town that Mizzi above all, with the 'airs and graces' which amused Alice at the time, would not give up until her parents agreed to the change. Friedrich Herz had hesitated at first, as the monthly fees were a lot more than the Bürgerschule. He must have known from the beginning that he would have to give way, for Irma had also taken her leaving certificate at the Lyceum. For a long time it had been seen as the best German-speaking girls' school in Prague. The classrooms were splendidly equipped, and the art room, music room, gym, chemistry and physics labs were fully up to date. There were about thirty children to a class, most of them from Jewish homes.

Alice was passionate about her teachers, who provided 'knowledge for life'. There was the French master from Belgium, the stenography mistress (Alice was top of the class), the history master Herr Pick, who had a talent for telling gripping stories from the past but most ably avoided talking about the current war still raging on three fronts. Politics was not on the syllabus and Alice never heard a single word about how the central powers were acquitting themselves during all her time at school.

One day the German mistress brought a vase full of spring

flowers into the class. The girls had to write an essay about spring. Alice and Mizzi sat together at a desk and used the same schoolbooks. Mizzi liked doing essays and wrote them fast and well, and often she had time left to help bring Alice's dull script to a rousing conclusion for her. This time, however, Alice was keen to write it all herself.

A few days later the teacher brought the schoolbooks back. 'Some of your essays are so interesting that I should like to read them out,' she said. 'I'll start with the most interesting.' Alice was very excited: it was not Mizzi's but her essay the teacher had selected! Alice had written about the months of joyful expectation of spring, and the happiness that man and beast feel when the sun finally arrives to provide them with warmth, and the buds burst and the birds sing.

Straight after Alice's essay, the teacher read Mizzi's out. She had also described how people waited for spring. She came to the conclusion, however, that every year nature was reborn ever more beautiful and luxuriant, while man had just one life, and was condemned to die. 'Observe the twins', the teacher said. 'One is an optimist and the other a pessimist.' There was no question about it: both essays were good, but all the children sensed that Alice's text was brimming with joy and happiness while Marianne's essay was imbued with melancholy.

The teacher made the two texts an excuse to talk about the different views of the world. Every pupil had to attempt to express the difference between optimism and pessimism in one line. The teacher started at the first desk and intended to proceed row by row, but the first girl she asked said, 'I can't do it.'

The teacher gave her a hand: 'Then tell me: what is the most striking difference between Alice and Marianne?' 'Now I know. Alice is always in a good mood and Mizzi is generally serious. Optimists are therefore happier than pessimists.' That broke the ice and almost all the girls were able to make something up. Daisy's contribution was particularly telling: 'Optimists are mostly gay, but pessimists can see the way.'

Alice and Mizzi were due to deliver their lines last. Alice got hers in first: 'Optimists always see the best; they spread happiness,' she said. 'Pessimists are the worst, they scatter gloom.' Mizzi had the last word and her line lodged itself in the girls' minds for days: 'Pessimists see the truth, optimists ignore it.'

That afternoon the twins talked about the lesson with Daisy and Helene. Helene was still in the Altstadt Bürgerschule, but she came round often to the Herzes' house and was an optimist like Alice. Sofie Herz listened carefully to the discussion and the girls liked it when their mother took an interest in what they had been doing. When Helene asked her whether she could explain why Mizzi, as opposed to Alice, was so anxious, pensive and always a little on the pessimistic side, Sofie answered frankly: 'Mizzi has certainly inherited my nature, as I also see the darker side at first. And Alice is very like her father, who has a joyful nature. For him the glass is always half full, for me it is half empty.'

Helene was not only hugely imaginative, she was also observant and it did not escape her notice that the twins were treated very differently. Mizzi had to be the little princess, and was rarely, for example, obliged to take part in the weekly cleaning. Alice, on the other hand, thought it only right to lend a hand. Helene felt this extremely unjust, but she did not dare raise the matter with Frau Herz. Nonetheless, she succeeded in stirring up trouble.

'There is one thing I always wanted to ask: why is it that Marianne has a pet-name, and Alice not?' she asked one day. Sofie's mother hesitated for a while before answering, then said: 'The explanation is quite simple: all Austrians shorten the name Marianne and say Mizzi or Mizzerl. There is no shortening for Alice, or do you think Alizerl is a fitting pet-name?'

The answer was unsatisfactory, and Helene would not give up. 'All children like to have a pet-name. I am also called Lene. And there is no reason that Alice . . .' 'You are quite right, but Alice is already so short and pretty that it is like a pet-name', Sofie riposted. 'Or do you have a better idea?'

Helene was a bit unprepared for this sharp response, but she refused to be intimidated. Alice's pet-name needed to have as many syllables as 'Mizzi' and sound similar. Suddenly she lit up: 'If the M at the beginning of Mizzi stands for melancholy, then Alice's pet-name must start with G for good-naturedness . . . That means Gigi!'

Sofie Herz smiled: 'That's a very good idea!'

From that moment onwards Alice's friends, and soon her relatives as well, began to call her Gigi. She was Alice only to her parents and Irma.

*

IN THE THIRD year of the war its effects were becoming obvious, even to children. The food supply had got dramatically worse soon after the beginning of the conflict and by the end of 1916 almost all food was rationed.

All through the war, Friedrich Herz was able to provide for his family reasonably well. He had important customers in the country who could supply him with potatoes, butter, eggs and every now and then a bit of meat – although the prices had soared. Luckily, Alice had a modest appetite and was happy with a small portion. She can't remember going hungry between 1914 and 1918 or having been noticeably colder than usual. Her father clearly always managed to find sufficient fuel to heat the two stoves in the kitchen and the drawing room. The bedrooms had never been heated.

By 1915 bread coupons were issued and the longer the war continued the more stamina was required to buy a simple loaf of bread. Many people waited all night outside a shop when a delivery was due. The Herz children took it in hourly turns to stand in the queue at their local baker's. The bread they finally acquired was a rough mixture of unidentifiable ingredients with a persistent taste of turnips.

And throughout these years of hardship there was scarcely a family who had not been touched by loss. Irma and Georg mourned their dead friends, and Alice and Mizzi grieved with their brothers and sisters.

By November 1916, when Georg had applied to work at the Skoda weapons and steelworks in Pilsen and he was taken on at a monthly salary of 280 crowns, when most of the healthy young men were doing war service, Georg was now twenty-eight and a confirmed rake. No one knows how long he held down his job, but a letter to Felix Weltsch of 27 November speaks volumes. Relations between father and son were icy: 'Can I ask you kindly to go to my father and get him to advance me 150 crowns so that I can last the first month here in Pilsen. I will then pay off the sum month by month.'[3]

Felix Weltsch carried out his brother-in-law's request and acted as an intermediary between him and his parents. He was always an even-handed negotiator and master of well-chosen words. Yet at the time he was facing some very serious problems, both in his professional and private life.

Russian troops had marched into eastern Galicia and Bukovina and their arrival had unleashed a monstrous tide of Jewish refugees who converged on the west. For most German-speaking Prague Jews it was the first time they had set eyes on these 'eastern Jews' culturally so different from themselves. They were mostly women, old people and children, for the young men had naturally been recruited into the armed forces. The German-speaking Jews of Prague veered between pity and repulsion at the sight of their poverty. Alice and her siblings saw Talmudic scholars on the streets of Prague for the first time.

While the Prague Czechs and even the Czech-speaking Jews kept their distance, the German Jews were deemed to be responsible for looking after the refugees. Life's necessities were organized, a Jewish soup kitchen opened, clothes were collected, shelter was prepared and a strange cultural life grew up including a refugee school at which both Max Brod and Felix Weltsch enthusiastically taught. Meeting the refugees proved traumatic to the young intellectuals; it made them more conscious of their Jewishness and confirmed their conviction that the Jews needed their own state.

Felix Weltsch took regular Hebrew lessons and gave courses

for refugees; the unpaid work seemed to make him happy. 'My father-in-law keeps saying that this is no use, that with my talents I should be giving my course on the Altstadt Ring Road before an audience of 2,000 people, and that it should be written up by the *Neue Freie Presse*, that I am starting out too modestly and on too small a scale etc.'[4]

At home, it was increasingly clear that Irma's temper, always fiery, was getting worse. His friends had seen it coming from the earliest days of their relationship. He felt trapped in his marriage, although he was ready to recognize that Irma's 'persistent and only occasionally interrupted angry abuse' was a sickness, 'Ninety percent of what she says consists of insults, which range at their most extreme form from hatred to the vilest nastiness imaginable. The most common epithets are murderer, crook, blackguard, corpse, brat . . .' It was one of the lowest points of Felix's married life.[5] 'You might even admire the linguistic creativity; she has a kind of genius when it comes to insult and belittlement.'

He remembered that his wife had exposed her negative character just after they had married in 1914: 'There was a terrible storm against her parents, which made me very concerned at the time. She called them "those dogs".' Irma had flown into a rage because in her opinion her parents were not sufficiently concerned about Alice, who remained strikingly small, while Mizzi was developing normally. To be fair, it must be said that Sofie had tried to obtain money from her husband to send Alice off to an orthopaedist. Irma had been present at this conversation and had bluntly argued Alice's case. After a battle of words, Friedrich Herz finally produced the money. For Alice the consequence meant regular and painful treatments, where she was stretched for hours in an orthopaedic machine with only limited success; she never grew taller than 1m. 52cm.

It is a mystery that the sickly Mizzi grew normally while the much more robust and independent Alice stopped growing early. For Irma, however, it was a good reason to fuss more about Alice in the next few years and to invite her round to the Kirchengasse more often – and not only to play the piano. For Irma did not just 'abuse, cry and lament' – she was loyal and protective as Felix Weltsch maintained: 'She is conscientious above all, upstanding and reliable in everything she does. Her hatred of me is a clear case of love-hate [. . .] She is no less anxious about me than she is about herself [. . .] She cares honestly and properly, right down to the smallest detail. She forgets nothing, and knows my smallest desire . . .'6

And it was precisely this exaggerated carefulness and punctiliousness of hers which manifested itself in such strange ways – as in this instance in July 1917. On the ninth of that month Kafka, now himself engaged to be married, dropped in to see the Weltsches with his fiancée, Felice Bauer. It was a short visit, as Kafka was expected at his sister's. Somewhere between the Kirchengasse, Kafka's sister's flat and his own rooms, Felice Bauer's silver handbag was lost. It contained at least 900 crowns. Anxious about the loss, Kafka immediately endeavoured to retrace his steps. He dashed back to the Kirchengasse, told Irma what had happened and added that Felice Bauer was absolutely certain that she had not left her handbag at Irma's.

Three days later Max Brod told Felix Weltsch that, fortunately, the handbag had been found the same day. Knowing how concerned Irma had been about the situation, Felix immediately sent a message home to tell her, too. As far as he was concerned the matter was closed.

When he returned that evening he was greeted by a completely distraught Irma. She screamed, bickered and nagged about 'the impudent Kafka' to whom she had already written a rude letter. Felix, who in their fifty years of marriage often thought about divorce and always rejected the idea, was baffled.

A few days later Kafka's polite answer arrived: 'Dear Frau Irma! . . . Shortly after I left you I found the handbag at my sister's. Miserable about the loss (I am so painfully mean) I returned straightaway to the flat which I had already turned upside-down and systematically poked around on my hands and knees in every corner and finally I found the bag quite innocently hiding under a suitcase. I was naturally very proud of my performance and would have been happiest if I had come straight back to you.'[7] In what was to be understood as irony and in conclusion he offered his excuses 'in sufficient number, possibly even too many. Had I not received your letter, I might have considered myself almost innocent. Since you had further thoughts about the bag and possibly looked for it again, these excuses are naturally insufficient, and I must stress that I bid you not entirely to remove the joy of relocating the handbag by being cross at my negligence . . . With best wishes your Kafka.'[8]

But Irma was by no means appeased by the letter and the 'affair of the silver handbag' was the cause of bad moods, arguments and disharmony in the Weltsch household for weeks. Four months later, in November, Kafka sent a letter to Felix Weltsch: 'Best wishes [to] your wife, with whom I have sadly had nothing to lose since the business with the handbag.'[9] Yet Irma continued to bear the writer a grudge over the affair, but by January 1918 Kafka, who was now suffering from tuberculosis, had put it behind him. He sent Felix a postcard from Zürau in which he enthused over his sanatorium: 'It is really splendid, however, and you could happily sacrifice a week in the library to come here. I will tell you a lot more funny stories when I see you . . . There is also a piano, Frau Irma!'[10]

*

THE AUTUMN OF 1918 was the bleakest Friedrich Herz had ever experienced. People had only good things to say about the philosopher and revolutionary commander Tomáš Garrigue Masaryk who with the blessing of the victorious powers declared the independence of Czechoslovakia on 28 October. In the course of many talks, Friedrich's son-in-law Felix had endeavoured to open his eyes to the advantages of democracy. The manufacturer, was prepared to listen, but remained loyal to the Habsburgs. There was no question that he was hard hit by the long-awaited truce between Austria-Hungary and the Allies. Five days later the war was well and truly lost. Friedrich Herz had invested a considerable part of his fortune in war loans. The money was gone. As he told his children: 'Now we have to start again from the beginning.'

The rebirth of nationalism brought on by the creation of the republic threatened to turn to hysteria. For the first time in more than a millennium the Czechs were to rule again in their own land, and many Czechs felt a desire for vengeance for the injustice they had suffered. There was a serious threat that this would be translated into a real, even physical danger for the German-speaking minority. German was frowned upon and already Alice got used to speaking Czech most of the time she was out in public.

At the beginning of November 1918 Alexander von Zemlinsky, who had been chief conductor at the German National Theatre in Prague, described the situation to his friend, pupil and later brother-in-law Arnold Schönberg: 'German culture is going to collapse here, if it is tolerated, and the theatre will go down with it. This might happen very soon; and what then?'[11]

There were still separate German and Czech universities, a German and a Czech National Theatre, a German and a Czech cultural world, but, as Zemlinsky observed: 'everything turns round the Czechoslovak state! Jews and Germans and Jews above all!'

Zemlinsky's fears for German culture did not immediately turn to reality, even though the Czech language and culture began to take pride of place. With his strong convictions President Masaryk abided by the victorious powers' wishes and protected the minorities of the successor states of the vanished Dual Monarchy. Immediately after taking office he gave his personal support for the future of the New German Theatre.

As the respected Prague Conservatory was made an official state institution, administered by a Czech directorate, there was no alternative for German artists but either to accept the situation or to found their own conservatory. This was easier said than done,

given the lack of funds. In the end Masaryk approved state
subsidies of 250,000 crowns per annum, which was about the same
amount as that given to a provincial elementary music school, for
the setting up of the German Academy of Music. For that reason
the project was underfinanced from the beginning and the fees had
to be set relatively high.

Food was still in desperately short supply and Prague was soon
afflicted by the onset of riots. 'Give over your potatoes or there
will be revolution,' cried the famished inhabitants of the big cities
during their strikes and mass protests. They vented their despair
on the familiar scapegoat – the Jews. On 1 December 1918 the
rampaging Czechs could no longer be contained and attacked
Jewish merchants in the streets of Prague's old town terrifying
them with cries of 'hang the Jews!' Masaryk's attempts to appease
them had very little effect.

The Herzes wanted to keep any echo of anti-Semitism away
from their children's ears, but 'Gigi', Mizzi and Paul were conscious of how muted the celebrations were that New Year's Eve of
1918. That night, Alice and Paul gave their parents a present of a
little concert and Friedrich and Sofie showed their heartfelt gratitude for the gesture. Then the young people left to visit their friends
and bring in the New Year.

*

SIX MONTHS LATER, in the summer of 1919, Irma and Felix
Weltsch spent their first holiday after the Armistice in the Salz-
kammergut. Alice, now sixteen, was allowed to go with them. They
travelled to St Gilgen on the Wolfgangsee, which Irma, as a passionate young pianist, had visited and fallen in love with because
Johannes Brahms went there year in, year out to visit his friend the
physician Theodor Billroth. Alice fell in love with the Alps, which
deepened when she later travelled there year after year with the
family of her piano teacher Václav Štěpán.

Surrounded by the beauties of nature, away from the daily
grind, the atmosphere was generally pleasant, even if Irma's fury

occasionally bubbled up and Alice had no alternative but to side with her brother-in-law.

Soon after the holiday Irma found she was pregnant and became particularly irritable. Things went from bad to worse. In July 1920 she gave birth to a girl, whom Alice looked after from the start. Irma's nervous disposition made it almost impossible for her to find the necessary peace of mind to feed little Ruth. At these times she would call Alice over to help her.b

'She is not feeding again, come at once!'

Alice broke off her piano practice and ran up Bělsky Street to the Sochařská – the Malergasse – where for the past few months Irma and Felix had been living at number 333. Friedrich Herz had sold the block of flats in the Kirchengasse in an attempt to halt the downward slide of the family finances. When Alice took her little niece in her arms, she immediately stopped crying and allowed her aunt to look after her. It was a defeat for her fragile mother, which did nothing to calm her down.

The longer that Alice was faced with Irma's psychological problems, the more she reflected on the secrets of a fulfilled life and, interested in philosophy even as a young girl, the more she felt drawn towards it, asking herself what causes man's happiness and unhappiness. It was probably Irma's difficult marriage and destructive attitude to life that gave Alice a powerful impulse to develop the opposite approach and to pursue it for as long as she could.

FOUR

Music

'He was still sober at nine...'

IT WAS MIDNIGHT and the grandfather clock was still striking the hour when Sofie Herz opened the door to the drawing room. Alice had been practising for five hours without a break. In her determined way she kept going over the difficult passages in a Bach partita.

Her mother went up to the piano and laid a reassuring hand on Alice's shoulder. 'It sparkles like a shower of crystal-clear water,' she said. 'It's perfect, not one single mistake. You are going to pass the audition. Don't you think you should go to bed now?' Although fatigue was written all over Alice's face, her eyes were still radiant with the inspiration which always seized her when she plunged into the adventure of conquering a new piece. When she practised she forgot about the world around her and lost her sense of time. 'Mother, you have never played before an audience. It is not enough to be able to play a piece, you have to know it a 100, no 200, or at best 400 per cent before you can step on to the podium. It has to belong to you in some way; it has to become part of you, body and soul.'

The Herz family and those members of it who still lived in the flat – Mizzi, Sofie and Friedrich – had learned to be tolerant of Alice's prolonged sessions at the piano. Grandmother Fanny had died before the end of the war and Georg had moved to Vienna after the final break with his father. Paul – against his will – was at the Military Academy.

Once again, it proved impossible to convince Alice to go to bed. Sofie therefore disappeared into the kitchen and returned with a cup of steaming chicken broth that she always had to hand, ready to reheat. It had become an affectionate ritual between mother and daughter and whenever the sixteen-year-old girl wanted to carry on practising well after midnight.

*

THE TWINS' TIME at the Lyceum ended in 1920. Without any hard and fast ideas about what she wanted to do later, Mizzi went to a school of commerce to learn about business. Alice had no doubts about what she wanted: she intended to be a pianist and she applied herself to the task with uncommon rigour.

Irma had told Alice that at the beginning of September that year the German Academy for Music and Drama would at last open its doors. The man who was carefully chosen as rector was Alexander von Zemlinsky, who had been born in Vienna in 1871. He was not just the most famous musician in Prague at the time, but was internationally respected as a composer and conductor. His teacher and patron had been Johannes Brahms who had had a high opinion of his abilities, so much so that he gave the then fifteen-year-old boy his grand piano. Zemlinsky, however, already knew that he was not going to become a peripatetic concert pianist, but wanted to remain at home in Vienna to conduct and compose.

In order to attract students from all over Europe, Zemlinsky created masterclasses for four disciplines: conducting, composition, violin and piano. Intended for trained musicians, they were none-theless open to any student who wanted to apply. Zemlinsky appointed one of the world's best violin virtuosi, Henry Marteau, to look after the violin class; when it came to the piano he tempted Conrad Ansorge from Berlin. Zemlinsky was hoping Liszt's former pupil would make a splash, though he himself would be taking the first two masterclasses.

Alice knew who Zemlinsky was but little more than that. Irma, on the other hand had a good deal to say about him. Outwardly an unattractive man, but brimming with wit and charm, Zemlinsky had, almost a decade before, taught 'the lovely Herz' for a year and during that time it was clear he wanted to be one of her suitors. In spite of this, encouraged by Irma, Alice decided that she would apply for a place.

The high fees were, however, a stumbling block and it was only with difficulty that Sofie Herz was able to convince her husband that Alice's happiness in life depended on his consenting to finance her studies.

*

THAT NIGHT ALICE carried on playing until one o'clock in the morning. The next morning at nine she was back at the keyboard. Around midday she emerged from her melodious world and went for a walk in the old town; this, too, was part of her usual routine. Alice loved Prague. She made her way directly over the Franz-Joseph Bridge (popularly known as the Elisabeth Bridge, later renamed the Štefánik Bridge) or she went the long way round through the narrow lanes of the 'Lesser Town' which lead to the inner city; or wandered around Wenceslas Square, enjoying accidental meetings with the friends and acquaintances who emerged from the midday throng. It was a necessary counterpoint to the solitary life of the pianist, for Alice was not solitary by nature – quite the contrary.

This summer afternoon in 1920 there were more people on the streets than usual. Happy with the progress she had made, Alice was swept along with the crowds and soon found herself in the elegant Wenceslas Square where the army was parading in dress uniforms. As a squadron of cavalry rode up she stood entranced: at their head was a strikingly well-built older man of majestic bearing – the president of the republic, Tomáš Masaryk, who fought so passionately for the new democracy and for cooperation between Czechs, Germans and Jews. How often she had heard his name in these last few months in her parents' home and above all at that of her brother-in-law, Felix Weltsch.

Alice gazed at Masaryk for a long time. Although she was aware that she was invisible in the crowd she felt as if she was meeting the president in person. In less than two years since the state had been founded he had brought national and international prestige to the new republic as a result of his humanistic and democratic thinking. His integrity was universally admired and it was considered that he would make tolerance between the different ethnic groups a central plank of his politics at home. His speech of 22 December 1918 in which he spoke of 'justice as the mathematics of humanism' was on everyone's lips.

Alice naturally knew that the former professor of sociology was also a passionate music lover. His wife Charlotte Garrigue had studied music in Leipzig, and his son Jan was not just a diplomat and, later, a highly regarded politician, he was also a pianist and composer. Surely the new German Academy of Music was directly attributable to his policies? Surely the fact that Alice was permitted to apply to the masterclass was thanks to him?

*

EVERY TUESDAY JUST after nine o'clock in the morning, and in the period before the audition sometimes even twice or three times a week, Alice interrupted her practice: Václav Štěpán was expecting her at ten. She liked the walk to his house, not just because it cost less than going by tram: she was used to going everywhere by foot, come rain or shine.

From her earliest days Alice had made Goethe's line her own. Prague was indeed 'the prettiest gem in the stone crown of the world'. There was always something new to discover in her home city. She made her long journey along the banks of the Moldau, past the heights of the Belvedere and through the Lesser Town, which allowed a full view of the castle, to the borough of Smichow. There, in a smart new building, not far from the Franzensbrücke Bridge, was Štěpán's apartment.

Alice had had plenty of fresh air on the way and was full of joyful anticipation when she went in and exchanged a few words with the good-humoured porter. The house belonged to a Czech musical society. On the ground floor there were offices and a concert hall in which Alice later performed often. A broad, curved staircase led up to the first floor where Štěpán lived with his wife Ilonka, also a successful pianist. She was the daughter of Wilhelm Kurz, who had been born in Lemberg, taught music in Brno and Prague and was a close friend of the composer Leoš Janáček.

Alice longed to be part of this world: she had been passionate about Czech music from the first and she was impressed that Štěpán had published regular articles on contemporary Czech musical history: on Josef Suk, Antonín Dvořák's son-in-law, and his friend Vítěslav Novák. He had also edited scholarly editions of Czech compositions and was the author of the piano version of Bedřich Smetana's *Dances*, music which fascinated Alice.

It was in this house that she was plunged into a proper Czech cultural circle for the first time. She had never known such groups existed before. Although Štěpán had perfect mastery of the German language, Alice spoke to him exclusively in Czech – and with no accent. From her teacher she acquired the view that a piano piece should be interpreted in such a personal way that it was equivalent to playing a new work, but for all that no changes should be made and the piece should be played as it had been set down in the score. In questions of rhythm in particular, Štěpán was categorical and he demanded total concentration. Despite this, the lessons were fun. Like so many Czechs, Štěpán was endowed with a particularly subversive sense of humour.

To get the best from her lesson, which was only forty-five minutes long, Alice took care to memorize all the master's little maxims. Afterwards she sat down on a step on the stairs directly opposite the door to Štěpán's flat and noted down everything from the class in a little notebook that she always carried with her.

One day when she was still sitting lost in thought on her step, the piano teacher came dashing out of his flat. He wanted to make a telephone call from the offices and tripped over Alice, and only in the nick of time was he able to prevent himself from falling flat on his face.

'But Gigi, what are you doing there?' he blurted out in shock while he clutched on to the banister.

Alice was embarrassed and showed him the notebook. Štěpán leafed through it page by page. For months Alice had been copying down every instruction down to the smallest detail. He had never come across such application.

'But why don't you take these notes during the lesson?'

'I don't want to waste a moment of the time we have together.'

*

FINALLY THE DAY of the audition came. Only thirty out of roughly twice that number would be given a place in the masterclass. The tension during the preliminary heats was unbearable. The famous firm of Förster had donated two grand pianos for teaching purposes which now stood like holy relics on the stage of the new hall. The examinees sat in a semi-circle around the stage while other students from the Academy sat in the seats behind them.

Alice sat down comfortably at the piano, knowing that she was well prepared for the day. Her playing impressed everyone present, including Conrad Ansorge. He whispered to his fellow jury members: 'This Herz is a really tremendous girl.'

Alice got in; she was the youngest member of the masterclass.

At the end of the auditions Ansorge gave his inaugural speech. He was not a talented public speaker but he nevertheless impressed his new pupils. His thoughts went back to the years 1885 and 1886 when he had been in Franz Liszt's masterclass in Weimar. On the first day Liszt had told the class that he felt not the slightest desire to talk about any problems of technique. Practising technique was like washing dirty linen, it was something you did at home: 'and that is precisely what I expect of you as well. I shall take it for granted now that you will apply all necessary diligence to perfecting your technique.'

His teaching was above all concerned with interpretation. 'I am convinced that most of you would be interested in what the great Liszt thought important,' Ansorge went on, 'and in recognition of your efforts the best of you will play at our twice-yearly public concert.'

During their three-year training the budding pianists would perform regularly. At the end of the third year a final concert would be given, to which the four best players of the previous concerts were admitted. 'The winner will be awarded a Förster concert grand,' Ansorge rounded off his speech before sitting down at the piano.

The effect his playing must have had on Alice and her fellow students is clear from a critic, who wrote in 1922: 'Ansorge is the Gerhart Hauptmann of pianists and as such the greatest at thoughtfulness, dreaminess and self-abnegation. Here in the adagio-style Ansorge offers shading with an indescribable whiff of ether and a celestial tonal colour. He plays the slow movements of the Beethoven concertos and sonatas as if detached from all earthly playing.' The members of his new masterclass thanked him with prolonged applause.

When Alice came home that day, laughing in a relaxed way that had eluded her for weeks, her friend Trude Hutter was waiting for her. 'I knew it,' Trude said, guessing the cause of her friend's happiness immediately, 'now tell me, how did it go?'

Trude wanted to know everything: what did Conrad Ansorge look like? 'Like an actor at the court theatre.' Had he impressed Alice? What had he said about her? And what had everyone felt about his playing?

Alice answered patiently, but when Trude asked her whether there were any good-looking men in the masterclass Alice shook her head in amazement. 'The very idea of it! I am not attending the masterclass to meet men!'

But Trude would not let her go. 'Do you mean to say that none of them took your fancy? Maybe there was one who was particularly nice or interesting?' Alice shook her head again: 'Trude . . . You are incorrigible.'

*

LESSONS BEGAN THE next morning. Conrad Ansorge announced that in future pupils should attend the class for three consecutive days each month. Every student then had half an hour of his attention to work on their chosen pieces with him.

Alice loved to listen to the others playing and to think about the master's comments. From the first bar in the morning until the end of the day she remained fully alert and observed what was going on around her.

It did not escape her notice that after an hour and a half Ansorge ordered a pause and left the Academy. Alice watched him from the window as he crossed the road and, without further ado, disappeared into a restaurant. He repeated the process at midday and after his return Ansorge was far less attentive than he had been at the start of the day. And he smelled of alcohol. In the afternoon he disappeared for a third time, after which it was clear that his ability to concentrate was yet further impaired.

Next day, when the drawing-up of a timetable was proposed, Alice put her hand up: 'I would be very happy, as the youngest member of the class, if I could always play first.' Ansorge agreed and for the next three years Alice had the privilege of opening the monthly course and playing to her teacher, who – at that early hour – was sober and able to follow what she was doing.

After six months, Conrad Ansorge gave out the names of those who would give the first masterclass concert. No matter how hard Alice worked, she was always critical of her performances. In her opinion at least half the students merited a chance to perform in the concert, but she was only really certain about one of them, the Hungarian Jenö Kalicz. Alice admired his ability from the start, and she liked his amiably reserved style and she found his accent funny.

The first time they spoke she had to laugh out loud. 'Alice why you make these dangerous leaps with the fingers?' he asked her. She needed to think for a moment about what he meant before she realized that he meant her fingering and had confused 'dangerous' with 'unusual'. Since then they had often discussed music together.

Jenö Kalicz was one of the six elected and so was Alice. After Conrad Ansorge called out the names, she ran home and began practising straightaway. There was just a week before the concert and in the intervening time her mother had to force food down her. The evening before the concert, she practised solidy, refusing to take a single break.

The German Academy of Music's first public concert was held at the beginning of March 1921. It was a success, not only for the Academy and Conrad Ansorge but also for the youngest pianist. Of all the pieces played it was Alice's interpretation of the Schumann *Abegg Variations* which left the most profound impression. The *Prager Tageblatt* wrote the next day: 'the prize for the evening goes to Alice Herz'.

*

ALICE HAD BEEN aware for a long time that the family piano was not up to the demands imposed by the masterclass. Sofie Herz and her two brothers had played on it as a child and she had brought the old instrument with her from Iglau as part of her dowry. A Prague piano tuner had made it clear to the Herz parents that the repair of the piano would be expensive and that it would be wise to buy a new one. But there was no money.

Alice, ever resourceful, found a way out of her predicament. At fourteen she had begun to teach a fellow piano student. Now she made the decision to allocate three afternoons a week to piano teaching so that she could save enough money for the new piano. In her precise calculations she totted up how many pupils she needed in order to be able to raise the necessary sum within nine months.

With characteristic strength of will she set out her plans. Her pupils were scattered throughout Prague, but she travelled the long distances on foot. When the time came the dealer took the old piano away and paid her a small sum towards its replacement: it was not new, but it had a much better tone.

Now, when she could, she practised for six to eight hours every day, and even the few hours left were given over to music. Alice was as happy to do her theory as she was to sing in the Academy choir, which relied on her alto voice. In the afternoons it was her turn to teach and several times a week she went to concerts, as the Academy regularly had free tickets to hand out. Standing or sitting right at the back Alice was able to hear the guest performances of many internationally known artists at the German or Czech theatres.

In her second year Alice was once again allowed to play in the spring concert. A week before her appearance the thirty-eight-year-old Wilhelm Backhaus gave a performance in Prague. One of the most famous pianists of his day, he played Beethoven's Sonata in A flat major, Op. 110 which Alice had been practising for weeks. Her fellow students advised her that it would be better to switch to another work at the last minute than beg comparisons with Backhaus. Alice, however, would not be put off, and obtained a ticket to the Backhaus concert – and she refused to change her interpretation of the piece.

As it was she withstood the baptism of fire. The day after her performance the Czech newspaper *Bohemia* wrote: 'We have heard this sonata twice this week, once from Backhaus and the second time from Alice Herz. Her interpretation measured up to that of her famous rival.'

The *Prager Tagblatt* not only praised Alice's progress which 'has revealed itself in this past year to be the most surprising [of all the students in her class]' but went on to say that beside her

'powerfully mature technical assurance' above all she possessed
'fire and passion, the will to create and an understanding rare in
someone of her years'. A year before 'there was scarcely the seed
of this to be seen, but now it has become a potent flower'.[1]

It was obvious that Conrad Ansorge shared the critics' views.
For a year he had been convinced that along with Jenö Kalicz his
youngest pupil would be playing in the final Masterclass Concert.

*

'ALICE WE ARE happy today and we should today clink glasses.'

After the concert a lively group of masterclass students repaired
to the Castle to celebrate. Jenö Kalicz ordered a bottle of Mosel,
but before he could pour some into Alice's glass, she put her
hand over it: 'Please may I have a glass of water?' she said, 'still
water.'

'But Alica,' Jenö exclaimed in his usual theatrical way, 'why
watair?'

'Just have a look at our Ansorge,' Alice said with a laugh. 'At
9 a.m. he is a real master, as he is still sober. At eleven he is tipsy
and inattentive. By midday he is useless either as a pianist or a
teacher. Don't you think playing the piano and drinking alcohol
are mutually exclusive?'

'My dear Alica,' Jenö said warmly, in the same melting tone
he had employed in the past two years and which for two years
had failed to have the desired effect, 'you lo-ove Schumann, and
Schumann lo-oved Clara and drink. Schumann was a regular, he
drank dai-aily in Leipzig's Café Baum. Go-ood wine, contented
mood, wonderful feelings!'

Alice liked a good joke, but when it was about drink she had
no sense of humour: 'Jenö, if you don't watch out you'll go the
same way as Ansorge!'

Later that evening Alice was glad that Jenö walked her home
through the dark streets. He pranced merrily backwards and
forwards between the road and the pavement and – as he thought
there was a chance this might have relaxed her – he turned towards

Alice and tried to bring down the proverbial wall she had erected around herself.

'Alica, you lo-ove Schumann, I lo-ove Schumann. You lo-ove playing piano. I lo-ove playing piano.' Alice agreed with a smile. 'Alica, I like you. You like me, not true?'

A shadow crossed Alice's face: 'Jenö, I am eighteen. How old are you?'

'Oh, my Alica, when Clara was sixteen years old, Robert Schumann was twenty-six. You know how the story finishes.'

They had now reached the door of her parents' home in Bĕlsky Street. The lovesick Jenö carefully stooped over Alice to take her in his arms. She was painfully moved but fought him off.

'Alica' started up, 'music . . .'

'I know,' Alice said in a slightly harsher tone than she intended: 'Music is love and love is music.'

Jenö had repeated this phrase countless times in the past two years – and he still wasn't thinking of giving up.

'Alica, I have read everything about Clara and Robert, and I will tell you now a secret from Clara's diary. These are the words: 'When you kissed me for the first time, I thought I was near to fainting, it went dark before my eyes, the light that should have guided us I could scarcely see.'²

Alice took a step backwards, and Jenö pursued her a last time: 'Alica, music is love and love is music. I like you, you like me, yes?' Alice nodded. 'Why I might not give Hungarian kiss?'

'Good night Jenö,' was Alice's response, and she disappeared through the door of her house.

Even in their final year Alice refused to go out alone with Jenö. But because Alice made him believe that an age difference of nearly ten years had to be a reason for caution, they arrived at a relaxed friendship, which would unite them from henceforth. In reality, however, Alice's heart was already beating for another man, who was not ten, but fifteen years older than she was.

*

LOOKING AT IT objectively, Rudolf Kraus was not a particularly attractive man. He was small and undistinguished, but Alice felt drawn to him. Everything about him fascinated her, everything he represented was in some way extraordinary – his charm and sophistication; his jaunty step; his boldness and sporting ability. She found even the way he puffed on a cigarette so individual that she tried taking up smoking herself, though she soon stopped – for good. There was no question about it: Alice was in love for the first time in her life.

The two had come together by chance. Rudolf's father was a dentist and he treated the entire Herz family including Alice, who was a friend of his daughter's. At weekends Trude Kraus often invited a large body of friends round. The Krauses' flat was next door to the surgery on the first floor of a solid patrician house in the City Park, not far from the German National Theatre. Alice used to sound out the pieces she was studying on Trude's guests.

On one such occasion she met Trude's elder brother Rudolf. He was a dentist like his father, already thirty-three years old and in the process of taking over his father's practice; and he was looking for a woman to marry.

The modest perfection with which Alice played immediately entranced Rudolf Kraus, even though, as he was the first to admit, he knew very little about classical piano music. The first time he took her out, Alice noticed, however, that he was naturally musical. He followed the current custom of taking her to a coffee house which turned into an intimate dance hall in the evenings.

When Rudolf asked Alice to dance, she was over the moon. She had never danced so passionately before, nor had she ever been so physically close to a man. To the strains of a piano and violin duet she danced waltzes, foxtrots and tangos late into the night.

From then on Rudolf and Alice went out together twice a week, usually ending the evening in that same coffee house. By that time it was often so late that there were just one or two couples left, and Rudolf and Alice had the dance-floor to themselves. Even when they paid calls on one another at home, sooner or later they began to dance. Rudolf had given Alice a recording of tango music which made distorted crackling noises when it was played on the gramophone but it moved her nonetheless.

With her success in the masterclass and her love for Rudolf, 1922 was the happiest year of her life so far. She might even have forgotten Jenö Kalicz's stubborn attempts on her virtue had it not been for an almost fateful encounter between the two of them at the final concert of the masterclass.

When Conrad Ansorge informed the four finalists (the others were Gisela Kettner and Margarete Lössl) that they had to put together a half-hour programme and that, if possible, it should focus on one composer and one of his most important works, Alice made it plain that she would play Schumann's *Fantasy* in C major, Op. 17. She had always loved Schumann's work above all others. The piece she had chosen was a sonata-like composition, but a freer, sensitively improvised piece, the three movements of which Schumann had so individually fashioned from a variation, a rondo and a song.

'Alica, I have correct heard, you will play the *Fantasy* in C major?' Jenö asked her one day. 'Do you know how piece written?'

As Alice did not reply, Jenö went on: 'Schumann wrote this Fantasy in 1836, when he was very much in love and in despair over Clara Wieck. Father had tried to prevent love. Clara had to travel, Schumann must stay at home. C Major Fantasy is infinite longing, infinite despair. How do you want to play Fantasy without one time kissing Jenö Kalicz?'

Alice laughed but Jenö would not be put off.

'How you play love piece without knowledge of love?'

'I am full of love: love of music, love of nature, love of mankind,' said Alice. 'Therefore I shall play this piece with a feeling of . . . love.'

But Jenö shook his head pensively and revealed to her that he was also going to play the *Fantasy* in C major. 'But I will not think of nature and of a lot of people. I will think of just one person, and who will win?'

On the night of the concert, the atmosphere was tense. All the members of the masterclass were present together with many students from the German Academy and their relations. It was now almost commonplace that Alice would finish her programme with bravura. There was no criticism raised about her technique, and she also produced a convincing interpretation of the *Fantasy*, but in Jenö Kalicz's music there was something that stood out, the sound of longing, something unfulfilled and despairing which gripped the audience.

The jury deliberated after the concert. Finally Conrad Ansorge walked on to the podium. 'It is the opinion of the jury that all four contestants have allowed us to hear outstanding performances, but our verdict is unanimous for all that. We will now ask this evening's winner to come forward and play his programme once more . . . on the Förster grand; applause now for Jenö Kalicz from Hungary.'

Jenö bowed low to the audience, and allowed his gaze to wander through the auditorium to Alice, and he stared at her for an instant. Then he sat down at the grand piano, his grand piano. This time Alice sensed that he was playing for her alone. And he played exceptionally beautifully, in dark, transfigured tonal colours, bringing out Schumann's intended mood of elegiac abandonment with something approaching genius. Even Alice, otherwise so optimistic, was gripped by a strange feeling of apprehension which left no room for what was actually the natural emotion of that moment: disappointment.

'You can only love one man,' she thought. 'And I don't love Jenö, I love Rudolf.'

*

AT THE BEGINNING of December 1922 much of the country was already covered by snow, and Alice and Rudolf went off to the Riesengebirge with a few friends. They took rooms in a hotel for a long weekend. They skied by day and danced by night.

They might have had a romantic time had it not been for the

fact that with every day there was an ever-growing tension between the couple, and Rudolf was getting increasingly impatient. He was a man in his prime and just dancing, however intoxicating, was not enough to satisfy him, but Alice would not respond to Rudolf's attempts to achieve greater intimacy other than with a quick kiss on the lips. The nineteen-year-old believed there was no question of giving yourself to a man before marriage.

Neither of them said anything about it at the time, but when the couple came to return to Prague their mood was troubled. A horse-drawn sleigh took Alice and Rudolf to the station and as time was short before the departure of the train, the coachman drove his horses at the gallop. Alice never understood why the horses then suddenly bolted, but the sleigh turned over and all three of them – Alice, Rudolf and the coachman – were thrown from their seats. Alice escaped with slight bruises, but Rudolf broke his right hand and could not practise for weeks.

From that moment onwards Rudolf was announced less and less at Alice's home. After weeks of uncertainty, she learned that he had developed an interest in another woman. Alice knew her: she was often to be seen at the Krauses' flat. She was not just a lot taller, but, in Alice's imagination, she was a lot more attractive and more flirtatious than she was. When Alice received the news of Rudolf's impending marriage she was devastated: 'How shall I live without him?' It didn't help that Rudolf's mother had told her privately how much she had been looking forward to having Alice as a daughter-in-law. Rudolf Kraus remained the great, unfulfilled love of Alice's life.

As had been so often the case, music provided Alice with the great support she needed, and all the more so when she learned that Alexander Zemlinsky was going to conduct Mahler's Eighth Symphony again and that he was going to bring in the student choir from the Academy. Over a decade before, at the beginning of his career as a conductor in Prague, he had put on the Symphony of a Thousand. It had been a dazzling success. Alice threw herself body and soul into the rehearsals. She had already finished with the masterclass, but she was continuing to study theory at the Academy. In the first few weeks Zemlinsky decided that the participating choirs should be divided. Two weeks before the performance the conductor took over the rehearsals himself, with a choir of over 200 male and female voices.

It was not just Gustav Mahler's music but also Zemlinsky's personality, capability and dedication which inspired Alice. On the other hand she had to get used to Zemlinsky's appearance: 'a caricature of a man, chinless, small and pop-eyed', was how Alma Mahler-Werfel described him, but his powerful expression led people to forget his unfortunate physical appearance. 'He always sings every phrase and performs every scene with theatrical expressiveness, the intensity and power of his characterization, his fullness of spirit, and the humour and the splendour of his colouration is astonishing,' was the view of Louis Laber.[3] The writer Franz Werfel (who subsequently married Mahler's widow, Alma, in 1929) also commented: 'As soon as he straightens his back and lifts his baton, it is music; the spark leaps into the air with the upbeat.'[4] And Igor Stravinsky, who was famously mean with praise, nonetheless characterized him as the 'most universal conductor' he had ever met.[5] Hardly surprising then that Mahler entrusted Zemlinsky with the first performances of two of his symphonies.

Under Zemlinksy's direction the choirs excelled, each member forging their voices together in powerful harmony. The performance in May 1923 of the Eighth Symphony was an outstanding success, so much so that two weeks later they had to repeat it. For Alice Herz it would be one of the most impressive musical experiences of her life.

*

IN THE WINTER of 1923, on Václav Štěpán's recommendation, Alice was offered the chance to make her debut playing Chopin's Piano Concerto in E minor with the Czech Philharmonic the following year. It was a great honour, but a monumental undertaking for such a young performer. Alice was still only twenty.

For months Alice prepared for the concert. For months she clung to more or less the same strict ritual – the ritual she kept all her life – while continuing to give piano lessons to her pupils. Perhaps it was for the best that her private life was now so uneventful. When she heard that not only was Rudolf Kraus happily married but that the couple were already expecting a child, she bravely dealt with the melancholy in her soul. She had seen nothing of the rather too amorous Jenö Kalicz; rumour had it that he was drinking more than ever.

But as she calmly prepared for the concert, suddenly there was bad news. A few days before Alice's debut, Moriz Rosenthal was due to appear with the German Philharmonic, and it was announced that he would be playing the Chopin's Piano Concerto in E minor, the same piece that Alice herself was studying so diligently. Rosenthal's explosive technique had led many to consider him to be the greatest virtuoso of his time. Alice knew the stories. He would apparently practise certain particularly difficult passages and sequences of notes for days on end, 'while at the same time some weighty tome of history or philosophy lay open at the desk and he was totally absorbed by its most difficult intellectual content'.[6] Alice's well-meaning friends were quick to advise her: there was no question about it – she had to choose another concerto. Why not the Schumann, which she had mastered so well already? Why tempt comparisons with the world's best at the beginning of your career? Why be so determined as to want the impossible?

Her friends and advisers clearly knew little about Alice's character and her ambitions. She was not planning to become famous. She played from passion and sheer joy in music – it was her door to paradise. She was not seeking direct comparisons with the maestro, but when fate decreed she was ready to rise to the challenge

'We will see if he works as hard as me,' said Alice to Irma with a hint of innocent cheek. Alice genuinely wanted to know how Rosenthal had become world famous. She found her answer in the Academy library: 'Moriz Rosenthal, born 18 December 1862 in Lemberg,' she read in Walter Niemann's *Klavierlexikon*: 'since 1890 (after his American tour), a phenomenal technician of world renown and a superbly intellectual musician.'[7] And in his book, *Meister des Klaviers*, Niemann wrote: 'With Busoni and Godowsky, Rosenthal fights for the title of the greatest technician of our time . . . not just the best from the point of view of technique, he is the master who in his purpose, goal and conception embodies the modern piano virtuoso at his purest.'[8]

In two respects Rosenthal was the born Chopin interpreter: firstly he was a pupil of Carl Mikuli, who for seven years was himself a pupil of Chopin, and secondly Rosenthal was influenced by his long-standing master Franz Liszt who could relay first-hand the views and playing style of his friend Chopin.

'I will play as well as I can,' she told herself. 'Not better, but not any worse.'

The moment for Rosenthal's guest performance came. He was as supreme as ever, true to Niemann's appraisal: 'Whoever hears Rosenthal play the adagio from a Chopin concerto today will take home the joyful certainty that he must be once and for all the undisputed and most eminent performer among piano virtuosi from the point of view of technique, and at the same time a truly great and soulful artist.'[9]

Alice's performance with the Czech Philharmonic came a few days later. Seats in the hall were completely sold out. Václav Štěpán and his wife Ilonka, Alice's parents and her sisters Irma and Mizzi were in the audience. Alice knew that Irma was attending with mixed emotions. There is no doubt that her elder sister felt pride and satisfaction; she had been Alice's first teacher and constant champion. She had taken Alice to Štěpán and given her the courage to leave the Lyceum and apply to the Academy. But mixed with the pride was envy, bitterness and dissatisfaction;

dissatisfaction with her own fate. Hadn't the great Zemlinsky smiled on her astonishing abilities at the piano? And what had she done with her talent? Why was she not giving concerts as Alice was doing? She had never been allowed a public performance. Felix Weltsch had an explanation for his wife's chronic discontent: 'It is my understanding that the constant excitement in which she lives is the problem, coupled with her constantly seething anger against mankind and the jealousy she bears every one or thing she can conceive of, from the meanest to the grand; not to mention disfavour, mistrust and incessant personal woes. Then comes practice, to which she applies herself with a mad determination.'[10]

But her determination to practise eventually slackened off and Irma finally gave up playing the piano. According to her long-suffering husband, 'Even if she is musical and has good taste, the bottom line is that she has no real feel for art. She plays the piano wonderfully, but she is self-obsessed. She spills her soul out on to the keys and fails to appreciate the work of art. The work is a means to express herself, or rather, her own unhappiness. That is what it was like before. She has long since given up playing the piano, as she has realized that she cannot "perform".'[11]

However tense Alice must have been on the evening of her debut, she gave no indication of it to the audience. She sat on the stage with a radiant smile on her face which gave the impression that she was not worried. Beside the great concert grand she looked delicate and fragile, and yet she was fired up with energy and conscious of her goal. The next day the *Prager Abendzeitung* recorded the 'unusually loud applause'[12] from the critical Prague public. The Czech paper *Česke Slova* admired 'Sureness, her brilliant technique in some passages and quite particular ability at bringing out the piano's finer tonal nuances.'[13] The *Prager Abendblatt* also praised Alice for 'the beautiful way she overcame the technical difficulties', going on to say: 'The tight composition of this difficult work comes to a natural flourish in the second movement and in the third breaks out into a mass of light-hearted trills. In the hands of this young virtuoso, a pupil of Ansorge's and

Štěpán's, it becomes brilliant and tender; she fetches up each motif with delicate force, and reveals the whole, exciting freshness of her youth.'[14]

The most respected of all the German-language papers in the city, with a Europe-wide reputation, was the *Prager Tageblatt*, which was more than content to compare Alice with her illustrious predecessor:

> An emerging talent on this scale has muddied the waters around Rosenthal's performance a few days ago. Alice Herz would not to be swayed from making her own interpretation and it has to be said of her that in the warmth of her sensitivity and the intimacy of her expression she surpassed her famous colleague. Also the sparkling clarity of her technique, which grew with the orchestra but retained her personal voice, made you sit up and listen. It announces a promising future for this young artist, who has already won considerable acclaim.[15]

Alice was exhausted when she stood up for the ovation, and for a fraction of a second she searched among the sea of faces for the figure of Rudolf Kraus, then just as quickly she put the thought away again. Her destiny was not to dance tangos, but to play the piano.

One of the first people who came to her after the concert to congratulate her was her teacher. 'Words fail me Alice. It was wonderful,' said Václav Štěpán. However, he had one small criticism, which remained with Alice for years. 'Nothing and no one is perfect, Alice! You forgot to shake the conductor's hand to thank him!'

*

IT WAS THE first day of the Christmas holiday in 1924. Alice was on leave until the New Year, she had nothing planned and had promised her mother that she would relax. She thumbed through the latest issue of *Selbstwehr* (Self Defence) which her brother-in-law Felix Weltsch had brought round. The Zionist periodical had been founded in 1907 and claimed to be an 'independent Jewish weekly' for the 'whole of Bohemia's Jewry'. It was a 'declaration of war against all that was rotten, half-hearted and lazy about the Jews'.[16] Felix had been its editor since 1919 and consequently had become well known in Prague.

'A call for you Alice,' Friedrich Herz called from the ground floor. Telephones had become part of everyday life and Friedrich Herz had been one of the first in the Seventh District to have one installed. The set stood in the director's office still, as Friedrich had decided that having one in his private apartment was an unnecessary luxury.

Alice ran down the stairs and picked up the receiver. The quiet voice at the other end belonged to Mr Klemperer, her friend Daisy's father. 'Something terrible has happened.' It came out in gulps. 'Daisy died yesterday. Quite suddenly.' Alice dropped the telephone and like a madwoman she ran out of the room and up the stairs. She didn't listen to her father who called out: 'For God's sake what has happened?'

Upstairs Alice collapsed. She was shaking all over.

'Daisy is dead,' she whispered between tears. And then over and over again 'Daisy, you have not died . . .'

When her mother came into the drawing room, Alice was crouched unconscious on the floor.

'Friedrich,' Sofie Herz called out to her husband in horror, but he had been standing next to her for a while. Together, they carried Alice to her bed.

The doctor diagnosed some sort of herpes attack. As a result of the shock her immune system had broken down. For two weeks Alice lay in a darkened room, lost to the world.

FIVE

Marriage

'I have married him, me!'

'GIGI, CAN YOU HEAR ME? Neither illness nor death takes us to paradise. It is only music.'

Alice opened her eyes. The face looking down on her had a comforting smile. Without taking her eyes off her friend, Trude reached for a cloth and dipped it into the dish of water on the bedside table.

'What day is it today?' Alice's voice sounded lifeless. Trude squeezed out the cloth and carefully dabbed the sweat from Alice's feverish brow. Earlier that day the family doctor had welcomed her back to life. His line, 'we have been very worried about you,' was still ringing in her ears.

'It is the seventh of January 1925,' Trude answered 'and you have been asleep for two weeks.' She sat down on the edge of the bed and grasped Alice's hand. The two friends looked at one another tenderly for a long while.

Trude hesitated before speaking again. 'You suddenly collapsed. I am so happy that . . .'

'Is Daisy really . . .' whispered Alice. Trude took a deep breath. She could hardly bear the pain.

'Go ahead and cry Alice,' said Trude, and she herself allowed the tears to roll down her cheeks. 'It was . . . very quick . . . just two days of high fever . . . inflammation of the lungs . . . no pain.'

It was less than three weeks since the four inseparable girls – Alice, Mizzi, Daisy and Trude – had last met and played music together. Daisy had been relaxed and happy and she had, like so many times before, infected the others with her mood.

'And now . . . gone.' Alice stared into the void.

'I was so terribly worried about you. I am so happy that you . . .' Trude said once more.

For two weeks she hadn't dared visit Alice. For a fortnight the same thoughts had been going through her head: whether there was any cause for her collapse other than Daisy's death? Whether things had been bad for Alice for some time, and that she had not noticed? Was it the disappointment over Rudolf Kraus? Or was physical exhaustion after weeks of practising Chopin's E minor Concerto the reason that Alice had become ill?

Trude had always found Alice so confident and strong. Was that just a facade? Was she in fact a much more fragile person than her outward demeanour would give her credit for? Had her friends been too little concerned about Alice because she was always interested in others, because she was always happy and always saw the best in everyone, and because she seemed always to know what she wanted?

'Do you know Leopold has written to me?' said Trude. Trude enjoyed a deep friendship (and a correspondence) with Leopold Sommer, a young man from Prague who had been living and working in Hamburg for a year.

'I'd like to read you his letter, Alice,' said Trude. 'He consoled me in such a lovely way. May I?'

Alice pressed Trude's hand. The letter's message made a lasting impression on Alice.

Dear Trude,

Why is it that someone must leave this world so early, before they have really even begun to live, while another might live to be eighty or more. Why do we have no reasonable answers to these questions? Or is it ridiculous to even ask them?

When I read your letter and sat down impotently for a while, I picked up all your old letters and read each and every one of them again. From your descriptions it was so clear what a likeable and joyful person Daisy had been. You often spoke of your excursions to the theatre and the concert halls and the countless books that you had read and discussed. And with what enthusiasm you played music together, Sunday after Sunday.

Think about it then: what profound pleasure a person can derive from a piece of music or reading a novel. Is that not an extraordinary gift, to be able to live with such intensity and with every experience become more mature and more humane? There is no question that Daisy belonged to the elect: people who are capable of the deepest relationships between human beings and yet who are endowed with the capacity to experience the miracle of true friendship.

Trude read reverently and emphatically as if she had read out the words many times before.

Does not the secret of true life lie entirely in the here and now and in the intense exchange of experiences with one's fellow man as well as in the consciousness of the daily miracle of this world? If we look at it like this, then your Daisy lived a fulfilled, happy and richly endowed life.

Using some unknown source of strength, Alice sat up in her bed so that she might hear better. With every sentence she became more excited and more alert.

Her death was not terrible for her, but for all those who were close to her. And for those people it should be the reason to examine their own lives. Don't more and more people measure the worth of their lives by outward success alone? And do they not define themselves by their money and their recognition by others? Don't we have to learn to see our

*lives in perspective again, to make the goal of life to render
people happy and keeping in step with those who are near to
us?*

*For me too the death of a girl whom I know only from
your descriptions is a challenge to re-examine my life; and a
warning not to give in to the transient, but to strive for an
alert and proper life day in, day out . . .*

'I have to meet him, Trude,' Alice burst out.

Her friend did not venture to ask why. Alice then spoke again:
'Did you say how old he was? He's going to be twenty? He must
be an extraordinary person to have so much wisdom and insight at
that age.'

Alice's unexpected recovery was so delightful to Trude that
she replied: 'You will meet him, Alice, he often comes to visit
his parents in Prague, and when he does he always calls on me.
Perhaps he'll even come in the spring, or in the summer at the
latest.'

*

LEOPOLD SOMMER'S LETTER performed a miracle: just a week
later Alice had recovered to such a degree that she was able to
resume her daily routine. She sat at the piano for four hours before
lunch, and in the afternoons she gave lessons. At twenty-one she
had not only made a name for herself in Prague, she was also
greatly in demand as a teacher. Although she lived with her parents
she was becoming financially independent.

Her evenings were spent almost without exception in the
standing areas of theatres and concert halls. What a pleasure it was
for her to sit at the top of the steps which led down to the seats
and to follow the music with the score in her hand. Quite rightly
Prague was recognized as one of the leading cultural metropolises
of Europe and musicians from all over the world were drawn to it.

After the performances Alice and her friends liked to wander
up to the castle. There were some evenings when she was lost in

thought, on others she was in a more jocular mood as she looked down on Prague and thought of all the reasons she loved her native city. Alice adored these walks at any time of year, but particularly on starlit winter nights when the fresh snow crunched underfoot. Her thoughts often turned to Leopold Sommer and his letter. Trude had to tell her what news she had of Leopold and bring a picture of her friend. The photograph showed a slender, carefully dressed young man, who gazed gently at the lens in a pleasant manner. Alice was all the more determined: 'I must meet him!'

It was a summer afternoon in 1925 when Alice met Leopold Sommer for the first time. Her heart beat loudly and once again she had to admit that she was susceptible to outward appearances. She was immediately struck by Leopold's impeccable teeth and elegant hands. On the other hand, at about 1.65m., slim and well-proportioned, Alice thought him rather small.

Trude Hutter had invited a large party of friends to a concert at her house, to be given by Alice. Knowing that Leopold would be there, Alice reflected long and hard over which piece would be fitting for their long-awaited meeting. She finally opted for Beethoven's Sonata in A flat major, Op. 110, which he had written in the spring of 1822 while he was completing his *Missa Solemnis*. Alice loved this late work and she played the jubilant finale with convincing panache, as if, Trude later recalled, she were pulling the notes out of the inner recesses of her soul. There was no question about it – she had reached Leopold's too.

When the two of them spoke towards the end of the afternoon it seemed as if they had known one another for years. Leopold was as enthusiastic as he was knowledgeable about art, and as precise in his judgement on music as he was in the visual arts. He had hesitated for a while about turning his passion for the violin into a profession, but he was put off by the thought of possibly demeaning his favourite recreation – making music – into his livelihood, and thereby making it merely a duty. He was also a realist and realized he did not have the talent to be a successful professional musician. So, together with his best friend, Robert Sachsel, he had

Sofie Schulz, c. 1883

Friedrich Herz, c. 1890

Georg and Irma Herz, c. 1897

Paul Herz, 1901

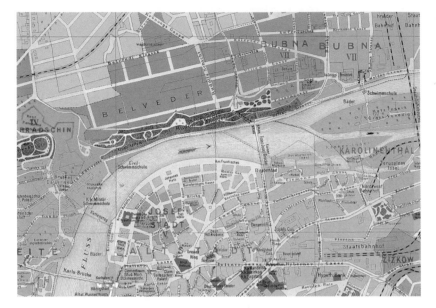

Map of Prague

The swimming school

Alice (on the left)
and Mizzi, with their friend
Helene Weiskopf, in 1911

Mizzi and Alice in 1916

Felix Weltsch

Franz Kafka

Max Brod

Oskar Baum

With schoolfriends, around 1917. Mizzi is second from the left, Trude Hutter, fourth, Daisy Klemperer, fifth and Alice is on the far right

Alice, aged twenty, with her great love, Rudolf Kraus

The brilliant pianist in 1924, the year of her debut performance
of Chopin's Piano Concerto in E minor.

Alice rehearsing at the
Music Academy

Alice with her baby
nephew, Heinz Adler,
in 1929

Dr Ernst Boronow in 1930

Leopold Sommer in 1935

Alice and Leopold
outside the registry
office after their
wedding

Alice's parents-in-law,
around 1933

opted for a school of commerce and an office-bound future. The two men had also chosen to take their first professional steps together. As they both spoke excellent French and English, they had joined a British import-export business in Hamburg.

Leopold Sommer was a reserved, modest man who was difficult to gauge at first sight: only those who took the trouble to get to know him saw how deeply he thought about things, and experienced his multi-faceted sense of humour. As if it were the most obvious thing in the world, he made a date to see Alice the next day. Until his departure for Hamburg, hardly twenty-four hours passed without the two of them seeing one another, and in the months until they met again they exchanged regular letters.

Ten days together in the autumn confirmed their feelings for one another. Leopold thought up a particularly lovely pretext to introduce Alice to his parents, brothers and sisters: he organized a musical soirée at his home. Before the break he played with his quartet; after the break, Alice came on stage.

From the beginning Alice felt at home in the Sommer household. Mother and Father Sommer exuded what many would characterize as 'aristocratic nobility' and received their visitors with such warm-hearted hospitality that everyone who came close to them felt special. His father, like Leopold, was pleasantly reserved. His mother was the outward-going person, with her infectiously open and refreshing manner. Alice kept in contact with her when Leopold was working in Hamburg; for even if it was not yet official she already felt part of the family. The weeks and months between meetings were a time of waiting and anticipation, even if Alice was by no means idle.

Alice was concerned about how she should develop her talents, and had been since she had finished at the Music Academy. Under Conrad Ansorge's directions, Beethoven had absorbed most of her time, followed by Schubert, Schumann and Chopin, but she had been limited to the nineteenth-century tradition. Václav Štěpán, who remained her most important adviser in musical matters, now made sure that she took an interest in modern Czech composers, above all Vítěslav Novák, Otakar Ostrčil and Josef Suk. The young pianist, however, was curious about the most recent developments in the world of music coming from Vienna, influenced by composers such as Arnold Schönberg and Alban Berg.

Alice listened to modern works whenever she could. In recent years, she had often witnessed the behaviour of conservative Prague audiences, who enthusiastically applauded the traditional works in the first half of the concert and then demonstratively left the concert hall in protest against the unfamiliar noises in the second half.

Alice had been struck by the experience of going to a performance given by the Polish pianist Eduard (or Edward as he was later known) Steuermann, who lived in Vienna. Among other things he played Schönberg's Chamber Symphony in a version made for solo piano. Steuermann had studied first with Busoni and then with his friend Schönberg. He was seen as a 'phenomenal musical talent', belonging to the much talked-about school of expressionism which, under the influence of war and upheaval, wanted to 'revolutionize piano music'.[1] Alice was struck as much as by his modern vision as his technical skill.

When Steuermann proposed the idea of teaching the younger generation of Prague pianists and suggested coming from Vienna to Prague once a month to give lessons, Alice seized the opportunity. Not only did Alice want to look at the modern repetoire for piano, she wanted to study a classical masterpiece with him so that she could compare Steuermann's version with Ansorge's, and a nineteenth-century view with one from her own time. Alice chose Beethoven's *Appassionata*.

After only a few hours of lessons Alice began to have doubts. Steuermann showed no real interest in his pupil, his teaching style was impersonal and uninspiring and Alice had the suspicion that he only came to Prague for the money. A year's lessons had been arranged and paid for in advance so Alice tried to make the best of the situation. At the end of the year, she was happy to see the back of Steuermann and even told him of her disappointment, though as a rule she went out of her way to avoid argument. Eduard Steuermann was shocked by what she said and told her: 'I simply don't know what you *want*! I taught you the *Appassionata* and now you are complaining.'

*

BETWEEN 1927 AND 1931 Alice spent a fortnight at least two or three times a year in Gräfenberg (Lázně Jeseník), in the Sudetenland, where her twin sister Mizzi now lived. It was a spa famous for the the quality of its air and waters near Freiwaldau (Jeseník) in the Reichenstein Mountains.

In 1927 Mizzi had married a Prague doctor, Emil Adler, who was three years older than herself. Up to then she had run an office for a leading firm of lawyers in the city, and done their accounts. Like Irma before her, she had celebrated her wedding with a modest ceremony and invited only her closest family to the registry office.

Even before their wedding, Emil, aged only twenty-six, had been appointed senior physician at the renowned Priessnitz Sanatorium in Gräfenberg. It was an ideal setting for invalids who could have all their neuroses looked after at the same time. In many mild cases, they could venture forth during the day, recover from exhaustion and see their time in the sanatorium as little more than a rest cure.

Alice arrived in Gräfenberg in the summer of 1927. She had promised she would visit soon at Mizzi's wedding. She was reconciled to the idea of not having a piano for the duration of her stay as Mizzi and Emil had more of an affinity with literature than music. As it turned out, their pretty house and garden in the middle of the doctors' compound was so small that it had not occurred to them to install a piano. In fact, despite the sisters' closeness, there was not even room for Alice, so Emil Adler reserved a room in the sanatorium for his sister-in-law.

Alice's fear that she would not be able to play music in

Gräfenberg proved unfounded. Right next to her room, in the common-room of the sanatorium, there was a decent grand piano and Mizzi had planned a small concert for doctors and patients for the evening of her arrival. She knew that Alice would not object, quite the contrary, and that she had a particularly wide repertoire which she could play by heart. Alice sat down at the piano and immediately put a programme together. After that, whenever she was in Gräfenberg, her weekly piano concert became a regular fixture. Even the first concert was so popular that Alice had to play three encores. When she finally closed the lid of the piano, she was approached by a man with deep-set, expressive eyes and a strikingly high forehead. Next to the girlish Alice he looked almost like her father although he was only a little older than her.

'Dr Ernst Boronow, music lover and dentist from Breslau (Wrocław). It is a pleasure.' Alice was astonished by his praise of the concert; she had seldom come across someone with such a deep love of piano music. At around ten that night Boronow asked Alice if she would play Smetana's *Czech Dances* once again, which was warmly applauded by the guests as well.

Over the next few days Boronow was always in the room when Alice came in to practise. He sat patiently there for hours, never interrupting her playing and even when Alice was not playing he stayed close to her. She enjoyed talking to him, and she did not refuse his invitations to go for long walks in the neighbourhood. When Alice discovered that Boronow did not work as a dentist at the sanatorium, but had been a frequent patient there, she was surprised. Boronow was so humorous, so spiritual, so well educated and so cultivated. However, since it was patently obvious he was harmless, it did not worry Alice in the slightest.

Another regular visitor to the Gräfenberg concerts was Joseph Reinhold, the director of the sanatorium. He had a passion for romantic piano music. He always reserved a seat for himself in the middle of the front row and regularly fell into a state of rapture when Alice brought the concert to a close with a piece by Chopin,

Schumann or Schubert and would carry on clapping long after the others had fallen silent. Reinhold would not ask for an encore so he carried on clapping until Alice played another piece – sometimes two.

Soon Alice was giving concerts at Reinhold's villa as well as at the sanatorium. Whenever she arrived at Gräfenberg, Reinhold would meet her to arrange the traditional house concert before a small, hand-picked audience. When the guests arrived there was a fire burning in the grate and they were treated to a impressive meal before the concert. Armchairs were then arranged around the elegant saloon in such a way that they could be close to the Steinway grand and have an unimpeded view of both the pianist and the hearth. Joseph Reinhold also offered his guests the chance to make requests and every one of them wanted to hear his or her favourites.

At one of the first of these fireside concerts Alice met the painter and graphic artist Emil Orlik, who had been living in Berlin since 1905 and was a regular guest at the Priessnitz Sanatorium.

Alice had heard of Orlik long before meeting him. A close friend of the poet Rainer Maria Rilke, he was the most successful Prague Jewish artist of his time. Moreover, Irma was a friend of Orlik's sister and was happy to recount the adventurer's innumerable journeys, which had taken him as far as Japan by the turn of the century. His experiences influenced the works he did for the Vienna Secession, to which he belonged from 1899 to 1905.

The artist was almost sixty when Alice met him, but he looked older. Orlik had grown up the son of a tailor in the ghetto and spoke fluent German, but with a heavy Czech accent which he never lost. No evening passed in his company without him recounting some amusing episode from his exciting life. His humour was basic, occasionally coarse and sometimes sarcastic, but he always carried his audience with him.

On one particularly amusing evening around the fire, besides Emil Orlik and the master of the house, Mizzi and Emil Adler and

Ernst Boronow were also present. A mischievous argument soon sprang up as to what pieces should be performed and which should be played first.

Joseph Reinhold was an indulgent host, and let his colleague Adler have first choice as he only rarely attended the concerts. Reinhold respected him as a highly cultured intellectual for whom reason always took precedence over sentiment. He was therefore not surprised that Adler decided straightaway that he wanted to hear Bach's Partita in B flat major. Boronow immediately protested. It was unthinkable to begin an evening by the fire with Bach: they had all come for a romantic evening, not an intellectual one. Besides this he wanted to sound off yet again about his view that Bach was overrated – 'when you come down to it he only wrote sewing-machine music.' He insisted on the first movement of Beethoven's *Appassionata*.

Reinhold found it hard to come to terms with such conflict at his cosy soirée and suggested a compromise, the first movement of the great Schubert sonata instead of the Beethoven. Emil Orlik, however, was enjoying the argument and provoked his fellow guests by proposing that the concert should begin with an atonal piece by Schönberg. All those present were all mature enough to appreciate the modern age, surely?

The guests' protestations amused not just Orlik but Alice too. Before he was able to put the guests in a bad mood she seized the initiative and played Schumann's *Fantasy* in C major. At last everyone was happy, except Orlik, who thought they were all too happy. He proceeded to torment them until late into the evening with a highly skilful imitation of how the distinguished gentlemen had listened to the *Fantasy*: Joseph Reinhold constantly wiping the tears from his eyes; Emil Adler, with the reflective features of the intellectual, benevolently nodding as a sign of his appreciation; Ernst Boronow, torn between being emotionally moved and physically tired, tossed this way and that, and finally shedding a few tears.

When Orlik wasn't busy teasing the others, he would take up

pencil and paper and begin to sketch. Even as a little boy in the ghetto he had caricatured the principal characters of Prague's old town with an astonishing gift of observation and wit. In Gräfenberg he made numerous drawings. To thank her for the music she played in the time they spent together, Orlik gave Alice engravings of Wilhelm Furtwängler, Igor Stravinsky and her master, Conrad Ansorge and, two years before his death in 1932, he gave Alice a sketch he had made of her, too.

*

FROM THEIR FIRST meeting a deep friendship developed between Alice Herz and Ernst Boronow. Boronow sent Alice frequent letters recounting his experiences of concerts in Breslau and she was happy to answer him because he always provoked fresh thoughts on music. When she left Gräfenberg after her first trip in 1927 he invited her to come and visit him as soon as possible in Breslau, so that she could meet his family and because he wanted to organize a concert for her in the great hall of the Breslau piano manufacturer's Scheitmayer.

In his letters to Alice he wrote of the negotiations with Scheitmayer and the support he sought from the city's Jewish community. Boronow also wrote about his wife and their two children and his work, so that when Alice paid her first visit to Breslau in the late autumn of 1927, she felt she was among close friends. Boronow's wife was not only an attentive host but she was gifted musically and played the piano well. Her brother, a successful conductor, suggested to Alice just after she arrived that both of them practise a duet and perform it at home. They played together all week long in the Boronows' house.

Alice's concert in the Scheitmayer Room was a great success, for both Alice and Ernst Boronow. He had volunteered to sell the remaining tickets because he wanted Alice to have the pleasure of performing to a full house. The evening began with Beethoven's 32 Variations in C minor, Op. 80, followed by Novák's *Eroica* Sonata, Op. 24, which was enthusiastically received by most of those present despite the fact they had little experience of modern Czech music. Alice had won over her audience by the time she reached the interval, so in the second half she rewarded her receptive listeners with a few Chopin pieces. Before she left she had to promise Boronow that she would warn him in good time if she were going to play the Novák concerto again in public.

Every year Alice gave three solo concerts in Prague. She frequently performed in the Mozarteum, an intimate space that held around 250 people. On 6 March 1928 Alice performed an almost identical programme to the one she gave in Breslau. Mizzi, who was eight months pregnant with her son Heinz, was sitting next to Ernst Boronow in the hall. This time the critic's chair was reserved for Felix Weltsch's old friend Max Brod, who reviewed the concert in the *Prager Tageblatt*:

> Every piece that she plays is interesting and seizes you with its particular, masculine lack of sentimentality and individualism . . . The technical perfection reveals the performer's particular class in the great crescendos of Novák's *Eroica* Sonata or in the stupendously difficult Prokofiev Toccata. There was a whole series of modern compositions in the second half. Alice Herz masters the tonal richness of the impressionists as well as she plays classics like Beethoven. She gives an example of this when she plays Debussy's *l'Ile joyeuse* with its evocation of a Parisian street singer. A Ravel Capriccio was striking in its strange guitar effects that made it seem blown in by the wind. The concert was as rich as it was beautiful and provoked the liveliest applause from every corner of the auditorium.

The day after the concert Ernst Boronow visited Alice at her parents' home. When he saw the simple wooden chair on which Alice sat to practise the piano he went straight to the Prague branch of the Sudeten German piano manufacturer Förster and ordered the latest adjustable, comfortably upholstered piano stool. It was one of many presents he was to give Alice over the next few years.

Boronow admired Alice and her art and, knowing that she had already decided that Leopold Sommer was the man she loved, was content with the role of avuncular friend and patron. He was loyal to her for three decades and for three decades Alice returned his loyalty.

*

AFTER MIZZI MOVED to Gräfenberg, only Paul and Alice were still living with their parents. Paul was approaching thirty and had abandoned his studies at the Military Academy. He had been a disappointing if well-loved cadet, and it was said that to the delight of the other cadets and his superior officers he played his violin every night in the mess. His father was worried that Paul lacked both the organizational ability and the ambition to take over the business after his death. His mother was also concerned that Paul showed no sign of giving up his bachelor life and his occasional lady friends were never brought home. From time to time, but a good deal less than when they were children, Paul and Alice found the time to play music together.

Of all the five children, it was Alice who worried the most about her parents. Both had health problems. Her mother suffered from a thrombosis and lived in constant fear of a life-threatening clot. Her father had had heart disease for more than two decades and had survived a heart attack before Alice was born. Although Friedrich never spoke to Alice about it, she was aware that he was regularly overcome by severe chest pain and shortness of breath. He was examined many times and each time the diagnosis was the same – his heart. Even as a child Alice had often lain awake at night and listened to her father suffering from an angina attack. Her mother regularly tried to alleviate the problem by alternatively applying hot and cold compresses. Later Alice took over and her anxieties about him often kept her awake at night.

At the end of the 1920s her father's health took a marked turn for the worse. One morning in 1930 he came out of the office and into the drawing-room at an unusual time. Alice was sitting at the piano and at first paid no attention to him, but when he went silently past her and hurried on into his bedroom with unusually heavy footsteps she leaped up and ran after him.

Friedrich Herz was pale. His mouth was open and his hands were pulling at his collar as if he was fighting off someone who was trying to strangle him. He collapsed on the bed. Alice tried to speak to her father, but he did not react. Terrified, she called out for her mother. Sofie Herz rushed from the kitchen and stared at her husband as if she had been preparing for his death for years, a death like this.

'Fetch the doctor.' She said no more that day.

Alice ran out in a panic, but the family doctor's door – which she normally entered unannounced – was locked, with a temporary sign on it directing patients to another doctor a few streets away for the duration of his holidays. Alice ran there, too.

'Please come at once, my father has just died.' Alice begged. The doctor clearly did not view a dead man as a patient. He said he had no time to come at the moment and tried to persuade Alice to leave, throwing her into a rage in the process.

'You say you are a doctor.' In shock, she screamed louder than she intended, but it had the desired effect. The doctor accompanied her to Bělsky Street, but there was of course nothing he could do.

At the funeral Alice walked arm in arm with her mother directly behind the coffin. Mizzi and Emil Adler had broken off their holiday in Sicily and hurried back to Prague. Alice had telegraphed the couple in Palermo and Mizzi received the news early in the morning: it confirmed a dream from which she had just awoken, in which her father had been dying.

Many more people came to the cemetery than Alice expected. Leopold Sommer stood beside her at her father's grave and his presence gave her great strength and comfort. Besides friends and relations all his workers and former colleagues from his firm wanted to say goodbye, the faithful Franta included. Clearly Alice's father was an exceptionally well-loved man, something about which she never gave the slightest thought.

It was this view of her father which preoccupied Alice after his death, far more than her grief at his passing. For so many years Alice had accepted her mother's opinion that one could hardly speak to such an uneducated man, and certainly not about art or culture. But through caring for him, she had been given the chance of getting to know her father properly at last and she realized that she had more to thank him for than she had ever known. Had he not been an example to her with his industry, his conscientiousness and his readiness to apply himself one hundred per cent? Were the two of them not very similar – much more similar than she and her mother?

Before the year was out Sofie Herz had sold the factory buildings, but she hung on to the living quarters for the time being. Paul still clung to his mother's apron strings and lived from day to day without much purpose except for his daily game of chess in the coffee house. Georg did not come to his father's funeral, nor afterwards. The family received fragments of news of his existence as a gambler and drinker in Vienna. He finally returned home in 1931, already a very sick man, and died soon after in a Prague hospital. He was not even forty-five years old.

*

LEOPOLD SOMMER NOW came more regularly to Prague than before. As often as he could afford it he got on the night train and spent the weekend with Alice. They played music in her parents' home, they invited friends round, they went to concerts; it was very clear they belonged together.

They had never spoken of marriage, but Alice was aware that Leopold had been looking for a job in Prague for some time. He obviously believed that he could only ask for Alice's hand if he had taken the necessary steps to provide for a family. It did not worry Alice much that it was not easy to find a job as a merchant. Her income as a piano teacher was sufficient to feed a family.

After a particularly lovely evening at a concert, the couple were standing on the ramparts of the castle look down on the sea of lights that was Prague, when all at once Alice blurted out:

'Look, I have something important to say to you.'

'What is it?' asked Leopold.

'We are going to get married this year,' she said.

Leopold was thrilled that Alice had the courage to speak so plainly.

'And you are completely sure?'

'Absolutely sure,' said Alice with a laugh, 'and we will spend our honeymoon in Hamburg. I want to see what you have been up to all these years.'

In the spring of 1931 the banns were published and Alice finally married her Leopold. After the ceremony in the registry office there was a small wedding party in her mother's flat. As in Mizzi's case, it was composed entirely of members of the family. Before they sat down to dinner there was a small concert in which the newly-weds themselves played. Their obvious empathy and *joie de vivre* brought even Sofie Herz out of her shell. She was happy with her daughter's choice and thought her son-in-law a wise man. After the meal she broke the habit of a lifetime and got up to speak. She handed Alice an envelope with a cheque in it and recounted in a few sentences how she and Friedrich had put the money aside some years ago for Alice's dowry. It was sufficient to furnish the three-room flat that the couple had rented at number one Sternberggasse right next to the exhibition hall, about half way between her mother's flat and Irma's home.

Leopold's parents also surprised them with a generous present. They knew that Alice had been saving up for years for a Förster grand and now they gave her the money she needed.

The imposing grand piano immediately became the heart of the Sommer residence. The married couple not only used the largest room to eat in but also for Leopold's chamber music evenings. Double doors led through to the piano, and another set of double doors led to the bedroom. Next to the small kitchen there was a cubbyhole, hardly big enough for the maid Anitschka to sleep in.

Alice lived her life to the full. At first marriage did not alter her everyday routine. She practised before lunch and taught in the afternoon. In the middle of the day she often looked after her mother and two nights a week she and Leopold had dinner with his parents. On Saturday nights there was music-making in the Sternberggasse and sometimes Rudolf Kraus and his wife came, for Alice, not without some effort on her part, remained on good terms with her first great love. On the remaining evenings Alice and Leopold often went to a concert or to the theatre.

Like Leopold, Alice was receptive to the ideas of the avant-garde. When Emil František Burian opened Theatre D 34 in 1933, they quickly became regulars. Leopold particularly loved Burian's cabaret-style one-man shows. The funnier Burian's comic attacks became, the more uncontrolled was Leopold's inimitable, almost girlish, high-pitched, squeaky laugh. The man from Pilsen had made his name as a composer, actor and director and he, too, was pleased when he heard that Leopold was in the audience, as his bursts of laughter were infectious, inspiring not only the rest of the audience but also the performer himself to greater comic heights.

One morning in March 1933, practising as she did every morning, Alice suddenly leaped from the piano stool, ran to her desk and started frantically searching for a letter from the secretary of the Vienna International Piano Competition. The competition had been announced months previously. It was to be the greatest piano competition of all time. The judges would be the best-known pianists and conductors of the period: men like Wilhelm Backhaus, Alfred Cortot, Emil Sauer, Moriz Rosenthal and Felix Weingartner, and competitors had to be under thirty.

Alice's thirtieth birthday was imminent, but she was still just eligible and had immediately applied, with a programme of three pieces that she had already mastered so well that she would not actually have to practise them for the competition. The organizers wanted a 'classical' work; she chose the Beethoven Opus 110 Sonata – a 'romantic' piece, Schumann's Symphonic Studies; and a modern work – for which she opted for Bohuslav Martinů's *Three*

Dances. She wanted to see for once in her life if her talent was up to international standards.

She finally located the letter and quickly opened it. A glance at the date and her watch confirmed her worst fears: at that precise moment she should have been sitting at the piano in Vienna playing Beethoven. Alarmed, she sped off to the post office and sent a telegram to the organizers of the competition, excusing herself for the lapse and asking if she might play the next day. She then took the next train to Vienna, where her mother's brother met her at the station.

Otto Schulz had lived in Vienna for years. Before the war, Alice and the rest of her family had often visited their uncle there and Otto also frequently visited them in Prague. He was horrified that she had forgotten the date of the competition, since he thought it was a great opportunity for her. The organizers, on the other hand, were more understanding. Alice was allowed to perform her Beethoven piece the next day, and her uncle, himself a capable piano player, was in the audience, watching nervously.

Alice played extremely well and went through to the second round. It was then she suffered her second misfortune. She was supposed to play Schumann's Seventh Symphonic Study, but instead she began the Eighth. The piercing sound of the jury bell interrupted her playing.

She was sure she had ruined her chances of playing in the final but, despite this mistake, she played the eighth variation majestically and was praised by the jury. Out of roughly 200 entrants, just 25 got through to the last round, including Alice. She did not win the competition, but the finalist's diploma she received was proof of an important achievement.

When she told Ernst Boronow he persuaded her to write to Arthur Schnabel in Berlin and to ask for a chance to play for him. Schnabel was then the most successful pianist in the world and since 1925 had led a masterclass at the State Music Academy. Two weeks later Alice received an answer from Schnabel: she was to come.

Alice travelled to Germany with mixed feelings. Hers was a musical world and she was largely immune to political events. Although the National Socialists had been in power for a few months and Jews had been banned from public life since 1 April 1933, Alice was less concerned about the boycott of Jewish businesses than by her anxieties about Schnabel. Her Berlin friends had warned her about him, not least that he was notorious for charging exorbitant fees.

Her general disquiet was not helped by her first impressions of Artur Schnabel. She remembers him being 'unaesthetic and squat' and felt that she couldn't breathe when she played for him. Throughout her performance he was wreathed in smoke, sucking in an unappetizing way on the cigar he kept turning in his fingers.

Alice played pieces from the classical, romantic and modern schools. After about half an hour Schnabel stopped her and said, with great goodwill: 'I cannot add anything to what you have already learned, either from a technical point of view or a musical one.'

He then named the price for this praise and Alice had difficulty keeping her feelings under control. She would have to teach for an entire month to pay his fee, but she controlled herself from making any comment and simply pressed the money into his hand, said the briefest of farewells and left his flat as fast as her legs could carry her.

Years later, by which time she could finally laugh about it, her friend Edith Kraus, a former masterclass student of Schnabel's, told her that shortly after his meeting with Alice he had emigrated to England and had possibly even bought his ticket before she played for him.

*

ALICE FIRST MET Edith Kraus on a damp and murky afternoon in March 1937. It had alternately rained and snowed all night, so the streets were covered in grey slush. Fortunately Alice had no need to venture out, but when there was a ring at the door and she opened it, she saw an enormous dog, whose naturally white coat was dripping wet.

'Yes, well who are you then?'

'This is Pucki,' said the well-dressed young woman who was holding the dog's lead.

'Putzi?' Alice asked in disbelief.

'No, Pucki.'

'Oh thank God,' Alice laughed, 'Putzi is what I call my husband.'

The visitor laughed, too, then introduced herself to Alice.

'I am Edith Kraus. Can we come in?'

Alice had heard of Edith Kraus, a pianist who had been born in Vienna and grew up in Carlsbad. As a five-year-old she had been able to play by ear all the pieces that her seven-year-old sister was practising; at eleven she had played Mozart's Piano Concerto in C minor with the Carlsbad Orchestra. The conductor Leo Blech was so impressed by her talent that he wrote to Franz Schreker, the then director of the Berlin School of Music: 'I think I would be doing you and your school a favour by sending you this great talent.' Edith started studying the piano at the Berlin School of Music at the age of thirteen. A year later she became the youngest member of Schnabel's masterclass.

'I have come to ask you a favour,' Edith said. In the meantime Pucki had sniffed out every corner and taken a sudden interest in the chaise longue. As Edith watched appalled, the dog leaped up on to the seat which Alice had just had covered in a beautiful pale fabric. Alice could hardly have been more relaxed about the muddy paw marks: 'He has a good nose,' she beamed. 'He knows the best place to sit.'

Edith quickly recovered her composure and explained the reason for her visit. 'I am preparing the Martinů dances,' she said. She had had no dealings with Czech contemporary composers before and was at a loss to interpret them. 'I wondered if you could play them for me. You have mastered them so well.'

Alice played them for her and by the evening, when Edith left, they were firm friends. Edith's visits became a regular occurrence and soon the two young women were inseparable, playing duets together for the sheer pleasure of it. There was never any thought of rivalry between the two friends. Their love of music was too great, and it was forever opening new horizons for them. Their meeting was to mark the beginning of the greatest friendship of Alice's life.

*

NOT LONG AFTER Alice met Edith, she and Leopold managed to get tickets for one of a series of concerts given by the Kolisch Quartet, from Vienna. The evening was later jokingly dubbed 'the night of the dancing handbag'. Alice was six months pregnant and before the concert began she put her leather evening bag on her stomach. As soon as the music began the baby started to kick in rhythm to the music and the handbag to jump, so that it 'danced' on her stomach.

'Leopold, look!' Alice whispered, and her husband, equally astonished, stared at the 'dancing bag'. Was the child going to be as musical as the mother?

Even before their wedding the Sommers had agreed that they wanted to have three children. They were not in a hurry, however, but Alice was now thirty-four, which at the time was considered rather old to have your first child. Given that she was also small and delicate, Leopold was worried that there might be complications and asked the advice of his brother-in-law, Felix Mautner, who was a doctor. Mautner suggested that the child should be born in a clinic, rather than at home, which was then the usual practice. Felix was at pains to secure a bed in the private clinic of a prestigious gynaecologist (he himself specialized in orthopaedics) but he wanted to be present at the birth.

At 10 a.m. on 21 June 1937 he took Alice into the delivery room. In order to pass the time between labour pains, he told her light-hearted anecdotes from his professional life. An amusing and extrovert man, Mautner was a master of the punchline. He called

Alice and Leopold the family's 'little idiots', while Leopold's brother and his wife were dubbed 'the big idiots'. The difference in size between the two brothers was a mere two centimetres. Felix happily told his stories all day long and succeeded in making not only Alice laugh, but also the nurses and the midwife too. The mood in the delivery room was so relaxed that the doctor kept popping in for a laugh. The birth itself was, as expected, complicated and in the end Felix Mautner had to help with the forceps. But finally, at about seven in the evening, Alice Sommer delivered a baby boy. When she saw the tiny creature for the first time she forgot her pains. There were still pieces of caul clinging to the infant's body; didn't people call that 'lucky skin'? Didn't old wives say that children born with this could expect particularly good fortune in life? And wasn't it also a good omen that he was born on Midsummer's Day?

When the door to her room opened and a colourful bouquet advanced towards her, Alice was already half asleep. Suddenly Leopold's beaming face emerged from behind the flowers and the nurse brought in the baby, swaddled in blankets and placed him in Leopold's arms. As exhausted as his mother, the baby went to sleep peaceably, but not before Alice and Leopold had named him Stephan, after her piano teacher, Václav Štěpán.

SIX

Occupation

'They came like vultures ...'

'HE LIED', ALICE THOUGHT, as she knocked the snow from her shoulders and opened the door. 'What is this man going to get up to next?'

She had scarcely entered the hall when Stephan ran into her arms. Alice knelt down on the floor, closed her eyes and pressed her child to her bosom for a particularly long time. She was tired. For two nights she had hardly slept.

'Door, Maminko,' said Stephan, who unwrapped himself from his mother's embrace and gave the door to the flat a kick. He chuckled as it slammed.

'It is shut,' said Alice with relief. What she had just suffered should remain outside. Worries about Hitler and the future should not be allowed to trouble her family's happiness.

Two hours previously she had hurried into the centre of Prague through the snow, having told the nanny she needed some shopping. This was not in fact true. What she wanted to do was to see with her own eyes what was happening to her home town. It was 16 March 1939. Exactly twenty-four hours had passed since the German army had occupied the city: 'This is the second ethnic German transmitter' began the radio broadcast announcing the invasion.

'The microphone is in the museum gallery on Wenceslaus

Square. The lower half of the square has just filled up with people who are singing songs of joy. German troops have entered the square . . . Everywhere hands are being raised in Hitler salutes. The historic moment has come: 10.40 a.m. on 15 March Adolf Hitler's soldiers have arrived at Wenceslaus Square, the heart of the city.'

This was propaganda. Prague was occupied by artillery, supply troops on motorbikes, army lorries and armoured cars and the Czechoslovak Republic had ceased to exist. The president, Emil Hácha had announced that he had placed the destiny of his country into the Führer's hands. The mist that hung over the city refused to disperse all day.

As Alice reached the Elisabeth Bridge, she heard an unusual noise coming from the centre of the city. Then, as she approached Wenceslaus Square, she saw soldiers everywhere. At the Graben she plunged into the crowd that was being pushed back by the police. She soon had to make space for a German unit wearing grey field coats and steel helmets which came thundering by. There were swastikas hanging from the German House, since the 1870s the meeting place of German associations, and they fluttered elsewhere too. Alice was distraught as she looked back and forth between the soldiers and the people behind the barriers. There were small groups of Germans and Sudeten Germans cheering the German soldiers. Only occasionally did anyone register a whistle of protest, a clenched fist or an attempt to sing the Czech national anthem. Most, however, remained silent, almost apathetic; they had been literally overrun.

Alice now saw that the marching soldiers were only the advance guard. A few moments later motorbikes drove along the Graben escorting a cavalcade of cars. In one open-topped vehicle stood Adolf Hitler, his right arm lifted in a 'German salute', staring blankly at the crowd. 'Where is he looking?' Alice asked herself. Only six months before, after the occupation of the Sudetenland, he had given repeated assurances that he made no claims to the rest of Czechoslovakia.

'He was lying all along. What will he do next?' But the white-

haired old man next to him made Alice even angrier: it was
President Hácha – 'that fascist' – who was raising his arm in
humble submission to 'the Führer'. What treachery it had been,
what humiliation!

Bewildered, Alice started walking home. Suddenly, she felt like
an outsider. Where did she actually belong? She was from Prague
and had grown up in a German world. From her childhood she
had looked up to Germany. It was the land of Goethe and Schiller,
Bach and Beethoven. Now the Germans had overrun her country.
She was not a German . . . or not any more. But was she a Czech,
because she took the Czech side? Or, even though she had never
taken any particular interest in her origins or in Jewish traditions,
was she first and foremost a Jew – a member of a race that provoked as much hatred from the Czechs as from the Germans?

'Come Maminko,' shouted Stephan, distracting his mother
from her thoughts and towards the piano. He hit two keys, gently
but properly, one after the other and then both at the same time.
'Listen Maminko!'

Even when Stephan was only a few weeks old, Alice had
noticed that the baby reacted unusually powerfully to music. Her
hopes had come true. Now, at nearly two, he listened to the music
Alice played with remarkable concentration, rare in one so young.
However, more and more frequently he went to the piano himself
and searched for notes and harmonies. Alice used to put Stephan
on her lap and together they went on a voyage of discovery through
the major and minor keys. Later Alice packed the child and his
nanny off to get some fresh air while she lost herself in her playing.

That night, when Leopold came home, he and Alice sat down
in front of the wireless set and listened as Hitler's foreign minister,
Joachim von Ribbentrop, read out the 'Führer and Reichs Chancel-
lor's Decree for the Protectorate of Bohemia and Moravia': 'The
ethnic German population of the Protectorate will become German
subjects and Reich's citizens according to the Reich Citizenship
Law of 15 September 1935. From now on they will be qualified
by German blood and German honour [. . .] The remaining

inhabitants of Bohemia and Moravia will become subjects of the Bohemian and Moravian Protectorate.'

There was no mention of the sovereignty originally promised to the Czechs and it was crystal clear to Alice and Leopold that the occupying power would discriminate against them as they did the Jews in Germany and the former Austria. Would it be weeks or days before the first anti-Jewish decrees were issued?

Alice was in touch with many of the Jewish artists and intellectuals who had found temporary exile in Prague. They had fled immediately after the Nazis' seizure of power in Germany and the *Anschluss* in March 1938, and many of them were preparing to flee again – to France, to England, even Palestine, the USA or South America.

Alice and Leopold had considered emigrating in 1938 when Hitler had brought the Sudetenland 'home into the Reich', but in the end had decided against it. They tried to be optimistic, telling themselves that 'it would not be so bad', but even Alice, who spent so many hours a day lost in her music, could not hide from the political reality, which from now onwards could only mean bad news for the the Jews under Hitler's influence. The brother of her friend Helene, Franz Carl Weiskopf, had returned from Berlin where he had been the editor-in-chief of the anti-fascist *Volksillustrierte* and had plenty of stories to tell of the National Socialist terror, and Alice's brother-in-law Felix Weltsch had written 'several articles against the new barbarism in Germany' in *Selbstwehr*.[1]

There were compelling circumstances which Alice believed required her to stay in Prague. On the one hand there was Stephan. Could she expect a child so young to make a journey into the unknown? On the other hand, there was her mother. Sofie's medical condition meant that she felt unable to emigrate to a country far away and Alice would not countenance leaving her behind. There was also a a third consideration: lack of funds. A visa for Palestine would cost Alice and Leopold the astronomical sum of around £1,000 sterling a head. Her sisters Mizzi and Irma had both decided to emigrate, but had difficulties raising the money, so the whole family chipped in. Sofie Herz gave both children their inheritances, albeit against her will and only after great arguments. Even Alice had given her sisters part of her savings.

On 14 March 1939, two days before Hitler's triumphant entry into Prague, the Adlers – Mizzi and her husband and their son Heinz, who was almost eleven – and the Weltsches – Irma and Felix and their daughter Ruth, who was now twenty – had set off with all their heavy suitcases for Palestine. Alice and Leopold accompanied them to the railway station to see them off.

*

'ON TUESDAY AT around 9 p.m. we arrived at the Wilson Station, the former Emperor Franz-Joseph Station . . . On platform two we found our train and many of our friends,' Max Brod wrote later.[2] Immediately after the Munich Accords in October 1938, Brod, like Felix Weltsch and a few other like-minded friends and acquaintances had 'decided on emigration to Palestine, which was then under a British mandate'. For Zionists like Weltsch and Brod it had been, as they put it, a 'life's intention' to one day emigrate to the Promised Land.

Yet they still saw no desperate reason to hurry. Hitler had said that with the takeover of the Sudeten German areas he had attained his goal. The French and British governments agreed to the secession; for Paris and London, the carving up of Czechoslovakia was the 'price of freedom'. It was a high price, since Czechoslovakia had lost not only most of its industry in the secession, but also its border defences. The Czechs themselves called it 'treachery' and 'horse-trading'. Before they realized what the consequences of the secession would be, the government ordered total mobilization: a measure that was as fruitless as it was futile.

Edvard Beneš, who had succeeded Masaryk as President of the Republic in 1935, resigned and went into exile in 1938, and Emil Hácha succeeded him in the November. According to Max Brod it was not yet 'life and limb threatening but to all extents and purposes' a shift to the right.[3] In the short term it was not going to get better for the Jews – after five years of National Socialism in Germany he was as certain of this as Felix Weltsch – and it might get worse. The intellectual climate in the so-called Second Czech Republic became increasingly reactionary, and strengthened the resolve of both journalists to leave their homeland. President Hácha had quite clearly modelled his domestic policies on Germany and proved that he could adopt even the Jewish policies of the German Reich. Intellectuals like Weltsch and Brod were particularly at risk.

Hácha issued a decree early in 1939 which proved the final straw for Felix Weltsch. His younger brother-in-law Emil Adler, Mizzi's husband still needed persuading. Mizzi and Heinz had returned to Prague from Gräfenberg in September 1938 before the signing of the Munich Agreement. They had returned for their personal safety. Emil was a man without illusions and realized that similar measures would be introduced against the Jews after the cession of the Czech border regions that had been imposed after the *Anschluss*. But after ten years as principal physician at the Priessnitz Sanatorium he neither would nor could leave at once, and for a while he commuted between Prague and Gräfenberg. At the beginning of January 1939, rumours of expulsion and killings of Czechs, so-called 'Sudeten' Jews and Gypsies in the border regions, forced his hand and he returned to Prague for good.

He arrived in Prague planning to open a private clinic and had rented a floor in an imposing house on the Moldau, which would serve not only for a clinic but was also large enough to accommodate the family. Although he was preoccupied with his plans he saw the many hurdles the authorities had put in his way. As a student he had come into contact with Social Democratic circles and at the German university he was elected president of the social democratic students' organization. This was now clearly held against him.

Then Emil learned that all Germans or German-speaking Czechs who had left the Sudetenland after 1 January 1939 were forbidden to practise their professions in Prague. Now he saw all too clearly that he had no future there. The measure was obviously targeting Jews, for the majority of the Sudeten Germans had rejoiced at the arrival of the *Wehrmacht* and saw no reason to leave.

Emil sought the advice of his brother-in-law. Felix Weltsch knew Palestine: one of his brothers had already been living there for ten years, working as an architect in Haifa, and Felix had been to visit him. Felix encouraged his brother-in-law to emigrate, telling him that Palestine needed good doctors and that they would be received with open arms.

Felix himself had waited for weeks before he received the necessary paperwork for himself and his family. The emigration forms were, according to Max Brod, exactly like Kafka's *Castle*: 'every sort of obstacle was put in your way. Long forms had to be filled out five or ten times. They contained innumerable questions and sub-questions: the number of silver knives and forks you owned and wanted to take with you, was for example of particular interest to those in authority. Just the numbers? No, they wanted to know the precise weight. Finally I had to submit permission to God-knows-how-many different offices to receive their various stamps, and testify that I had paid up all the taxes on my dog, and I had never owned a dog.'⁴ The emigrants were keenly aware that their mother country did not think it a duty to help them to leave the danger zone, but instead, with complacent laziness and pettifogging bureaucracy, spun more new webs in which to entangle them.

Finally, all the forms were completed. The Weltsches, together with the Adlers and Max Brod and his wife Elsa Taussig, were in a party organized by the Prague Zionist Society of around 160 families which would leave Prague on 14 March and would arrive in Romanian Constanza at 1 p.m. on the 17th to catch their ship. The *Bessarabia* would take them via Istanbul, Pireaus, Crete and Alexandria to their goal, their worldly goods having preceded them on the long journey weeks before.

There were huge crowds on the station platform. Hundreds of

people, including many children, friends and relations, were there to say goodbye. The grown-ups were tense and anxious: the news-papers that morning carried reports that President Hácha had gone to Berlin for a meeting with Hitler. As long as they are talking, nothing can happen, said some, while others feared the worst. Scarcely anyone, however, thought it meant they were on the brink of an invasion. Songs were sung in the hurly-burly, turning everyone into one massive family. Alice was sad and moved: when would she see her dear ones again? Most importantly, would she be able to visit Mizzi? 'Write immediately,' she told her twin sister.

At 11 p.m. the train rolled out of the station. When it reached Mährisch-Ostrau (Ostrava) on the Czech-German border at four in the morning, the Germans had already occupied the town and were heading for Prague. Many of the passengers had no idea what was going on, even when they were faced with soldiers wearing swastika armbands. 'It is hard to explain why this sight caused me no fear,' Max Brod said. 'I think it was because I was so tired and had thought I was still dreaming.'

The soldiers had orders to let the train go. Later they learned that it had been touch and go. In Cracow they heard that Prague had been occupied. While the train was still crossing Galicia, members of the Gestapo were forcing their way into the offices of *Selbstwehr*.

'Where is Felix Weltsch?' they demanded.

'He left last night.'

Mizzi's first letters from Jerusalem sounded confident. As a farewell to Europe they had visited the Acropolis and except for Felix Weltsch everyone had been seasick on the way to Palestine. Alice needed good news. Since the occupation of Prague, the city rang with rumours of Hitler's next move. Since Poland had rejected the Führer's demands to hand back Danzig (Gdańsk) and allow the building of motorways and railway lines to connect East Prussia with the Reich, everyone was simply waiting for an attack on Poland. Would Hitler dare to march into Poland? How would the

British react this time? Would they finally hit back? Alice remembered the Great War and thought with horror of the many million dead.

However uncertain the situation was there was no doubt about one thing: the threat to the Jews in the Protectorate. One by one, their rights were stripped away. One sunny late afternoon in 1939 Alice made a spot decision to go swimming, and leave Stephan alone with Leopold. Since her earliest childhood Alice had been passionately fond of swimming. She counted it among her greatest pleasures. Fumbling for her purse outside the swimming pool she spotted a sign written in German and Czech: 'Forbidden to Jews'. Shaken, she retraced her steps.

A few days later, after the German invasion of Poland on 1 September, Britain and France declared war on Nazi Germany. It was war, a war which affected everybody. On 23 September 1939 all Jews were required to hand in their wireless sets within the next few hours. It seemed quite silly, as there were bigger things to worry about, but Alice could not help feeling bitter as she saw Leopold heading off with the object under his arm. She felt cross that she would be cut off from the news from now on, and, even worse, she remembered all the concerts she had given for Radio Prague during the past six years.

The next blow was the decree that Jews might not own telephones any more. One day there was a dialling tone, the next one not. The next step came a few days later. It was a normal working day but Leopold came home before lunch. Alice was sitting at the piano as usual when he walked into the room: 'I have lost my job,' he told her. For several years he had been working for a Prague chemical company. It was well paid and they could afford to run a car. 'More and more people are going to be dismissed.'

In moments like these, Alice was always strong and she tried to comfort Leopold: 'It can't last much longer. And while it does we can live from what I get from teaching the piano.' Alice had risen to become one of the best-known and most sought-after piano teachers in Prague. Even at the age of nineteen she had taught around twenty children a week. Now she could choose her own pupils, who came from the richest families in Prague. She earned a good living.

'Sadly, Alice, it means you too. From now on Jews may not teach non-Jews,' Leopold told her.

'But that cannot be,' Alice cried in fury, 'how will we pay the maids?'

'That's a redundant question, Alice,' Leopold replied, making an effort to sound sarcastic. 'From now on Jews are not allowed to employ Aryan servants.'

Alice's world literally fell apart, the world she had constructed for herself in order to apply equal intensity to practice, teaching and performing, and which was still so important to her.

She had taken on Anitschka, a Czech the same age as herself, immediately after her wedding. She did all the housework. She went shopping, cooked, cleaned and did the washing. A few months after Stephan was born Alice decided to look for a German-speaking nanny. She appointed Marianna, a sixteen-year-old Sudeten German girl. She took Stephan out in the pram, cooked his meals and played with him. Both girls lived in the Sommers' three-room flat. Anitschka set up her camp bed in the kitchen every night, and Marianna slept in the tiny cubbyhole next door. The two girls were treated like members of the family and although it was crowded in the flat there was a warm and pleasant atmosphere.

As they dined together that night Leopold explained the situation that had been forced on them. It was a sad farewell. Anitschka had run the household for eight years. She left the house the next day in tears: 'I have had the happiest time of my life with you.'

*

THE YEARS BETWEEN 1939 and 1942 were a time of farewells for Alice, saying goodbye to possessions, friends and freedom. The fact that bit by bit the Jews were deprived of their material wealth made her angry, but she was not too shaken by it. As early as 21

June 1939, on Stephan's second birthday, all Jews in the Protectorate were ordered to sell their gold, platinum and silver jewellery
and objects to the state-owned agency Hadega; needless to say,
way below their market price. All shares, letters of credit and other
assets had to be handed over to the bank. Cash had to be lodged
in a closed account, from which the owner could only draw out a
limited monthly sum, which was hardly enough to manage on.

So as not to leave themselves with nothing, Alice and Leopold
had kept a few things: three oil paintings, a few carpets, a gold
watch and Alice's valuable necklace. Alice was particularly sad to
say goodbye a pretty ring, set with two diamonds, as it symbolized
the close ties she had with her mother-in-law: 'This ring should
always remind you that you are the most beloved of my children,'
Leopold's mother had told Alice when she gave her the ring shortly
before her marriage to Leopold.

It hit Alice harder that gradually more and more friends and
relations were saying goodbye. In the course of 1939, even Alice's
best friends from school left the country. Helene Weiskopf, whose
brother had inspired her leanings to communism, emigrated with
her third husband to Sweden. Trude Hutter had received a visa to
enter the United States with her husband Paul and their nine-year-
old son Bruno. Out of approximately 120,000 people in the Protectorate of Bohemia and Moravia defined as Jews by the Nuremberg
Laws, 26,000 left the country legally or illegally before the doors
were closed to them in October 1941.

Alice left the house less and less. Freedom of movement for the
Jews had become more and more restricted; there were curfews
and they were not allowed to go to the theatre or concert halls.
Also, until the Jewish Community office finally set up a kindergarten, Alice had to spend all day with Stephan. During this time she
rarely played the piano, but Stephan was determined to try out
various scales with just one finger and to play tunes, often for
hours on end. He particularly enjoyed Bach's Concerto in E minor
which Leopold often played. Stephan patiently sought out the first

note of the concerto. He hit key after key until he got to E. He was beside himself with happiness and called out to his mother: 'Maminka, I have found it!'

One morning when he was about three Stephan dashed out to the piano in his pyjamas to try out the major chords. His hands were still too small to hit all three notes of a chord – the first, third and fifth of a scale – simultaneously. For this reason he needed to play two notes with his left hand and one with his right. He began with C and played the C major chord. Then he went one further and played the D major. Then he repeated it with E, F, G and A. At B major he suddenly became troubled – the chord did not come out in the usual way. Stephen tried once again but still couldn't get it to sound right. Alice was in the kitchen preparing breakfast while he was playing the piano and Leopold was shaving in the bathroom. They dropped what they were doing and hurried into the drawing room to listen to their son properly, Leopold's cheeks still covered in shaving soap.

'That doesn't sound right,' said Stephan and looked at his parents with a puzzled expression. He was right too. In contrast to all the others the B major chord requires going twice as high: that is from D to D sharp and from F to F sharp. Alice and Leopold looked at one another in amazement. That their child had worked it out all by himself showed that he had an extraordinary musical talent.

From then on Stephan often demonstrated to his parents how musical he was. As the Protectorate's Jews were officially banned from using public transport, Alice and Leopold used to put their little son in his pram when they went to other parts of town – although he had long outgrown it. Once a week they visited their new friends whose son, like Stephan, was at the Jewish kindergarten. To do this meant three-quarters of an hour's walk across Prague. The route went past several churches.

At around six they were walking home. Just as they walked past a church, the bells chimed. 'G flat' piped Stephan from his pram, and pointed to the church tower. When the bells rang in the next church: 'D flat', said Stephan decisively.

'Listen to that, Leopold, he has perfect pitch.'

Alice had to rely on pleasures of this sort to make life bearable, as the German occupiers had ever new forms of bullying and humiliation up their sleeves. Part of Stephan's daily routine was a trip to the playground in the Baumgarten Park near their home. He loved it there. He could climb, swing and dig. At the beginning of 1940 the Nazis hung up signs at the entrance to the park: 'Forbidden to Jews!' in both German and Czech. Alice had to make a considerable effort to suppress her anger when she saw the sign for the first time.

'Let's go back Stephan,' she said with sangfroid, 'the park is closed.'

'But I want to,' answered Stephan with childish insistence and squeezed Alice's hand.

'There is sadly nothing I can do, my love.' Alice tried to convince her son: 'Look, the sign, it is written there.'

'What's written there?'

'It's being rebuilt,' Alice lied. 'That means the park is going to be repaired.' She couldn't bring herself to tell her son the truth.

'Go on, stand over there,' she said, rather than taking Stephan away, and she made sure he was standing next to the sign. Alice took out her camera, which she often carried with her when she went out for a walk with Stephan. 'We'll take a picture for papa.'

At the time Leopold Sommer was in Belgium. In the autumn of 1939, he had travelled to Brussels with a friend. The anti-Jewish laws, the ban on employing Jews in the Protectorate and the news of the first deportations (to 'retraining centres', as they called them) had made it only too plain to the Sommers that they and their child were in danger in Prague. Belgium was a neutral country, and at that point it looked as if it would remain neutral for the rest of the war.

A friend had convinced Leopold of the potential of joining

forces and starting up a business dealing in cigarette and sweet machines for stations. Leopold's aim was to bring Alice and Stephan over as soon as he had earned enough money either to offer them security in Belgium or even to emigrate to another country, possibly South America or Palestine. He borrowed the money to start up the business from his mother-in-law. Although Sofie Herz was mistrustful by nature she knew Leopold Sommer was a fundamentally decent and exceptionally reliable man. The sum she lent him was a fortune for her: a large part of the money remaining from the sale of the factory and the inheritance she had given Mizzi and Irma before they emigrated. While Leopold was away Alice rented out the flat in the Sternberggasse and she and Stephan moved back into her mother's flat. The rent, together with her income from the few Jewish pupils she continued to teach, was just about enough to live on.

With every passing month it became more difficult to obtain food and other provisions necessary for everyday life. From September 1939, sugar, tobacco and textiles could no longer be sold to Jews. Ultimately National Socialist civil servants introduced ration cards with the unwieldy name of 'Lebensmittel Bewirtschaftungs Bestimmungen' (literally 'Food management requirements') stamped with the letter 'J', with which, from then on, Jews had to do their shopping. There were coupons for everything. Everything, meant potatoes and bread. Meat, eggs, biscuits, fruit, jam, cheese, milk products, fish, poultry, game, yeast, stone fruits, sauerkraut, onions, garlic, alcoholic drinks, honey or sweets were all forbidden to Jews.

In their despair the Jews turned to their Czech fellow citizens. Some showed themselves ready to help and provided their Jewish neighbours with food, but quite a few of them made money in the process. Alice was glad that the porter's wife in the Sternberggasse had offered to get her 'anything she needed'. It was only later that Alice realized that she was charging precisely twice the market price. It wasn't long before a large part of the hidden Herz and Sommer family money had been used up.

Alice went to Brussels to visit Leopold at least once while he was there. She used the opportunity to give a concert and paid for the journey with the fee. But when she got there, the news was less and less encouraging. Leopold's venture had failed and his mother-in-law's money was lost. Sofie Herz took the loss badly and showered Leopold with accusations. As Alice later said, whether it was down to Leopold's character (his high-mindedness or his lack of fighting spirit) or the arrival of the German army in Belgium on 10 May 1940, Leopold was forced to return to his family as quickly as possible.

*

BY 1942, SOFIE Herz had been living in a Jewish old people's home for some time. For the first time in her life she was away from her family. She had been forced to sell her property in Bělsky Street against her will and for less than its value, and moved just two streets away to Veverka Street to live with her son Paul, but relations between mother and son were not good. Paul had married a Hungarian woman, Mary, who was poorly educated but made up for it with her decisiveness. She was the caretaker of the block of flats they lived in, had left her first husband and child behind in Hungary, and shared Paul's love of gambling and drinking. Sofie could not put up with their lifestyle and moved out, first to stay with Alice for a few weeks, and then to the old people's home. Sofie's opinion of Mary was not influenced by the fact that Paul, like 7,000 other Jews in the Reich, was by virtue of his marriage 'related to Aryans' and thus (at least for the time being) protected from deportation.

Alice visited her mother in the home twice a week and each time found her weaker and more depressed. When she arrived on the morning of 11 July 1942 Sofie could not even manage to say hello to her daughter. Instead, she silently pressed a letter into her hand: it was a deportation order for Theresienstadt (Terezín). Attached was a list of the objects she could take with her in a rucksack

Alice read the letter over and over again. When a transport had taken Edith Kraus away a few days before, Alice was able to console herself that her friend was being drafted into some sort of work. When, a week before, Leopold had accompanied his mother and her sister to the prescribed collection point at the Exhibition Hall, Alice had cried. Her mother-in-law was seventy-five, Leopold's aunt two years older. What sort of work service could they do? And now her own mother: a woman suffering from a thrombosis. Mechanically, she helped her pack.

Alice returned the next day to take her mother to the Exhibition Hall. The enormous building, like a railway station, was only a short distance from the old people's home.

'You will need your coat,' Alice said, even though it was summer outside, and she picked up the heavy object. As she did so, her eyes fell on the yellow star with its black, Hebrew-style letters: 'Jude', which had been neatly sewn onto the left breast. Sofie Herz had always been meticulous with her needlework.

Jews had had to wear the Star of David for nine months, and every time Alice set eyes on it she was incensed. At the beginning of September 1941 all Jews from the age of six had to obey the order to obtain the yellow star and to carry out the regime's instructions 'to handle it carefully and with due attention and while sewing it on to the article of clothing to attach the border at the same time.' No decree upset Alice quite as much as this one. She felt humiliated; chosen from the pack by the Nazis, isolated and outlawed. Her one consolation was that Stephan did not have to wear the star.

Mother and daughter walked down the street arm in arm. Few words passed between them. Alice carried the heavy rucksack and when she reached the collection point she draped it over her mother's shoulders. They stood among hundreds of mostly elderly people who had obeyed the call and fumbled for words of encouragement, which they had difficulty in finding.

It was over seven months since the first trainful of deportees had left Prague for Theresienstadt on 24 November 1941, to be followed by regular transports to the camp; not just from the

Protectorate, but also from Germany, Austria, the so-called Sude-
tengau, Holland, Denmark, Slovakia and Hungary. The timetable
and number of passengers were worked out in Adolf Eichmann's
'Jewish Section' in the Reichssicherheitshauptamt* in Berlin. The
Jewish communities themselves decided who was to go.

Leopold Sommer must have known what lay ahead for his
mother-in-law, since by then he was working for the 'organization'
of the Jewish community.[5] One of his several jobs was to draw up
the lists for deportation. He never spoke to Alice about it and she
never asked him. They both made every effort to protect their son
and she was glad that Leopold was bringing money home regularly,
if only in modest quantities. Nonetheless she constantly tried to
prepare herself for the fact that when Leopold had finished his
work they too would be placed on a transport and deported from
Prague.

In the agonies of parting, Alice quickly pressed her mother
to her breast. Sofie said goodbye in her own way: 'Give my love to
Marianne.'

On 13 July 1942 Sofie Herz was deported to Theresienstadt.
On 19 October the same year she was moved to the extermination
camp at Treblinka. All trace of her has been lost.

*

THE NEXT FEW days were the nadir of Alice's existence. She
was now thirty-nine. She could not sleep or eat; she could not
think clearly. Physically she was allowing herself to go to pieces.
No one could bring her out of the depths of her despair; not her
little boy, not her loving husband, not the trusted family doctor.
Even her beloved piano, which for three decades had been the
source of her strength and confidence, was now standing cold and
silent in the flat. Alice could not play.

* RSHA or Reich Security Main Office was the office created after the amalgam-
ation of the Security Service and the Security Police. It came under the authority of
Heinrich Himmler. From mid-1941 one of its tasks was the technical implementa-
tion of the final solution

Leopold took Alice to see a specialist, but even he could only tell Alice that she needed time. The next day she was wandering aimless and depressed through Prague's streets when suddenly an inner voice spoke to her: 'Practise the 24 Études, they will save you!'

Frédéric Chopin's work was famed as the perfect combination of great virtuosity with musical genius. Alice had always been familiar with it. The ability to master all of the 24 Études and then to perform them on stage was, in her opinion, a proof of the highest achievement and seemed for her personally quite unthinkable. Even the most famous Chopin-interpreter of the twentieth century, Arthur Rubinstein, fought shy of performing them all his life; indeed, as he once let it be known, they struck fear in him.[6] 'In the end I had performed pretty well the entire corpus of Chopin's works, with the exception of the Études. I had played many of them in concerts, but there were some I always left out, because I didn't think I had them right.'[7] In truth many of the Études border on being unplayable.

After graduating from the Music Academy, Alice had gone to a concert performance of the Études with Václav Štěpán. Alice was amazed by the American pianist Alexander Brailowsky's performance, and she was shocked too: 'I will never attain this level,' she told Štěpán. 'I think it would be best to forget about my hoping to become a concert pianist. I should give up straight away.'

Initially Štěpán had reprimanded her; then he appealed to her conscience. It was not important to become the world's best; the most important thing was to be able to play the piano for your own pleasure. 'And when you can make yourself happy, you will make others happy too.'

The 24 Études became the life raft on which – by her own strength and by the power of music – she was able to save herself from the wreck of despair. She began practising immediately and, after a few weeks battling the most difficult cycle ever written for the piano, she had regained her inner balance. Every day she made progress, and with each step forward her strength grew; precisely because she was constantly playing to the limits of her abilities, mental and physical. The circumstances under which Alice played brought her life into danger. A while ago the Jews had been required to hand over their musical instruments and her Förster grand had been confiscated. The SS men, however, had overlooked her piccolo piano and, although such oversights carried the death penalty, Alice had not owned up. It was also strictly forbidden for Jews to play. Even the Sommers' regular house concerts were now illegal.

Every Sunday afternoon Alice and Leopold assembled as many as twenty music-loving friends in their drawing room. Chamber music or the piano was played, or there was singing to a piano accompaniment. Stephan sat with the adults for hours on end, listening open-mouthed. Once, when a newcomer to the circle was introduced to him as 'Gustav' the five-year-old sprang to his feet and asked 'Gustav Mahler?' One of the regular guests at the house concerts was the composer Viktor Ullmann, a pupil of Arnold Schönberg. Alice particularly valued his *savoir-vivre* (he always kissed the ladies' hands) and extraordinary knowledge. On 8 September 1942 Ullmann was deported to Theresienstadt.

Not long after that, when Alice was playing, there was suddenly a loud and sustained banging on the drawing-room ceiling. A German officer and his family had been billeted on the floor above. Had her playing disturbed the officer? Was he going to report her? Alice was so terrified that she didn't play another note all day. Until, that is, the caretaker's wife came up and gave her confidence to sit down at the piano again: 'Herr Herman who lives upstairs from you likes your music so much and he is really sad that you have stopped. He had been led to believe that you had already been sent away.'

*

OVER THE COURSE of the following year, Alice learned all of the 24 Études to concert-performance level. The first one she tackled was the C minor Étude, the so-called 'Revolutionary Study'. The deadly menace and rebellion in the music can easily be explained by the circumstances of its creation. In September 1831, when Chopin wrote it, he must have been in a mood similar to Alice after she bade farewell to her mother. He was living in Stuttgart at the time, and it was there that he learned that the Russian army had suppressed the Warsaw Uprising.

Chopin was as introverted as he was distinguished, and unable to express his feelings except through music. He committed his thoughts about the fate of Warsaw and his family to paper only once, in the diary that musicologists refer to as the 'Stuttgart Sketches':

> Where are you mother, father, my brothers and sisters? Are you still alive? [. . .] The outlying districts have been destroyed, burnt to ashes and Jeannot and Wilus most certainly perished on the barricades. Oh God, are you still there? Will you not avenge us? Have there not been enough outrages? Father, dear Father, are you starving, maybe you cannot buy bread for Mother? My sisters, have the soldiers slaughtered you in their fury? Mother, if you have survived your daughter [Emilia] you must make sure that her grave is not defiled . . . And what is happening to her? Where is the poor girl? Perhaps she is in the hands of the Muscovites? Are they murdering, strangling or killing them? I am idle here. Sometimes I sigh and confide my sighs and despair to my piano. Oh God, destroy this world . . .'

Chopin translated all his passionate rage, his crippling pain, and his burning hopes into music when he wrote the 'Revolutionary Study'. Alice, too, was spurred to attempt the Études by the pain of loss, and by doing so she transformed impotence into protest from the very first. It was her own way of resisting the Nazis and preventing them from depriving her of her dignity.

*

THE TIME CAME when the Sommers were told that on 3 July 1943 Alice, Leopold and Stephan Sommer were 'to leave on a transport'.

The Protectorate was almost 'free of Jews' and the administrative work of the Jewish Community office was to be wound up. Most of its staff would be deported with the Sommers. In the past Leopold had never troubled his wife with details of his work, and certainly he had never mentioned his crises of conscience or the worries that tormented him. When they took him on they made it clear to him that the Jewish Community had no other choice than to follow the dictates of the SS.

At the beginning of June 1943 Leopold had to prepare Alice for deportation. There were various forms to fill in before the journey, and above all the new situation had to be gradually explained to Stephan. He was coming up to his sixth birthday but Alice decided to postpone his party until a 'better time'. She carefully explained to her son that in a few days the family would be giving up their flat and that they would be moving to the ghetto in Theresienstadt. Stephan's subsequent questions and her attempts to answer them only led to increasing doubt.

'Why can't we stay in our flat: it is so nice?' 'Why do all the Jews have to leave Prague?' 'What are Jews anyway?' 'When can we come back?' 'War? Who's at war? When is it finally going to end?'

Alice tried to comfort him. 'We are coming with you, my love. In a few weeks, possibly a few months, we will be able to come home again.'

Alice took infinite pains to involve the child in the preparations for the journey. She made him a special shoulder bag. He helped her to sew the prescribed numbers onto the rucksacks and name-tags onto blankets and articles of clothing. Together they collected utensils, tin knives and forks and three pocket knives. Stephan had his own water bottle, tin bowl, mug and pocket knife, which he found really exciting. A few days in advance they rehearsed the packing of their rucksacks. They had to have a warm blanket each, as well as underwear, a pullover, bed-linen, ear-muffs and gloves and enough food for five days.

'Daddy said that it will only be a few days before our train is ready,' said Alice. Once again she put the rucksack on the scales, unpacked it and packed it again, as there was no question of exceeding the maximum weight.

The night before their deportation neither Alice nor Leopold could sleep, but Stephan slept in the next room until it was time to leave. At four in the morning the caretaker's wife suddenly burst into the flat and scrutinized the few remaining objects of value. She looked straight through Alice and Leopold, then she disappeared again. A short while later she returned followed by several neighbours. They dragged off anything they could move: pictures, carpets and furniture, fighting over the best bits.

'Just look at them Leopold, how like vultures they are,' Alice whispered and held her husband's hand. 'It is unbelievable.'

'I think,' said Leopold in resignation, 'that for them we are already dead.'

SEVEN

Theresienstadt

'Maminko, why can't we go home . . .'

'MY DEAR, GOOD MIRACLE-RABBI; please, please help me, so that my mother comes home this week as normal and is not sent on the transport. Thank you. Your Dita.' This note written in a childish hand was found in 1946 at the opening of a collection box at the grave of the famous Rabbi Löw in the old Prague Jewish Cemetery.[1] It is a reflection of the fear that presaged the receipt of the deportation order. Between October 1941 and March 1945, 46,067 Prague Jews were torn away from their homes.[2]

The 'transport' led the Jews into a sinister future in either the Theresienstadt ghetto or in one of the concentration camps in the east. The word 'transport' was in itself enough to inspire fear, for many of those affected already knew that it stood for the breaking of all previous bonds and the loss of all possessions.

When he had gone to work for the administration of the Jewish Community Organization in 1942, Leopold had known that as soon as he had completed the job he and his family would also be despatched to Theresienstadt. A few weeks before their deportation Otto Zucker, a leading member of the Autonomous Jewish Administration in Theresienstadt, had sent word to Alice that soon after her arrival in the ghetto she could be giving her first piano recital. This consoled her somewhat as they got ready to leave. 'If they can organize concerts there,' Alice said to Leopold, 'it can't be such a terrible place.'

In the early hours of the morning of 5 July 1943 the Sommers had to be ready to stand on parade in the Exhibition Hall, which was guarded by the Czech police. The sky was heavily overcast and it was drizzling. Stephan was too tired to ask questions. He trotted sleepily between his mother and father down the street. The three of them with their heavy rucksacks looked rather like a family setting out for a holiday in the mountains, wearing warm clothes and sensible shoes. The three rucksacks were counted as 'hand luggage'. The main luggage – what they were allowed to ship – had been fetched a week before. Everyone was allowed to take fifty kilos, reckoned as two middle-sized, fully packed suitcases.

The Jewish Community Organization in Prague was obliged to work closely with the Autonomous Jewish Administration in Theresienstadt. Leopold was fully aware of what was waiting for him and his family in the ghetto, and he had told Alice to carefully plan the contents of the 'hand luggage' and to put in absolutely everything that was necessary for survival. He had been informed that for some time the SS had been impounding the main luggage and leaving the prisoners with just their hand luggage.[3] For that reason Leopold, Alice and Stephan's rucksacks were bigger and heavier than most of the other prisoners'.

At the 'assembly point' in the Exhibition Hall Leopold pulled three bits of cardboard threaded with string from his shoulder bag. They bore the transport and prisoner numbers. Around Stephan's neck he hung the card DE 164 and around his own, number DE 162. Alice's number was DE 163.

Alice caught sight of dozens of lavatories separated only by wooden partitions. Here you were obliged to respond to the call of nature outdoors, and in full view of those present. 'That can't be right,' Alice murmured. 'They want to strip us of our dignity.' It was the first shock. The second followed immediately after they entered the building.

The hall was a wooden exhibition shack, gloomy, ramshackle

and unheated. Rain seeped through the ceiling. Alice, Leopold and Stephan stood in a long queue which had formed before the 'registry'. This consisted of five tables behind which officials from the Jewish Community Organization were sitting dealing with bureaucratic formalities under the watchful eyes of SS guards. The men knew Leopold; they had worked together for several months. They all knew that they too would end up being deported to Theresienstadt and were particularly friendly to Alice and her son. But Stephan was not to be distracted either by kind gestures or jokes. He stared rigidly at the people around him who sat or lay dejectedly on straw sacks. Many of them were in tears. The lad pulled his mother close.

'Mama,' he whispered in her ear in German, 'Let's turn round. I want to go home.'

'Stepanku,' Alice replied in Czech, 'I am afraid we can't do that.'

The six-year-old switched effortlessly into Czech. 'Maminka, who is forbidding us from going home?'

Alice discreetly indicated two SS men standing nearby: 'Those ones, there in the black uniforms.'

Stephan would not let go: 'Please ask them why we can't go home we haven't done anything naughty.'

'Stephan, it is forbidden to ask questions. They will punish us straightaway if we ask them.'

Stephan was clearly finding it hard to understand this harsh new world, but how could he?

She embraced him tenderly. 'In a few weeks maybe it will all be over. Until then we must make sure that we never lose one another. And we are going to speak only Czech from now on. Do you hear that Stepanku? That way, at least they won't understand what we're saying.'

They were allocated beds 162, 163 and 164. They would have to spend the next few nights lying on these filthy, worn-out, dusty straw-filled sacks. Leopold, Alice and Stephan took their rucksacks over to their bedding before reporting to the first of the five registry tables when their numbers were called out. There the key to their flat was given the code DE 162–164 and confiscated. This happened comparatively quickly, but at the second table the queue had come to a standstill. This was where permanent food cards were issued and the remainder of the ration cards for potatoes, eggs and soap had to be handed back.[4] Papers were minutely examined to see that they had been filled in correctly and that the coupons had been used as intended. It led to ugly scenes and even beatings. The queue became longer and longer and there was no thought given to the children, the old, the sick or the frail who were standing in line. Alice, Leopold and Stephan queued for over four hours before their cases were dealt with.

At the third table they had to hand in a 'declaration of possessions'. This was an eight-page questionnaire which they had received a week before the date of their transportation and which had to be painstakingly filled out for every member of the family.[5] At this table, too, people waited for hours, as every questionnaire had to be minutely examined. Stephan watched silently as people were made to count out and to hand in their remaining cash. Most of them had little money on them, but a few had wallets filled with notes. One man counted out all his money from a shoe box. The humiliating business had already lasted more than five hours. Stephan occasionally rested on a portable folding chair which Leopold had had the foresight to bring with him. At last, like all the other future residents of the ghetto, it was Alice and Leopold's turn to sign the declaration. All their savings were appropriated in the interests of 'emigration funds'. Needless to say the process had been 'voluntary'.

As the hours dragged by, more and more people lost their tempers. There were anxiety attacks, bouts of hysteria and fits of tears. Stephan felt increasingly insecure and only perked up when the evening meal was served. It was bread and soup; and pretty basic too, but in the circumstances it was more nourishing than Alice had expected.

Exhausted, they lay down on their temporary beds. Stephan fell asleep while Alice was telling him his bedtime story. During the day Alice had been utterly tense and her back hurt, so it made her feel better to stretch out on the straw sack. 'Leopold,' she asked, 'what is going to happen to us?' Instead of answering, he pressed her hand tenderly and looked at her in a pensive way that told her: 'We have to survive; above all else we have to protect our Stephan.'

Suddenly, Alice's head and body started to itch. During the day she had seen cockroaches scurrying about the hall, but the nasty stinging and burning which was now tormenting her had to be down to fleas, bed bugs or lice. The only time Alice had seen such creatures was in natural history books. When she then saw rats scuttling between the straw sacks she began to understand why so many people were reluctant to lay down their heads, and why they preferred to sleep sprawled across them or sit bolt upright. She could see only too clearly the bitter inevitability of her position. She had been delivered into the jaws of the National Socialists.

The next day the humiliation continued. By the early morning they had taken their place in the queue for the fourth table where they were to hand over their valuables: gold coins, jewellery and silver. They were questioned very closely, almost as if they were being cross-examined. Some of the SS squads descended on the straw sacks to check whether the Jews had indeed handed in all their jewellery, money and tobacco. Anyone who tried to hide anything of value was beaten. Some of the SS men seemed to derive real pleasure from hitting their defenceless fellow men. Alice could not distract Stephan who watched these brutal scenes in horror.

Besides the wedding rings that they were allowed to wear, Alice and Leopold had wisely carried no jewellery with them. Even so it was late afternoon before they stood in front of the last table. Here the 'certificate of their citizenship' was cancelled: they had lost their status. Now they had 'ghettoisiert' (committed to the Ghetto) written diagonally across their passports: the formal recognition of the long-premeditated withdrawal of Jews' civil rights.

In the early hours of the third morning the 603 prisoners on transport DE were lined up on parade. They had to stand up straight for hours in the courtyard of the exhibition complex, and several old and sick people collapsed and were carried away on stretchers. At last the order was given to move towards the nearby suburban railway station under the watchful eyes of Czech policemen and members of the SS. In the order of their code numbers, fifty to sixty people at a time were crammed into each of the railway trucks. It was almost three hours before the train was ready to depart.

*

AFTER DAYS OF hanging around in the Prague assembly point the two and a half hour journey to Theresienstadt came as something of a relief. The closer the train got to its destination the prettier the landscape between the Elbe (Labe) and the Eger (Ohře) became. The garrison town lay where the rivers met, just sixty kilometres from Prague, surrounded by moats and two high walls. In 1780 Joseph II had built Theresienstadt in honour of his mother, Maria Theresa, and as a bastion against the Prussians. There were eleven great barracks along the mighty perimeter walls, originally built as accommodation for 3,500 soldiers. Inside the fortress walls three rows of houses were arranged around the central square. These had once been billets for the officers and homes for the civilians who provisioned the town. Its outward perimeter ran to 1,200 metres and it could only be entered through two closely guarded gates. For this reason the deputy Reichs Protector of Bohemia and Moravia, SS-Führer Reinhard Heydrich, believed it was the best place to create a ghetto conveniently close to Prague – and for as little money as possible.[6] In November 1941 he gave orders to the soldiers to vacate the place. Shortly after that the civil population living there was also rehoused.

*

UNTIL JUNE 1943 all transports had stopped at the station in Bohušovice, three kilometres away from Theresienstadt, so that the heavily laden new arrivals had to struggle the rest of the way on foot. Since then a new railway line had been constructed, and Alice, Leopold and Stephan's train brought them directly into the camp.

From the train window Alice could see Czech policemen, who, with their mounted bayonets, inspired fear and horror. The next moment, however, it became clear to her that they were not in danger from them, but rather from the SS. When they were not being observed by the SS, many of the policemen sought to allay the fears of the prisoners and cheer them up. On the other hand an SS man kicked one of the deportees and another repeatedly slapped an old man so often that he collapsed. Most people managed to keep their insecurity and growing fear in check, but faced with the inhumanity of the situation some lost control and began to sob.

On the platform Alice kept repeating to her son that he was not to run away and that he was to keep hold of the rucksack he was carrying on his shoulders. Exhausted by the days and nights at the assembly point, Stephan had slept for the whole journey. Now he sat on his father's rucksack completely bewildered.

'Why don't we go back home?'

Stephan persistently asked the question because he was not satisfied by any of the answers his parents gave him. Alice took him in her arms and whispered: 'Stephan, it will certainly not last long. And then we'll go back home. But until then you must never leave our sides. Do you hear that? Never! You must always hold my hand, always.'

*

THE PRISONERS WERE left standing by the train for two hours before they received the order to march across the tracks: 'Form up in fours!' They went through the 'lock' next, a sort of inspection and reception point which also served to place them in temporary quarantine. It generally took two days for a transport of over 1,000 people to be accommodated in the main camp.

Alice was horrified to see that the contents of their rucksacks were being randomly checked. The Czech gendarmes were looking for medicine, food, torches, candles, matches, lighters, batteries, cosmetics, bedpans, thermos-flasks and chocolate: lifesavers great and small which might render the ghetto more bearable but were banned.[7] Alice tried, but to no avail, to stop them taking not only her vacuum flask, which still contained a little bit of coffee, but also various tubes of toothpaste and pieces of soap. She was fortunately carrying her big water bottle in her handbag and by pure chance neither this nor Leopold's rucksack were inspected.

It was in the 'lock' that questionnaires had to be filled in for the labour exchange. While he was still in Prague, Leopold had heard that being some sort of craftsman might make life in the camp easier, which was why he had trained as a locksmith. Alice gave her profession as 'pianist'. The medical inspections, which came next, were long and drawn out and trying, as were the 'hygenic measures': this was because the ghetto was full to bursting and infections spread like wildfire. On the lock roof, newcomers had to strip to the waist. Without a word of explanation, they were all given injections. Those between the ages of three and sixty-five were inoculated against typhus and children and adolescents between six months and eighteen years also had to be inoculated for diphtheria.[8] A worried Stephan hid in his mother's skirts, but he was quickly grabbed by an orderly while another injected him directly in the chest. The boy screamed with pain and cried bitterly, but before he could recover from the shock he was jabbed again.

The following night was their last together. Like hundreds of their fellow sufferers, Leopold and Alice spent it sitting on a mattress. Stephan slept peacefully, his head in his mother's lap.

*

NEXT DAY, THEIR last in the lock, the new arrivals were assigned to their quarters. Men and women were separated and children over the age of twelve were put in children's homes. Stephan could stay with his mother. Leopold promised to visit as often as he could.

The way from the lock through the streets of Theresienstadt opened Alice's eyes to what she had to expect. Never in her life had she seen so many people in such a small space. With over 44,000 prisoners, people ran here, there and everywhere through the streets as if they had broken out of an ant-heap.[9]

It struck Alice that the houses had been built to an identical design, just like the eleven barracks, solid, gloomy buildings with, as she was soon to learn, badly functioning and wholly overburdened sanitary arrangements. Most of the one-storey buildings were dilapidated with stark, chilly backyards into which the sun never shone.

For the prisoners who had already spent some time in the camp, the arrival of newcomers was an event. They often had prior information as to whom they might expect to see on the next transport from Prague. People lined the streets waiting for acquaintances, friends and relations. Suddenly someone cried out Alice's name loudly. When she turned round she could hardly believe her eyes. It was an old friend whose voice sounded familiar enough, but who looked so thin and exhausted that she was hardly recognizable. The two women quickly exchanged a few words, but Alice did not dare stop. As she walked she spoke to various Prague acquaintances. They all appeared to have aged several years. A cart, borne by inmates and loaded with jute sacks, came towards them, giving off an unpleasant smell which made them feel queasy. Alice gripped her son's hand harder and dragged him on. It was the first time that mother and child had seen men used as beasts of burden. Alice had immediately understood that the men were drawing a hearse.

*

THE ATTIC FLOOR of the barracks was large, gloomy, filthy and airless, as there was not even the tiniest opening in the roof. The only thing that was an indication that people might be lodged here was the number of mattresses on the ground. The prisoner who brought the newcomers to this place comforted Alice. In a few weeks there would be a new space provided for mothers with children. The man knew that since July 1942 the barracks had been full to bursting. By the August all the other houses had been overflowing too, and from September 1942 they had even used stables and corridors to house the prisoners, as well as the window-less attics which were perishingly cold at night and often intoler-ably hot during the day. In the end even the underground casemates of the fort were used to house prisoners. Being put in these was often tantamount to a death sentence, for the rooms were musty, cold and damp.

When Alice and Stephan scaled the many stairs to the attic, the place was already so crammed that they could barely find any room at all. More than a hundred mothers and children had been herded together, with less than one and a half square metres each. The filth and the stench, the miserable whining of the inmates and the bawling of children gave the place a terrible atmosphere. When Stephan needed to relieve himself Alice discovered that the attic had neither latrine nor running water. After a prolonged search Alice eventually found two lavatories in the vast building from which emanated a foul stench. Dozens of people were standing out-side, and no one allowed Stephan to skip the queue: they all had problems of their own.

On the first night Alice could not close her eyes. Stephan was mercifully so tired that he nuzzled up against his mother and took in little of the chaos around him.

The next morning many of the children who had newly arrived fell ill. One of them had arrived with scarlet fever. The boy on the next mattress but one, with whom Stephan had played that after-noon, was struck down with a high temperature. Alice grabbed her son and rushed down the many steps where she asked after Dr Felix Weiss, who had looked after Stephan since he was a baby. She knew from Leopold that the paediatrician had been living in Theresienstadt for some time. After more than two hours she eventually found him and described the situation to him. The unexpected meeting seemed to give Stephan confidence, as he knew the doctor well and liked him. Alice was relieved when the doctor explained that Stephan had survived so many ailments in his first year of life that he was not only immune from many childhood diseases, but scarlet fever as well. If Alice was still worried about his condition, she should go to the doctor's surgery immediately. The surgery, however, was just a dark room with a table, a chair and a shortage of medical instruments.

The next problem came three days later. Alice went down with a fever and she was diagnosed with tonsillitis. The illness mercifully saved Alice from the 'hundreds'. Every new prisoner had to do manual labour for a hundred days before being assigned to the sort of work for which they were qualified.

Stephan felt responsible for his feverish mother and scarcely left her side. Always an observant child, he quickly found out how he could provide her with clean water and nourishment. He went to the kitchen to join the queue. When he reached the front, he told the person serving how ill his mother was. The man was sympathetic and gave him an extra ration.

For six days long Stephan organized special portions. At dawn he fetched the brown broth they called morning coffee and at noon soup, potatoes or, occasionally, a simple pudding. The evening meal was made up of ersatz coffee, sometimes with a little biscuit or gruel. Alice quickly regained her strength. As soon as she could stand up and fetch her own food she went back to the standard ration, which was scarcely adequate.

The prisoners were always hungry. Some of the older inmates told Alice what had happened the previous summer. On 18 September 1942, the overcrowded camp had contained 58,491 prisoners.[10] The few kitchens in the ghetto were capable of dealing with 10,000. Bread was baked too quickly to try to meet demand, but it rapidly went mouldy. Despite this, bread, together with rotten potatoes, was the prisoners' principal form of nourishment. Those performing heavy labours received a double ration at midday and more food all round, at the expense of the old and the sick who had to beg for watery soup or sift through piles of spoiled scraps. The guards' response was brutally practical. In just ten days between 19 and 29 September 1942, more than 10,000 prisoners were transferred to a Polish extermination camp. After that the conditions at Theresienstadt marginally improved.[11] At the time, the remaining prisoners could hardly have imagined that their fellow sufferers had paid with their lives.

*

THE NEWS SOON went round the camp that the well-known and well-loved Prague pianist Alice Herz-Sommer had been admitted. As early as the beginning of her second week, on around 15 July 1943, a member of the 'Free Time Organization' brought her the news that she could give her first concert the following week. Once Alice knew that she would be able to play every day and give a concert once a week her confidence grew. Leopold also brought her some news. She also heard that Leopold had finished his 'hundred'. Every morning he had had to march twelve kilometres from Theresienstadt to the construction site at Leitmeritz (Litoměřice), where the prisoners were building a shooting range for German soldiers. All day long, without a break, he had to shovel earth into a large wheelbarrow and then run and tip it onto an artificial wall before running back to fill the wheelbarrow again.

During the morning march Leopold got to know Rudolf, the twenty-two-year-old son of Ota Freudenfeld, the legendary director of the Jewish Orphanage in Prague. Rudolf told Leopold of the plans to stage Hans Krása's children's opera *Brundibár* in Theresienstadt, which had first been performed at the Orphanage in December 1942, with rehearsals starting at the end of 1941.[12] The conductor Rafael Schächter had originally been in charge of the project, supported by Hans Krása himself. When Krása and Schächter were deported to Theresienstadt in 1942, the set designer František Zelenka took over the staging and Rudolf Freudenfeld directed the small orchestra of piano, violins and percussion. That first performance of the work had, of course, been illegal as music by Jewish composers could no longer be publicly performed. The invited audience of some 150 people had to arrive at the Orphanage discreetly, so as not to excite suspicion from police patrols.

Rudolf and his father Ota, together with some of 'his orphans', had arrived at Theresienstadt at the same time as Alice, Leopold and Stephan. The news that Ota Freudenfeld had arrived spread quickly among the children who had been deported before him. That very day Rafael Schächter (or Rafik, as his friends called him) organized a concert performance of Smetana's *Bartered Bride* in an attic with a piano replacing the orchestra, in honour of the man the children called 'the chief'. That night, too, the idea of performing *Brundibár* was discussed. Rudolf Freudenfeld had managed to smuggle the score into the camp.[13] He knew Alice from her Prague concerts and he had also heard of Stephan's extraordinary musical talent. Would the six-year-old like to audition for a part?

*

WHEN LEOPOLD ARRIVED for his evening visit Stephan was already waiting for him on the stairs.

'Stepanku,' Leopold called out to him with a smile. 'I have a big surprise for you.'

'Where is it then?' Stephan wanted to know and tried to look for it in Leopold's trouser pockets.

'Wait until we have found Maminka.'

In his excitement Stephan hopped like a kangaroo all the way to his mother's sickbed. 'Maminka,' he burst out, 'Dadinka has brought a big surprise with him.'

His father sat down next to Alice, sitting the boy on his lap and began to tell the story: 'Just imagine Stepanku, from tomorrow you can take part in the rehearsals for a children's opera; a proper opera for children with principals, a choir and orchestral music.'

It sounded fantastic but Stephan had a problem imagining what sort of role he could play in it. His father tried to explain: 'The opera tells the story of two poor children who are foully abused by the hurdy-gurdy man Brundibár. But with the help of a dog, a cat and a sparrow the children win the fight against the evil man.'

Stephan's eyes lit up as he continued: 'Now they are looking for children for the choir as well as for the principal roles. The first rehearsal is tomorrow, and then we shall certainly learn more about it.'

That night as a bedtime story Alice told her son about the composer Hans Krása. She knew him from Prague, because she was a friend of his sister Fritzi. It was a long time before Stephan finally calmed down and went to sleep.

Alice was still weak from her illness but at six the following evening she took her son up to the attic of the Dresden Barracks. There they were already waiting for the choirmaster Freudenfeld to return from his 'hundreds' to begin the rehearsal.

Alice was pleased to see Hans Krása. They had lots to talk about and he told Alice the story of the opera's creation, which, in turn, she would use over the next few days for Stephan's bedtime story. The main roles for the piece had already been cast.[14] Rafael Schächter had chosen two experienced young singers who had sung in the production of *The Bartered Bride* for the roles of the brother and sister Pepiček and Aninka: Pinta Mühlstein and Greta Hofmeister. The roles of dog, cat and sparrow had also been filled. The dog was being sung by Zdeněk Orenstein, a thirteen-year-old boy, who later became an actor. The cat was sung by Ela Stein and the sparrow by Maria Mühlstein. But the undisputed child star of Theresienstadt was Honza Treichlinger, who could jiggle his stuck-on moustache so beautifully and stole the show as the hurdy-gurdy man.

Both Freudenfeld and Krása needed more children for the choir, and particularly musical ones as understudies. Rudolf Freudenfeld, therefore, played some short tunes on the harmonium and the children had to sing them back to him. After Stephan's turn, Freudenfeld and Krása were unanimous in their praise of his extraordinary musical gifts and agreed that his sweet voice would be ideal for the role of Sparrow.[15] So, in many of the later performances, Stephan changed places with Maria Mühlstein.

After the rehearsal Stephan was beside himself with joy and

collapsed onto his mattress, demanding the plot of the opera for his bedtime story. Alice began to tell the tale that he had heard for the first time only a few days before: 'Once upon a time, there was a brother and a sister called Pepiček and Aninka. They lived together with their mother; their father had been dead a long time . . .'

'Why was the father dead?'

'I don't know,' Alice replied, 'perhaps he had had a bad childhood. Whatever the reason it was bad for the mother and her two children to survive without a father. When their mother was ill in bed, Pepiček and Aninka worried a great deal. To get her strength back she needed milk, but the children couldn't find a single coin in the house to buy milk with. When they saw that people threw coins to the hurdy-gurdy man Brundibár when he played music, the children had an idea: they would go out on to the street and sing pretty songs. Perhaps people would then give them money.

'The voices of the two children, however, were too quiet; no one could hear them so they received not a farthing. When the hurdy-gurdy man saw them, he became very angry and chased them away. In the night the animals arrived – the dog, the cat and the sparrow and told Pepiček and Aninka to get together as many children as they could find and to sing with them. Then their voices would be loud enough for people to hear, and they would be better equipped to protect themselves from Brundibár. The three kind animals helped summon the schoolchildren. Together they sang a beautiful lullaby, and the people stopped dead in their tracks in admiration and tossed penny after penny into the hats. Suddenly, however, the evil hurdy-gurdy man jumped up and stole the money. After an exciting chase the children managed to clinch a final victory over Brundibár and at last Pepiček and Aninka could buy their mother some milk. Their mother got better and everyone was happy ever after because they had all proved themselves more cunning that the wicked hurdy-gurdy man. And if they are not dead, then   '

Stephan did not hear the last sentence: he was already happily sleeping at this mother's side.

*

FROM THEN ON the children rehearsed several times a week. The songs were simple and so catchy that after a few days Stephan knew them all by heart.

On the evenings when there were no rehearsals Leopold visited his family in their quarters. Exhausted from his 'hundreds' he usually sat in the corner of the attic listening to the children. He did not like to talk about his work, but Alice was aware that he must have been working like a slave in those first hundred days. Leopold was a small and delicate man, but tough, so the physical labour took less out of him than many of the others. He mentioned in passing that he had been moved on to agricultural work. Alice noticed, however, that in the evening he was more tired than ever.

The couple had decided between them that they would celebrate Stephan's sixth birthday after the next rehearsal. On the evening in question, Stephan sat waiting on the stairs when his father arrived punctually for his visit. Stephan was bubbling over with stories from the rehearsals that he wanted to tell his father. The two of them made their way past more than a hundred beds and heaps of luggage to Alice's mattress, where Stephan declared that the final chorus – when they sing of their victory over the evil Brundibár – was particularly lovely. In his enthusiasm Stephan immediately sang the song to his father:

> *You must rely on friendship*
> *And make your way together.*
> *Trust in strength and kinship*
> *And keep your ranks forever.*

Alice listened silently to her men. For a brief moment she was completely happy. Leopold took a cloth out of his pocket and carefully unfolded it: 'Today we three are going to have little parties,' he told Stephan, and as if by magic produced two tins of sardines in oil from his shoulder bag. In Theresienstadt these were an enormous treat. To this he added bread that he had saved from his lunchtime ration. Next to that he took out two packets tied up with pretty ribbons.

'What are we celebrating today?' asked Stephan.

Alice hugged her son and said quietly: 'Your birthday. We are celebrating your sixth birthday today.'

'Is it my birthday today?' said Stephan incredulously.

'It is not actually today,' said Leopold, 'but when your birthday came round in June we were in the midst of preparing to come here and we both thought why not have a party here.'

Alice was proud that Leopold had been able to smuggle the presents into the camp. Stephan was excited about pulling the ribbons. He carefully untied them and gave them to his mother, as he had been made well aware that every possession was of value in Theresienstadt. The bigger packet contained a volume of William Busch's best children's verses. Books that could be read aloud were absolute treasures. The second packet contained two bars of chocolate.

'It's not a party without music,' said Leopold to the contented but quiet Stephan.

'How can we make music without instruments?' stuttered Stephan.

'Perfectly simple,' his father said. 'You sing the final chorus again from *Brundibár* and I'll play second fiddle.'

Stephan looked at his father doubtfully.

'Just start and you will hear in due course.'

The boy began to sing.

> *You must rely on friendship*
> *And make your way together . . .*

Leopold winked at Stephan, and started to hum a second part. With a fine sense of comedy while he was doing so, he began to drag an imaginary bow over an imaginary violin so effectively that Alice began to clap her hands in rapture. The duet sounded so splendid that the neighbours applauded spontaneously and they had to repeat their performance, not once, not twice but three times. By the end many people were humming along and some of the children were clapping in time. From a secret little birthday party it had developed into a full-blown celebration with many guests. And because it made everyone so happy, Stephan also sang the lullaby from *Brundibár*. It might have sounded funny coming from the mouth of a six-year-old, but for the mothers of Theresienstadt, it was like a knife through the heart:

> *Mother, how you may sigh,*
> *Childhood has now passed by.*
> *You ought to know*
> *How quickly all our bodies grow.*

*

IT WAS WEEKS before Alice was able, at some level at least, to come to terms with the horrible conditions she was obliged to live in. From the first day, however, she wanted to find out what had happened to her mother. Since she had said goodbye at the assembly point in July 1942 she had had no word from her. Had she died here? Had she been moved on to one of the camps in the east soon after her arrival? People here spoke of such things in fear.

Most of what she knew had come from Edith Kraus who had come up to the attic a few days after her arrival to say hello. It was a great pleasure to see her again, but Edith had told her terrible things about what had been happening in the camp, and although she knew nothing concrete about Sofie Herz's fate, what she did know gave little cause for hope. The present regime was almost paradise compared to what conditions in the ghetto had been like at the beginning.

Now, for the first time, Alice learned something of the history of the concentration camp at Theresienstadt.[16] It had begun on 24

November 1941 with the first transport of Jewish prisoners: a total of 340 young Jewish artisans and workers had been given the job of turning the small garrison town into a camp. On 30 November and 2 December a further 2,000 prisoners – men, women, children and old people. They were followed on 4 December by another 1,000 young workers, who were sent to bolster the construction team.[17]

From then on life in the camp was regulated by a flood of commands and edicts: 'men may not meet women'; 'it is forbidden to send letters home'; 'the smuggling in of letters is punishable by death'; 'it is forbidden to speak to the non-Jewish population'; 'smoking will be punished'; 'all prisoners must have their hair cut off'; 'no one is permitted to walk on the pavement'; 'any one in uniform must be saluted'.[18] Besides these, as one prisoner later recalled, it was forbidden to:

> whistle or sing in the streets, to pick up chestnuts, to pluck wild flowers or to shake a chimney sweep's hand to bring luck. Prisoners had to hand in all money, stamps and writing paper, cigarettes, tobacco, preserves, medicines and much more. Small demeanours were punishable by ten to fifty strokes of the cane; major ones by several months in the dungeons. Corporal punishment was the norm, performed by other prisoners under the supervision of the SS-man Bergel, who was also more than happy to hit the prisoners himself. If the prisoner who was administering the punishment did not hit hard enough he received the same number of stripes as the man who had been sentenced.[19]

The few ghetto inmates, who had deluded themselves into believing they would survive the war in Theresienstadt in half-way decent conditions, were shaken by the executions which took place in January and February 1942. For trifling infringements of the camp rules – for instance, a short private conversation between a wife and her own husband who she had visited in his quarters, or a prisoner sending a secret report to his mother – nine inmates were hanged on 10 January 1942. This macabre spectacle was repeated on 26 February 1942 when seven more prisoners suffered a similar fate. One of the guards had assured them they would not be punished if they told the truth.[20]

Events on 9 January 1942 showed all too clearly that Theresienstadt was neither intended to be an old people's home nor a show camp. It was then that the first transport of 1,000 prisoners left for an extermination camp in the east. From that day onwards the thought of the next deportation hung over the prisoners like the sword of Damocles. Even though they were unaware that those who had been sent away would be gassed, they sensed the horror of what was happening. The final figures speak for themselves: of the over 89,000 people deported to Theresienstadt, at the most 3,500 survived.[21]

EIGHT

Happiness

'Two spoonfuls of soup for a Bach partita...'

LIKE ALL THE OTHERS in the ghetto, the room on the ground floor of the Magdeburg Barracks was tiny and shabby. It looked more like a box room than a place to practise the piano. Plaster was coming off the walls and the only furniture in the room was a pair of chairs and an old piano which an expert had carefully tuned. The sole window was stuck and two nails in the door served as hooks. In spite of this, the pianists in Theresienstadt were grateful for the chance to be able to play undisturbed, if only for a very limited time. So many professional pianists had arrived in the camp that they could only be allotted half an hour each day to practise.[1] Many of them were internationally known names:

Alice's friend Edith Kraus, a former child prodigy thought to have been one of Artur Schnabel's most talented pupils.[2]

Gideon Klein from Prague: a fantastically multi-faceted talent who was irresistible to everyone as a result of his good looks and his kindness. Klein was in charge of the music section in Theresienstadt together with the 'Free-Time Organization'. He was also heavily involved in 'Youth Care' and the education of children.[3]

Bernhard Kaff: the pianist and music teacher from Brno, who gave lectures on Russian music in Theresienstadt. He played so sublimely that he had the reputation of bewitching his audiences even when he played on the worst instruments.[4]

Renée Gärtner-Geiringer from Vienna: who gave a record thirty-two different concert programmes in the ghetto.[5]

The composer Viktor Ullmann: a pupil of Arnold Schönberg who in the two years before his deportation to Auschwitz wrote twenty new compositions, including the opera, *The Emperor of Atlantis*, which would later be world-famous.[6]

In the third week of July 1943 Alice sat at the piano in Theresienstadt for the first time. Her daily practice time was fixed for 9 a.m. and, as ever, music provided great solace. She might, too, have been prey to the odd touch of self-deception; it made life more bearable. That morning, and on many future occasions, she kept returning to the remark she'd made to Leopold in the Exhibition Hall in Prague: 'If you can perform concerts in Theresienstadt it can't be all that bad.'

The joy with which her son embraced the rehearsals for the children's opera was like a ray of light, which also distracted her from her overwhelmingly sombre existence and provided her with reserves of courage. Somehow, even in the camp, she clung on to her principles, always managing to be hopeful and see the positive side of things.

A few days before, Stephan had started at the ghetto kindergarten where children of seven and below secretly learned the basics of reading, writing and arithmetic.[7] The SS had forbidden formal education, but the Autonomous Jewish Administration's 'Youth Care' organization catered for the needs of the more than 15,000 children in the camp, although they were officially only allowed to pursue artistic activities: singing, drawing and crafts. Stephan really enjoyed it, not least because on his first day he rediscovered his best friend there – Pavel Fuchs – who was the same age as him and who had been at the Jewish kindergarten in Prague. They both liked acting as class lookouts. Whenever the SS approached they issued a musical whistle and all teaching material was put away while the children broke into a song.

*

IN THE MONTHS before Alice, Leopold and Stephan arrived, much had changed at Theresienstadt. From the autumn of 1942, Theresienstadt was often referred to as a 'ghetto paradise', as the SS endeavoured to mislead the increasingly disapproving outside world by presenting the camp as a normal town with contented citizens. Gone were the guards outside the barracks; now the prisoners were free to walk the streets without prior permission.[8] The powers that be never tired of saying that in Theresienstadt senior citizens could live out their days in security and that distinguished people were granted additional privileges according to the services they had provided to society. It was an inspired move on the part of the SS not only to allow prisoners to organize their own cultural and musical activities, but also to positively encourage them. In March 1943, the clever and dynamic engineer Otto Zucker took over the directorship of the Free Time Organization (FZG) and became responsible for the most enriching aspect of cultural life at Theresienstadt: music was to be brought to the masses.[9]

Alice had not expected to find that the Free Time Organization would organize the musical programme so effectively and professionally. Otto Zucker had asked her to draw up a list of her repertoire. Alice put together a total of four concert programmes from the extraordinary number of works she could play almost all by heart and handed the list to one of the women responsible for the weekly concerts. They advised her to come along to the Magdeburg Barracks on Monday morning. It was there that the programmes were displayed so that people could see where and when they would take place. When she saw the lists for the first time Alice realized that in some ways it was an ideal situation for a pianist. She was astonished by the variety of concerts offered. 'No organization to do, just practise every day and give a concert at least once a week. What more can an artist actually desire?'

Her first concert was to be given just over a week later and she had chosen three very different works for it: Beethoven's *Appassionata*, Bach's Partita in B flat major and a selection of Chopin Études. The *Appassionata* seemed particularly appropriate to Alice because there is scarcely any other composition for piano that is both so grippingly dramatic and has such fascinating tonal qualities.

For Alice, the Bach Partita in B flat major was the ultimate expression of musical creativity and she especially loved its spirituality. Years before she had read in Johann Nikolaus Forkel's famous 1802 biography of Bach, that anyone who plays the partitas well 'can make their way in the world with it'.[10]

She did not only want to play the Chopin Études because they had been an anchor to her these past twelve months, capable of lifting her out of her depression, but also because – in some strange way – they were the musical representation of the highs and lows of human existence. Far more technically demanding than the other pieces, Alice began to practise the Études first.

One day, while she was practising with great concentration, the door opened without her noticing and Hans Krása came in. He sat down on one of the chairs and listened attentively. As one of the most important members of the Free Time Organization he played a pivotal role in the planning of the concerts.[11] He also composed and accompanied many musicians on the piano. He had intentionally arranged his practice time to follow on immediately from Alice Herz-Sommer's.

Krása, knowing the concert was coming up, was well aware of what was on the programme and, as he particularly liked Chopin, he was hoping that she would play some pieces for him. When Alice stopped playing he stood up and clapped. Startled, Alice turned round, but when she recognized Hans Krása she was delighted. He was considered one of the most talented composers of his time, but one who had made comparatively little of his tumultuous gifts. Alice distinguished herself by her limitless industry and a clear sense of duty. Krása was the opposite.[12] He was only four years older than Alice and before the occupation of Prague he had lived the life of a prosperous bohemian.

In Prague Krása used to get up at about midday, by which time Alice would have been practising intensely for four hours. In the early afternoon he generally looked in on the Czech Theatre for an hour or two, where he was engaged by the hour as a tutor. After that he would visit a friend who edited the literary section of the *Prager Tagblatt* for a chat and their daily game of chess. Later he would go out with his friends and the evening would end in a party of wine-induced gaiety. Nonetheless, Alice had a lot of time for Hans Krása. His jollity was as catching as his charm was winning.

'Most esteemed Alice, might I ask a favour? Would you play me Chopin's B minor Scherzo?' It was his favourite piece.

Chopin's atypical scherzo, thought Alice, was appropriate for Krása's character in a quite particular way. It was brimming with humour, gaiety, energy and joy, whilst also having its dark and dramatic moments, which fascinated the composer.

If there were any flowers in Theresienstadt, Hans Krása told Alice, he would have picked her the most beautiful bouquet to thank her. As he left he asked if he could pop in to her rehearsals from time to time. Of course he might, said Alice, but the next four mornings she really needed to be by herself as she had to prepare for the concert. Krása respected her wishes. He let Alice practise in peace for the next few days, but after that he came over and over again and listened quietly, lost in his own thoughts. He frequently asked her for a particular piece; more than a dozen times this turned out to be the Scherzo in B minor.

Three days before her first concert Alice inspected the room in the former town hall that had been recently made available. For a week the ghetto guard, a body of around twenty-five men from the Autonomous Jewish Administration, led by Kurt Frey, had been restoring the place from top to bottom.[13] There was a new stage and curtain, benches with backs to them, even electric light. In addition there was a luxury that was sought in vain elsewhere in Theresienstadt – lavatories and running water had been installed for the audience.

*

ON THE DAY of the concert Stephan was proud and excited when, his hand in his mother's, the man at the door let the two of them into the concert hall ahead of everyone else. Alice wanted to show him everything, so they had got to the venue half an hour early. Before she disappeared behind the curtain, Alice promised him that she would give him a quick glance just after her bow, so that he could wink back: 'Then I will play particularly well,' she told him.

At the very last moment, Leopold arrived to take his place next to Stephan.

There was no backstage in the town hall, so the performers had to come in through the public entrance and walk down the central aisle to the stage. As Alice made her way through the audience she felt a profound sensation of happiness, tension and nervousness, which she always experienced just before a concert. She could feel the expectations of her 300 listeners. As she bowed, she noticed Stephan trying to wink at her, a blissful smile on his face. Her boundless optimism infused the audience and she began to play the Partita in B flat major.

Alice's playing rang out crystal clear and her magisterial performance was rewarded with rapturous applause. Then came the *Appassionata*, whose three movements express in turn a tortured mind, its consolation and reflections on man's strength. The conductor Rafael Schächter was sitting in one of the front rows. He was so inspired by Alice's performance that a few days later he told his choir: 'If you want to know what passion really is, go to Alice Herz and listen to the *Appassionata*.'

After a short interval, the second half began with a selection of the Études. Chopin had conceived these pieces as exercises, but his genius had transformed them into masterpieces of unfathomable strength and beauty. At the end of the concert Alice played the

'Revolutionary Study', which begins with a powerful chord followed by a veritable storm of passages in the left hand, while the right plays the solemn theme.

Alice played the lilting, undulating left-hand passages in a breathtaking tempo while her right hand allowed the central theme to ring out. The theme is almost a fanfare with its few rousing notes. When the tonal colour alters, the chords become yet more powerful and more passionate. The melody starts out sounding threatening and violent but halfway through takes on a triumphal character. The victory of the hopeful mood does not last long, however, and yields to a feeling of great agony. Finally, this pain-filled motif reverts to the pathos of the introduction, only more passionately, until the tension that has been mounting throughout gives way to exhaustion. At the end, the Étude rang out like an explosion in the concert hall. Alice's hands slid furiously over the keys; zig-zagging up and down from the heights to the lowest registers, with the four final chords ringing out, like so many shrieks of despair.

The audience was so profoundly moved that they hardly dared breathe. When the applause finally came it seemed to go on for ever. People Alice had never met embraced her with tears in their eyes. She couldn't get to her two men, who had stood up in their seats and were clapping with the same enthusiasm as the others. It was only at her second attempt that she was able to reach Leopold and Stephan and take them in her arms.

Standing a little to one side, one of the inmates who worked as a doctor in one of Theresienstadt's sickbays was watching the excited audience. Choosing his moment he walked up to Alice: 'I cannot express the feelings and reminiscences you have evoked in me. I thank you from the bottom of my heart.' He then offered her the chance to come to his sickbay once a week with her son to have a hot shower. This was an extraordinary privilege in the over-crowded ghetto, and Alice gratefully accepted.

The day after the concert Alice lined up at noon as usual with her tin plate, waiting to receive her lunch with Stephan at her side.

A young Czech had the task of dishing out the same sized portions to everyone. When it was Alice's turn he began to gush over Alice's interpretation of the gigue in the Bach partita. He particularly loved that piece. To thank her he gave her not one, but two ladles full of soup.

*

A FEW DAYS later, it must have been the beginning of August 1943, Alice and Stephan were on their way to receive their midday meal as usual. Stephan was babbling away cheerfully when he suddenly let go of his mother's hand and stood glued to the spot. He began to stare at two men with bright red faces who were pulling what was obviously a tremendously heavy cart. The load was covered with a black cloth under which lifeless arms and legs spilled out. Alice tried to get her son to move on, but he was literally speechless with horror and would not budge. The minutes felt like an eternity before the cart moved off in the direction of the crematorium.

'Maminko,' asked Stephan many times that day, 'how did those dead people come to be on the cart?'

'They are mostly old people who die here. They die of old age or malnutrition.'

'And where do the diseases come from?'

'There is too little water to wash with. There is filth everywhere. That makes people ill.'

'Why can't the old people have a shower?'

'Because there are far too few showers.'

'And why is it that we can have a shower and others not?'

'Because the doctor was so happy with my piano concert that he wanted to do something nice for us.'

'Was it because of us that the dead people on the cart could not have a shower?'

'No Stepanku, we have not taken anything away from the people. Certainly not. They did not get enough to eat.'

'But why not?'

'Because the camp authorities think that manual labourers and children should have more than old people who can't work any more.'

'Do the old people have to die because the children eat their food?'

The tone in Stephan's voice began to drive her to despair, but Alice wanted to give her son an answer, however difficult she found it: 'Stepanku, the children can't do anything about it. There is not even enough to feed them properly.'

By then the two of them were standing at the table where the food was dished out and Stephan was clearly thinking about the fact that his mother had received a double portion in gratitude for her first concert: 'Maminko, if the boy gives you more soup today, does some old person have to go hungry?'

'No, quite clearly not. Everyone gets soup.'

But that day a different prisoner was serving and Alice was pleased that she got the same amount as the others.

Stephan would not give up. After the meal he asked where the dead were going; why little children died too; what a crematorium was; and what happened to the ashes. In the end he also wanted to know why people were locked up here; when they could finally go home; why the war hadn't finished yet; and who was to blame.

In the next few weeks and months Alice was on her guard to prevent such occurrences whenever possible, but she did not always succeed. Death was part of everyday life in Theresienstadt. Over and over again there were outbreaks of infection which quickly spread, killing the weaker inmates. In July 1942 an average of thirty-two prisoners died each day. The figure rose to 75 in August and to 131 in September. When Alice and her son arrived in the camp at the beginning of July 1943 hygiene had improved but still there were thousands dying of infectious diseases. Between August 1942 and the end of March 1943 there was a total of 20,582 deaths – more than 2,500 a month.[14]

*

IN THE MIDDLE of August 1943, after nearly six weeks in the attic, mothers with children were moved to one of the 'blockhouses' in the Seestrasse. A room measuring just twelve square metres contained three two-storey bunks for twelve people, a small iron stove, a window, and no place to set up a table or chair. Such luxuries had to be 'organized' first, anyway. Alice had to make an instant decision: top or bottom? The bottom bunk was more airy, and it was easier to get out, especially at night when there was no electricity. She was lucky enough to get the bottom one by the window. Stephan inspected the bunks with interest, as up until then they had only slept on thin mattresses on the floor.

Stephan disappeared on his first attempt to lie down. The bunks were constructed like deep, narrow boxes, about sixty-five centimetres wide. At one end there was a sort of storage area, but even this was too small to accommodate the few trifles they had been allowed to keep. The rest of their things stayed in the rucksacks which were shoved under the bed. Unlike the barracks, the single-storey blockhouses had no washrooms, just one sink for everyone.

*

EVERY EVENING FROM six until quarter to eight the men were allowed to visit their wives and children. With every father who made his way into their narrow confines the noise became more deafening. Over Alice's head children squealed with excitement at their fathers' stories. The little boy in the next bunk kept climbing onto the side of the bed and jumping off again making an awful noise in the process. A few mothers tried to discipline their children by hissing at them. One of the couples spoke so loudly to one another it sounded as if an argument had broken out.

One evening, when the noise became so loud that she could no longer hear herself speak, Alice jumped to her feet and bellowed in a piercing voice that one could hardly believe could come from such a fragile-looking person: 'Attention, all children,' 'Attention, all children,' 'Attention, all children.'

Her outburst was so unexpected that everyone fell silent immediately. Then into the stillness Alice spoke in a gentler voice that was both firm and friendly: 'Every child must now take a doorknob in his hand and as quietly as possible close the door.'

They all looked baffled, and one of the mothers whispered: 'My God, now she has gone mad!'

But in the next moment Alice repeated her request, grasping, as if playing charades, an invisible handle and quietly and slowly turning it. Alice repeated her mime until all those present understood and were imitating her, all the children too. Alice's outburst left its mark. Whenever it looked as if it was about to get too noisy during the evening visit, one of the mothers would cry out: 'Close the doors!'

Alice's fellow residents also took up her suggestion that the room had to be cleaned out as much as was feasible twice a week; the mattresses had to be taken out into the courtyard and beaten and the beds and floors scrubbed. Once or twice they dismantled the beds, as the insects that preyed on them concealed themselves in the cracks in the wood. Relations between the women in the block got better and better as they learned to live and work together: this support and cooperation was a small but important lifeline for them all. The rest – hunger, the threat of disease and death – remained unchanged. And, as soon as the lights went out, the women and children were incessantly attacked by insects. The bugs, fleas and lice were never defeated.[15]

*

ALICE WAS AWARE of her privileged position in the camp. The five women who shared the room with her had to go off to work for up to twelve hours, either in one of the camp factories or in maintenance – the kitchens, sickbays or administration. Their children were sent to 'activities' (kindergarten until they were seven and the childrens 'home' thereafter)

Alice was spared physical labour from the start. Otto Zucker had exempted Alice from work and she was accepted as a member of the Free Time Organization with the task of preparing solo concerts and chamber music. The fact she had to look after the six-year-old Stephan was also taken into account. Alice could therefore pick Stephan up at the kindergarten at midday, and she often collected his friend Pavel, too, and looked after them both.

In Theresienstadt Alice had just one purpose: to protect Stephan, provide him with warmth and prevent him from suffering. Night after night he slept in his mother's bed. Snuggled up to her he felt an obvious sense of security. Every day she had three problems to overcome: to spare him from boredom, fuss and hunger. The saddest thing for her was when her son asked for food and there was none to give, and he had to go hungry. When she earned a little bread or margarine from a concert, she would naturally hand it on to Stephan. And even that often did not stave off the hunger for long.

Once – the only time in her life – Alice was driven to theft. It was one of the rare occasions when none of her fellow lodgers was in the room. Stephan was crying with hunger, but Alice had nothing more to give him. Then she spied a piece of bread on a neighbouring bed, and grabbed it.

*

STEPHAN WAS ALWAYS so tired in the evening that he went to sleep immediately his father left. On the other hand he woke shortly after five in the morning, long before the others. To some extent this was an advantage for Alice and Stephan as it allowed the two of them to wash and dress in peace. After six, people had to form a long queue: a torture for all those suffering from the camp sickness, diarrhoea. A lavatory watch was formed on a daily basis and was supposedly responsible for order and cleanliness.

Until the official reveille Alice and Stephan had the best part of an hour to while away. As there was nowhere to sit down, they would go back to bed after their wash. While Alice would have loved to go back to sleep, Stephan was bored. One morning he had an inspired idea: 'Let's count'. Alice was amazed, because she knew that he hated counting, and she sympathized. She had never felt much affection for arithmetic but was happy to do sums with him from that moment on. Over and over again they repeated their tables in every possible way they could and at the same time they did multiplication and division, which taxed not only Stephan, but Alice too.

*

AT THE BEGINNING of September 1943, Alice experienced her first outbreak of panic in Theresienstadt. The cause was an order issued several weeks before by SS Command. On 24 July 1943, it was decreed that two barracks had to be cleared as quickly as possible,[16] so that a group of SS officers from Berlin could prepare the empty buildings to house the archives of the RSHA, the Reichssicherheitshauptamt (Reich Security Main Office), the subsection of the SS created by Heinrich Himmler in 1939 to fight 'all enemies of the Reich'. Within thirty-six hours 6,422 prisoners had to find temporary accommodation in other buildings. Leopold was also affected. He later told Alice about the speed with which the prisoners had had to assemble the little they had left – and what was essential for their everyday lives – before they left their billets.

As Theresienstadt was already filled to bursting, the 6,422 prisoners were divided up among the attics and cellars. From then on every nook and cranny of the ghetto was occupied. The evacuated buildings stood empty for three weeks before they could accommodate the archives: documentation of Nazi crimes.

The SS had a quick and lethal solution to the chaos they had caused: thousands of prisoners would be transferred to camps in the east. The first selection was to be made from people from Bohemia and Moravia no older than sixty-five, a criterion which fitted around 12,000 prisoners. Another thousand had to be available as reserves: one in two prisoners from Bohemia and Moravia was under threat.

The camp was in uproar. No one knew precisely what went on in the eastern camps, but there was much speculation. The name Auschwitz was known to the prisoners, but so far there had been no rumours of mass murder or systematic gassing. One thing was certain, however, and that was the conditions would be worse and more difficult than they were in Theresienstadt.

The atmosphere in the camp changed overnight: people crept nervously through the streets and all social contact was marked by mistrust. Fear became a reality when the SS finally informed the Jewish elders that they had to draw up the deportation lists. The Council of Elders had to meet immediately and make their choices. A secretary typed the lists, with carbon copies: first the number of the person, then the number of the transport, then the first name and surname, followed by date of birth and address in the ghetto. Finally the carbon copies were cut up so that each name appeared on a thin strip of paper. Messengers took these strips directly round to the the elders of each block and they in turn had to inform the chosen and hand over the piece of paper.

The final composition of the transport was put together by a 'commission', which was appointed by the Council of Elders, and each of the sections of the Autonomous Jewish Authority was more or less equally represented. On the days the commission met there was frantic activity on the staircase of building B5, where the chancellery was housed, as once the list was made known it could become a death-sentence.[17] Many people appealed to the commission, giving reasons why their names should be struck from the list.

All the sections produced lists of exemptions in four categories: indispensable, relatively indispensable, relatively dispensable and dispensable. A strict 'transport protection' was only applied to two small groups in the camp: to some of the 'celebrities' who were chosen for various reasons but generally because the SS showed a special interest in them. The artists affiliated to the Free Time Organization were exempted in this way. Around 120 people fell into this category – a pathetically small number[18] who would be spared the gas chambers. Alice was one of them. Leopold Sommer was not. Also protected were the members of the Council of Elders and those who enjoyed a similar status as members of the Autonomous Jewish Authority. These two privileged groups had the right to draw up their own lists of people to be protected. They were limited to thirty people, but on some of their lists there were up to seventy names.[19]

The SS Commandant Anton Burger exploited the situation to clear the camp of people he disliked. He also had many of those who had been brought in to construct the camp deported although they had been promised that they would be ineligible for deportation. As Burger feared that there might be resistance on the part of the Jewish ghetto guards, he ordered that the majority of them be transported too. On one day alone, 6 September 1943, 5007 prisoners left the camp including 327 children under fifteen. Of these only 37 survived.[20] But for the time being, Leopold, Alice and Stephan had been spared.

*

THREE WEEKS LATER, the mood in the camp was lifted by the first performance of *Brundibár*. Rehearsals had continued even during the ghastly period which preceded the transport to the east. Stephan often returned from the rehearsals singing happily and when he opened the door all those present joined in. He once climbed up onto the top bunk in order to conduct the choir – his choir – of mothers and children, using a cooking ladle as a baton.

At the beginning of July 1943 everyone had agreed that *Brundibár* would be accompanied on the piano alone. But soon after, they received the exciting news that the SS was going to allow them to use confiscated instruments, and they were permitted to create a small orchestra. This surprising decision was not for any altruistic reason but only because Adolf Eichmann was intending to allow a delegation from the International Red Cross to visit Theresienstadt and wanted to mislead them into believing that 'Jews here enjoy every liberty'.

Ignorant of this, Hans Krása was filled with enthusiasm at the chance of working with an orchestra and he frantically wrote out the parts for the newly available instruments A number of well-known musicians put themselves at the orchestra's disposal, among them Karel Fröhlich, Fredy Mark, Romuald Süssmann, the Kohn brothers, Fritzek Weiss and Gideon Klein.[21]

The premiere of *Brundibár* took place on 23 September 1943 in the mess hall of the Magdeburg Barracks. Hundreds of prisoners attended the performance. Rudolf Freudenfeld remembered decades later that it was a 'festive premiere . . . Zelenka had the opera performed in front of a wooden fence covered with posters representing the animals in the cast. Kamilla Rosenbaum was the choreographer. The orchestra had to find room in front of the stage which was reached via the aisle. She glanced warmly at all the children; it was a smile pretending that nothing bad could happen from now on, that it was all going to go smoothly, then the lights went out and off we went! I went through the little door to the orchestra, and at this moment I forgot that I was a prisoner; that we were all prisoners. For a while we forgot everything and for a moment we children experienced things we would never forget.'[22]

The children's opera was a huge success. *The Bartered Bride* had been put on thirty-five times, but between September 1943 and September 1944 *Brundibár* was performed fifty-five times.[23] Every time the room was so full that one could hardly breathe. Soon all 'Theresienstädter' knew *Brundibár*. It was a story pregnant with symbolism, and the infectious enthusiasm of children singing and dancing, and the alluring playing of the orchestra, were balm to the souls of thousands of prisoners. The final chorus became a sort of secret hymn.

Come let's beat the drum
Victory is ours . . .
Because we will not let them defeat us,
Because they will not, cannot frighten us.

*

ON 9 NOVEMBER 1943, during the 'census', the SS accused the former president of the Council of Elders, Jakob Edelstein, of falsifying the number of prisoners in his daily report. Edelstein and three of his colleagues were taken down to the bunker, where they were imprisoned and later shot. As if that were not enough, two days later, the SS showed yet again just how ruthless they could be and no survivor will ever forget what happened.[24]

At about four in the morning of 11 November, all the prisoners were forced from their houses. Alice dressed Stephan in the warmest clothes she could find, and put their rucksacks on her shoulders. The march to the Bauschowitz Valley lasted over an hour. The entire area was surrounded by Czech gendarmes with their machine guns pointed at the prisoners. For more than seventeen hours 40,000 people were forced to stand there in the cold and rain. With every passing hour the children became more fidgety and more distressed, crying and begging for somewhere to lie down.

Alice had a little folding chair and an umbrella with her. She had Stephan on her right knee and another child on her left. She told the two of them one story after another and for a change, read verses from Stephan's Wilhelm Busch book out loud until they had learned them by heart. All day she looked for Leopold, but she failed to find him in the sea of people. When night fell, SS officers ordered the prisoners to line up in rows of ten. Alice took Stephan in her arms. She assumed they were about to be shot. She was not frightened. She was very close to her child and there was a black curtain before her eyes, as dark as pitch.

But the gendarmes did not shoot. Suddenly a loudspeaker announced in Czech: 'Back to the ghetto!' Everybody ran through the darkness towards the ghetto in complete panic. No consideration was shown towards the weak. It looked as if children would be trampled to death and their despairing mothers tried to protect them.

It was after midnight when the valley was finally emptied. Empty that is but for the bodies of the old people who had collapsed and died from exhaustion. Around three hundred people perished that day. Heaven and hell are just round the corner from one another, thought Alice.

NINE

The Gates of Hell

'The noblest specimens of degenerate art . . .'

ALICE WAS SITTING in the practice room in the Magdeburg Barracks wearing fingerless woollen gloves, a cap on her head and a warm winter coat over her cardigan. She was rehearsing for the premiere of her fourth Theresienstadt concert programme. It consisted of Ludwig van Beethoven's D major Sonata Opus 10, Schumann's *Fantasy* in C major, which she had played in her final concert at the Academy of Music, and Smetana's Dances, which her teacher Václav Štěpán had so brilliantly transcribed for the piano.

In January 1944, Theresienstadt was covered in drifts of snow and it was icy cold. In their miserably inadequately heated rooms, the prisoners were subjected to the full force of the weather. It was a blessing that Alice had been prudent and packed some fur-lined lace-up boots before she left Prague, even though it had been mid-summer at the time. So Leopold at least could keep his feet warm in his freezing locksmith's workshop and Stephan practically ran to his 'day home' because the warm shoes felt good in the snow and during break they were allowed to go skating.

In the ghetto the relationship between Alice and Stephan had become even closer. They went to bed at the same time, got up at the same time, and except for the time he was at school, they spent the whole day together. Even when Stephan went to concerts on his own in the evening and was temporarily not with to her, she always had the feeling he was holding her hand. As long as he could feel secure, feel he was held, his world was safe.

Alice's previous concert programmes had been received by the audiences with great enthusiasm. In the past few months Alice had had to repeat them many times. Leopold had been encouraging his wife to do the Beethoven Sonata with its famous D minor Largo for ages, because the piece seemed to reflect the situation of the prisoners of Theresienstadt.

As ever, Alice threw herself into the task. When she prepared for a concert she perfected the pieces she was going to play for weeks in advance. In Theresienstadt she also added two of Chopin's Études to her daily exercise. Every day she tackled two different ones, because she wanted to bring this difficult repertoire up to concert standard in case she was called upon to play them.

Today was no different. After the last notes of the sonata had died away she took a little time before she decided on the E major study. Stephan loved this Étude. In Prague Alice had played it while he was going to sleep. Even here in Theresienstadt she would hum the theme to him at bedtime.

Alice began to play. The piece starts peacefully. Chopin once revealed to his pupil Adolf Gutmann that he had never written a melody to compare with it.[1] The Étude affects the listener like a dreamy, melancholic story with a shocking event in the middle. Step by step the emotion mounts, and the tension rises with it until it becomes almost unbearable.

Suddenly a darker thought distracted Alice from her playing: 'My son is in great danger, now, at this very moment,' shot through her head. As she passed the dramatic highpoint of the piece the worry became too much for her and she leaped to her feet and ran to the door, driven by an anxiety she had never felt before. She knocked over the chair and the lid of the piano came crashing down. Alice ran as fast as she could.

When she got near to the kindergarten she saw Stephan first only in profile: a boy with a white cloth wrapped round his head, a temporary dressing. She knew at once 'That is my Stephan!' She was breathless when she reached the people who were giving her son first aid. He had hit a tree on his toboggan. Blood was flowing from a nasty-looking wound on his nose. She thanked the helpers, put Stephan back on the sleigh and set off to the surgeon who had come to every concert she had given so far. He calmed Stephan and consoled his mother, but even though the wound looked worse than it actually was he had nonetheless broken his nose and he needed stitches. Alice was told to leave the room. After a tortuous quarter of an hour's wait the door to the surgery opened again and Stephan appeared with his cheeks wet with tears and a dramatic-looking bandage round his head. He mustered a brave smile. He bore the scar of the accident for the rest of his life.

Leopold was amazed when he visited them that evening.

'How did that happen?' he asked Stephan.

'We were having a race.'

'But you must have done something. There is enough room on the hill outside the kindergarten to go to the left or the right of the tree.'

'True, but the person who comes closest to the tree comes down the hill fastest. I was doing some great tobogganing.'

'Maybe that was a mistake. Life is not just about doing better than others or forcing them to do things. That is not real happiness.'

'Should I not have been on the sleigh?'

'Sleigh racing is fun, isn't it? But when the competition becomes too intense then the fun is gone, isn't that so?'

Stephan thought about it. 'I don't understand.' He went on, provocatively: 'A little competition, but no proper competition?'

Inwardly Leopold was pleased that Stephan was arguing with him. 'All right, I'll explain it to you in a different way. Your mother likes playing the piano above all else.' Stephan nodded. 'But she never gives a concert in order to be better than others. She plays simply for the love of music and for the joy it gives others to hear her. She is in competition only with herself when she practises every day. She wants to play as well as she can. But on stage there is no competition.'

At this Stephan turned to his mother: 'Maminka,' he said. 'At home there was a big certificate hanging over the piano. You told me that you had won it at a piano competition in Vienna. You have been in a race then. Isn't that true?' The word 'race' sounded so odd that they all three began to laugh out loud. 'Yes,' said Alice, 'but I did not crash into a tree.'

*

TWO DAYS LATER Alice paid her weekly visit to Hannah Eckstein, a Prague acquaintance more or less her age whose two sons she had taught to play the piano. The two women liked one another and Alice had asked Frau Eckstein to come to several of her concerts. The Ecksteins had managed to send their two sons, aged twelve and fourteen, to Sweden just before the deportation. There they lived as 'long-term holiday children' with a kind peasant family. Whenever they could, they wrote to their parents in Theresienstadt. As the post was very irregular, it was often months before they had a letter and then they might receive three or four postcards one after another.

Alice appreciated the calmness that Hannah Eckstein had developed in Theresienstadt, but that morning she was agitated. A few days before she had fallen asleep and woken suddenly with a piercing cry. In her dream she had seen her twelve-year-old boy fighting for life in deep water. Now she had received a letter in which he described how he had been ice skating and gone through the ice and nearly drowned.

Alice told Frau Eckstein how she had jumped up in the middle of playing the piano because she felt that something terrible was happening. 'How does this sort of intuition come about? Perhaps the love between a mother and a child can be so great', she said looking for an explanation, 'that something intangible happens.'

Rational to a fault, neither Alice nor Leopold had time for supernatural interpretations. However, they frequently spoke of these two events in the subsequent weeks. Alice also reflected on the singular effect the Chopin Études had had on her. She was actually more inclined towards Robert Schumann than Frédéric Chopin, but it was not Schumann's romanticism that had pulled her from the jaws of despair. At last, she decided to play the twenty-four Études in one concert. First, however, she had to continue practising her fourth concert programme.

*

THE HALL WAS as packed as ever, and Leopold and Stephan were as usual sitting in the front row. A few seats further along sat the composer Viktor Ullmann with paper and pencil in his hand. For Theresienstadt's music lovers, Viktor Ullmann's critiques of the concerts were a minor sensation. Between 1943 and 1944 he wrote a total of twenty-six of them. Even in the ghetto he demanded an incredibly high standard and judged everything by the toughest criteria, just as if the concerts had taken place under normal circumstances. [2]

The premiere of Alice's fourth programme was a colossal success from the audience's point of view. What, however, would Ullmann write? While Alice played he had been scribbling furiously on his sheet of paper. He typed out his articles in the office of the Free Time Organization. There they were duplicated and then delivered to his readers.

'She is a friend of Beethoven, Schumann and Chopin's; for years and here in Theresienstadt we have thanked her for so many delightful hours. Alice Herz-Sommer at the piano means stark, clear, intensive playing with moments, often whole movements, which show off the masters' genius quite perfectly.' [3] Thus Ullmann began his review.

It is difficult to say whether Ullman was writing at his own initiative or at the behest of the Free Time Organization, [4] although without the approval of the Autonomous Jewish Authority it would hardly have been possible to distribute the reviews. Shortly before he was transported to Auschwitz on 16 October 1944, Ullmann gave his collection of reviews, together with his compositions, to his friend Emil Utitz who had taught at the German University in Prague before the war. Utitz had a worldwide reputation and in Theresienstadt he had built up the ghetto library and delighted audiences with lectures on history and psychology.[5] He survived Theresienstadt and in 1946 he gave Ullman's articles to Hans Günther Adler, who wrote the first complete study of Theresienstadt.[6] Adler himself spent thirty-two months in the ghetto and also survived Auschwitz and Buchenwald.

Another survivor, the writer and musician Thomas Mandl, called the rescued Ullmann pieces 'Gold nuggets found in the devil's test-tube: the so-called ghetto of Theresienstadt[7] . . . They allow us to reach conclusions about a culture the destruction of which was a painful loss, and to imagine what the human spirit is capable of in the face of extermination.'[8]

One of these 'nuggets' is Ullmann's review of Alice's fourth Theresienstadt concert programme, which continued:

> . . . for [Alice Herz-Sommer] reproduction is actually creation; she identifies with the work and its creator. She contributes her eminent technique and great knowledge to the service of the work; she does not belong to the world of piano devils for whom virtuosity is both a goal and a form of self-satisfaction; she has more warmth than flashiness, more innate quality than brio. In the last few years her style has markedly clarified and developed; for this highly-gifted artist was once a virtuoso who specialized in temperament herself. From what everyone says she was made for the romantics, and this is true. She is perfectly accomplished, for example, when she plays the indescribably lovely final movement of the C major *Fantasy*, Schumann's Opus 17; this gliding, rapturous piece of high romanticism slides towards the captive listener and he forgets that in the March Scherzo that preceded it the artist had

slipped away from the notion of time; you cannot play this movement too quickly, and this wholly musical interpreter deals with its problems and rhythmic monotony in a natural way. The starkness of the 'ineffective' Beethoven is close to Alice Herz-Sommer's heart. In this Sonata Opus 10 No. 3 the Schubertian D minor Largo is always an experience and it was a highpoint for our musician. At the end Frau Herz-Sommer gave us Smetana's *Czech Dances*: delicious and innocent and with the famous 'Furiant' in which the Czech popular soul meets Franz Liszt.[9]

Demand was such that Alice had to play each of her programmes anything up to twenty times during the two years she was in the ghetto. Having premiered her fourth programme she now began to practise for her fifth, the Chopin Études. She had hesitated for almost a year before playing these pieces to her fellow prisoners, but now that she had practised them so intensely, she understood why. As she herself has said, she needed several months after her arrival in Theresienstadt before she could build up the necessary inner strength to face the extreme physical and mental challenge imposed by the Études. The challenge was not just technical, it was mental. Alice associated the Études with the despair she had felt at the time of her mother's deportation in July 1942. In the end, however, the excitement of playing all of the 24 Études conquered her despair. For Alice, every one of them was 'a world in itself. There is everything in them, everything: all human life and all sensation.'

In his Études, Chopin had expressed pretty well all the basic forms of human perception: mourning, complaint and despair, along with sadness and longing, passion and heroism, even gaiety, mischief and humour. There was even mystery and fantasy. The power of musical expression hidden in the Études is astonishingly original. It is music that 'belongs to some of the most accomplished music history has ever known'.[10]

But what is it that makes the Études such an extraordinary test of even the greatest virtuosi? In the early nineteenth century European composers competed with one another to stretch the pianist's virtuosity and Chopin took this process as far as it could go. Even though he remained faithful to the practical purpose of an étude – the study of particular hand movements, practising and perfecting technique – he nonetheless revolutionized the concept. He was not just interested in improving certain hand movements and increasing the speed of fingering. He wanted to unleash new styles of pianistic effects and sounds that had never been heard before. In reality technical mastery is not an aim in itself, but is above all at the service of the music. In the Études, Chopin was influenced by the compositional severity of Bach's *Well-tempered Clavier*, which he particularly admired. In each of his preludes and fugues, Bach used a standard structural formula which he shaped into splendid musical units. Chopin followed suit, whilst striving for something entirely new, which he would make completely his own. If his Études are played in a slow tempo, they reveal their perfect construction and infectious logic. The melodies are beautiful and the harmonic twists are bewitching. The complexity of the single figures reveals – especially when played slowly – their extraordinary originality.

Since the Études were written, few pianists have ever performed all twenty-four in one concert. Some people maintain that the Études should remain just that – studies – practice pieces which should not be considered part of the concert repertoire. Others feel that a few of them can be integrated into a concert. But perhaps most of all it is the sheer physical challenge that deters most pianists from taking on such a daring project.

When a pianist does decide to perform all the Études, they normally opt to begin with the Opus 10 set of twelve, which Chopin began writing in Warsaw in 1831, continued in Vienna, Munich and Stuttgart and finished in Paris. After the interval, the second cycle – Opus 25 – is performed, written almost entirely at the beginning of Chopin's Paris period between 1834 and 1835.

This is precisely what Alice did in Theresienstadt on 29 July 1944. The prisoners experienced what was for many of them the most impressive of all the concerts they heard in Theresienstadt. Despite all the humiliations they had suffered, despite the inhuman conditions in which they toiled, despite the constant threat of deportation and of death, the prisoners, after hearing Alice play, could look to the future with renewed hope.

A few survivors who witnessed her performances – some still alive today – have given an account of what they heard, such as the pianist Edith Kraus in Jerusalem, the writer Zdenka Fantlová in London, the piano and song teacher Anna Hanusová-Flachová in Bratislava and the writer and violinist Herbert Thomas Mandl in the United States and Germany. There are also a handful of contemporary accounts which have come down to us.

The Heroic: Op. 10 No. 1 in C major

Willy Mahler came under the spell of the C major study from the first moment. It begins with a powerful wave of sound which flows over the proud bass. The music was bold and truly heroic, he wrote in his diary, and he felt that the keys came to life in Alice's hands: 'They rant, disturb, narrate, illustrate, calm you down, let you forget, and put you in an almost narcotic mood of goodwill.'[11] The solemn, majestic melody played by the left hand in the bass had moved him so much that he compared it to something carved out of stone: mighty and immutable. He was fascinated by how

Alice's right hand went up and down the keyboard in waves; it was enough to make you dizzy.

Mahler, then aged thirty-seven, could feel the strength he was absorbing from the music. Like the majority of those present, he belonged to an experienced, educated, middle-class musical public who had filled the concert halls of Prague, Vienna and Berlin in the years before the war. Before being deported to Theresienstadt on 13 June 1942 he had worked as a journalist on the Czech paper *Lidové noviny* and was thoroughly knowledgable when it came to classical music.[12] He did not miss the fact that there was an extraordinary similarity between this study and the music of Johann Sebastian Bach, especially with the first prelude of the *Well-tempered Clavier*, which is also in C major. Chopin had stressed this in his own study, but while Bach's piece is played in the middle of the keyboard, Chopin extends the chord all the way down, invoking magical effects which would have been impossible on a baroque keyboard. Chopin not only pushes the manual difficulties to heights never achieved before, he also creates a fullness of sound and polyphony that had never been heard before, in which the right hand covers the keyboard with fractured triplets. As an experienced listener Willy Mahler noticed that the pianist was bringing out the effects with the careful use of the pedal, as if the music had eight, ten or even twelve voices. The result was ravishingly beautiful music: varied, rich in ornament and brilliant in tonal colour.

But what did the Theresienstadt audience hear in this first Étude? Willy Mahler's diary says it all:

> I gave myself utterly to the effect of the music . . . I totally forgot where I was. Afterwards it was only with difficulty that I became conscious again that I was in a modern, twentieth-century ghetto, sitting next to my then girl, among a lot of people designated by six-pointed stars inscribed with the word 'Jew'. Opposite us there was an old couple. He had to be about sixty, she perhaps seven years younger. She clutched his hand and pressed her tear-stained face into it. It was moving,

A happy moment in occupied
Prague, 1939

The proud mother with her son,
Stephan, in 1938

Emil and Mizzi Adler (on the left) sailing to Palestine

Stephan (far left, back row) at the Jewish kindergarten in Prague in 1941

'Jews Forbidden' – Stephan at the entrance to the park in 1940

The last photograph of Sofie Herz, taken in 1942,
just before she was deported

One of the Sommers' house concerts at Sternberggasse in 1941.
From left to right: Paul Herz, Leopold Sommer, Jöši Haas, Erich Wachtel

Stephan (front row, fourth from left) in the children's opera, *Brundibár*.
The performance was recorded in a Nazi propaganda film of 1944.

A ticket for what
was probably Alice's last
Theresienstadt concert.

but it was also an expression of weakness, obviously brought on by some lovely memories.

Artists like Alice Herz-Sommer and music like the C major Étude gave the prisoners the strength to cling to their belief in the ultimate goodness of mankind and the consciousness of their own worth.

The Puzzle: Op. 10 No. 2 in A minor

The prisoners were still revelling in the might and magic of the first study when after a momentary pause the second began like a gentle breeze. In the traditional sense this A minor Étude is lacking a melody. Instead you hear a serpentine series of chromatic notes, which become ever more disturbing and more unravelled, making the listener almost dizzy. The music critic Joachim Kaiser said once that this study was not only the most complicated chromatic ballad ever written, but that it also stood at the limits of playability.[13]

As Alice was bowing before the audience at the beginning of the concert, her friend Edith Kraus recollected their first meeting in 1937, when she had gone to see Alice to ask her about her interpretation of the Martinů dances. Alice had been heavily pregnant. Her son was born just two months later. Now he was a child prisoner, sitting a few places away from her and listening intently to his mother's music.

Edith had one of the Études in her own repertoire. When she heard the staccato like chords accompanying semiquaver figurations she remembered that she had been saved from being deported to the east by the music of Bach, Mozart and Chopin. Edith had arrived in Theresienstadt much earlier than Alice and her name had been on the transport list as early as 1942. Someone advised her that she should suggest putting on an evening concert for the prisoners.[14] At this time there was no officially sanctioned cultural life in the camp. Performers had to make do with an old, clapped out, and even legless piano, which the physician and music-lover Rudolf Pick had painstakingly put together with Gideon Klein. Edith's suggestion of putting on a concert was taken up. The legless piano was carried round to the Magdeburg Barracks and put on some boxes, and the pianist gave her first concert in Theresienstadt, a programme of works by Bach, Chopin and Mozart which she played by heart. Her name was struck off the transport list and in the months that followed she gave many more solo concerts.

The Ineffably Beautiful: Op. 10 No. 3 in E major

With the third study in E major the audience heard a tender, dreamy melody full of melancholy. Once, when Adolf Gutmann, Chopin's pupil, played it to the composer one day, the latter raised his hands in prayer and cried 'Oh my country!'[15]

The melody begins in a peaceful and comforting way. Only in the virtuosic middle-section does it explode with unbounded passion. Alice was a gifted raconteuse. In her interpretation of the shocking drama, she allowed the tension to grow note by note through a cascade of chromatic sixths, playing with both hands spread out in both directions as she reached the dramatic high-point. All at once the storm broke, the tension abated and softly and tenderly the opening theme was heard once more, the contrast making the melody even more intense and melancholic.

When Zdenka Fantlová, then eighteen, listened to the music she had already suffered a particularly bitter experience. In 1940, she had met the love of her life: Arno was good-looking, sporty, had soft dark hair and brown eyes:

> We looked at one another and it was like lightning: love at first sight . . . When he came to fetch me he would whistle up to my window a few notes from Dvořák's symphony 'From the New World'. When I heard our signature tune I dropped everything and ran to Arno's arms. The world seemed like paradise to us. The German occupation disappeared from view. We were alone in our world and perceived no dangers. And even if — we had no fear that love's light wings would surmount all difficulties.[16]

Their good fortune did not last long. Two years later the lovers were taken to Theresienstadt on different transports.

Zdenka arrived at the camp on 20 January 1942 together with her mother and brother. At that time romantic meetings between prisoners were still strictly forbidden. Zdenka knew, however, that Arno had to be somewhere in the ghetto. The thought that her lover was nearby, that he lived and breathed and thought of her as much as she did of him gave her courage. One day she heard their tune loud and clear. As if struck by lightening she rushed to the second floor window and very nearly fell out when she saw Arno in a group of six men sharing out potatoes. Like a madwoman she ran down the stairs and queued up behind the other women reporting for potato-peeling. 'We were only a few paces away from one another. In despair we sought to get close, but how and where?'[17]

At great risk to their lives, they met in an empty cellar that was accidentally left open: 'Right behind the door and in pitch darkness we began to kiss and cuddle one another passionately. Everything else disappeared: not just the barracks but also the Germans, time itself and Theresienstadt. Only we were there; now together; one mind, one body; alone in the world.'[18]

Suddenly they heard footsteps.

Jackboots: there was no doubt about it – it was a German patrol. Judging by the sound there were three of them. Then we heard their commanding voices. It was clear that we were standing before an abyss. If they found us here we would be punished by death . . . They opened the first door and peered into the room, then the second. Still in one another's arms we pressed ourselves against the wall. It was our turn now. They were surprised that the door was not locked. 'What is going on here?' one shouted, tearing open the door. The edge of the door banged against the wall in the narrow room, but there was a triangle of darkness into which they could not see, and that was where we were, still in one another's arms. We stopped breathing. The SS man stepped into the room. We could see his shoes. Only the door stood between us and death. 'Bring some light here', came the order. Our hearts stopped beating. The light of a torch circled round the room. It seemed to go on for ever. The dust they had aroused went up my nose and I wanted to sneeze. With the greatest effort I stopped myself and thereby prevented the greater catastrophe. 'Let's go on', came the order.[19]

But disaster was not to be averted. Arno was one of the 2,000 condemned to death in revenge for the assassination of Reinhard Heydrich and was despatched to Auschwitz on 13 June 1942. At about four in the morning, shortly before the transport left, he came to Zdenka one last time to give her a small tin ring he had made himself and on which he had inscribed 'Arno 13 6 1942': 'This is our engagement ring. It will protect you. If we survive I will find you somewhere after the war.'[20]

Zdenka never saw Arno again. None of the 2,000 deportees survived.

Elemental Force: Op. 10 No. 4 in C sharp minor

After the dreamy sense of longing of the Third Étude, it is hard to imagine a starker contrast with the fourth. The C sharp minor Étude is full of energy and vitality. It is insanely quick, but with an implacable clockwork-like rhythm. Right from the beginning it has a monstrous power, lending the music a wild, demonic character and all the tension of a brewing storm, which never breaks but becomes more and more menacing. The music seems to give off sparks; despite its dark colours it is filled with elemental force, power and confidence.

The Czech bass Karel Berman carried his unstinting power through Theresienstadt and on to the extermination camp at Auschwitz. Berman was transported to Theresienstadt just a few weeks before Alice on 5 March 1943.[21] There he had to work in the rubbish dump. His fellow prisoner, the conductor Rafael Schächter, chose him for his opera group and a deep friendship evolved between the two of them. They studied Mozart's *Zauberflöte* together, prepared numerous concerts and forged plans for what they would do when they were freed from the concentration camp and when the war was over.

Alice knew Berman from Prague. It is almost certain that he attended Alice's performance of the Études together with his friend and highly respected colleague Franta Weissenstein. Both singers appeared in the Theresienstadt performance of Smetana's *Kiss*

Weissenstein sang Lukasch and Karel Berman sang Paloucky and both were sent to Auschwitz on 28 September 1944 together with 2,497 prisoners. 'On the ramp at Auschwitz [Weissenstein] was just in front of me. With his thumb, the SS doctor Mengele pointed him to the right, me to the left,' Berman, who survived Auschwitz, later wrote. 'We took leave from one another in silence, staring for a long time into one another's eyes. Then he got onto a lorry. The death machine was already working overtime.'[22]

The Humoresque: Op. 10 No. 5 in G flat major

The Fifth Étude has gone down in musical history as the 'black key study'. It is a veritable firework display of brilliant piano music. As in a humoresque, there are several abrupt changes between forte and piano from one bar to the next, which lends the Étude a somewhat boisterous and carefree character, while retaining its distinguished and elegant style. 'It is gracious, has a refined wit, is a little malicious, sly and mischievous and has an excellent power of invention.'[23]

Thanks to its insinuating melody, infectious rhythm and dazzling playfulness, it is one of Chopin's most frequently performed works and one which breaks with convention. While most piano works use all eight notes in a scale, Chopin limits himself to the five black notes, a pentatonic scale. Moreover, the joyful character of the piece suggests that Chopin himself was happy and relaxed when he composed it, and playing it made Alice happy, too. The sadness in so much of his music affected her profoundly, but the Fifth Étude is wholly optimistic.

The 'Racked by Pain': Op. 10 No. 6 in E flat minor

The sixth study in E flat minor is steeped in melancholy, pain and deepest mourning, ringing out like a piece played slowly by night, or a 'dark, accusatory nocturne'.[24] The melody is almost a lament. With increasing dissonance and chromatic sequences of notes the music builds to a climax, until 'all that remains is the impression of an aimless wandering in despair'.[25] Even when the piece finishes with a reconciliatory major chord the impression of utter hopelessness lingers.

Otto Sattler had arrived in Theresienstadt in September 1942.[26] In the 1930s Sattler was one of the best-known and best-loved violinists in Prague and by November 1939 was still playing at the Elyse, a luxurious bar which, after the occupation, was popular not only with Prague's wealthy citizens, but also with high-ranking German officers.

Sattler's faithful companion was the pianist and harmonica player Kurt Meyer. Their ability was legendary and their virtuosity reminded people of Hungarian gypsy musicians. Perhaps because of this they were able to play in the plush surrounding of the Elyse long after Jews had been banned from going there. When their position there became untenable, they then moved on to the Litze coffee house, the only restaurant in Prague still open to Jews, and performed there until it was finally shut down in autumn 1942.

When Sattler and Meyer arrived in Theresienstadt in September 1942 they were asked to perform publicly that very week and their fame spread through the ghetto. They played in cellars, in attics, in sick rooms and in the shabbiest places; anywhere where people hungered for the solace of music.

When a 'coffee house' opened in Theresienstadt, Sattler and Meyer were seen there almost every day. They always played without a score and they were always prepared to improvize any melody someone cared to name. In the course of an evening they played not only Russian romances but also English, Danish, Norwegian and American popular songs. More than anything else, however, they played what the audience most wanted to hear: the Jewish songs that had been prohibited by law.

Sattler and Meyer's musical talent ensured that they were protected from deportation, but it could not protect them for ever. On 28 September 1944 first Sattler, and a few days later Meyer, was transported to the east. But their reputation had even reached Auschwitz and the 'Kings of Bar Music' were forced to play day and night at SS parties. It saved them from the gas chamber, but it drove Otto Sattler to attempt suicide. His father had starved to death in Theresienstadt and his wife and three children had been murdered in the gas ovens of Auschwitz soon after they arrived there. But when Sattler tried to throw himself on the electric fence in impotent despair, a guard held him back, saying 'You have more music to peform for us!'[27]

At the beginning of 1945 Sattler was sent to Sachsenhausen and from there he was later sent on a death march to Dachau, before being liberated on 29 April 1945.

The survival of his comrade-in-arms was equally miraculous. When Auschwitz was evacuated in January 1945, Kurt Meyer was sent to Buchenwald where, soon after, he contracted typhus. Some weeks later, thinking that he was already dead, the guards tossed him onto a heap of corpses. He lay there for days before an old friend from Carlsbad found him and saw that he was still breathing. It was 11 April 1945 – the day the Allies liberated Buchenwald.

The Mysterious: Op. 10 No. 7 in C major

'There are times when this study seems like light dripping through the trees of a mysterious forest . . . Were ever Beauty and Duty so mated in double harness?' was the American music critic James Huncker's enthusiastic response to the Seventh Étude in C major.[28] But its lightness and grace can only be truly conveyed when the pianist has both a voracious appetite for the piece and great technical accomplishment.

Both were true of the young violin player Thomas Mandl, who arrived in the Theresienstadt ghetto when he was sixteen. He was one of the youngest members of the Free Time Organization and played in the orchestra. He liked Alice and her radiance impressed him. 'She was a breath of fresh air and joy in Theresienstadt . . .'[29] She had none of that 'depressed mood of the normal, so-called ghetto-inmate'.[30] As Mandl often helped on the door, he was rewarded with the chance to hear the concert.

Thomas Mandl's fate was tragically similar to that of Leopold Sommer. Both were shipped off to Auschwitz, both survived the selection on the ramp, and both were later transported to Dachau. Mandl's description of his journey from Auschwitz to Dachau is a vivid evocation of what he and his fellow prisoners suffered during it: 'One day in Auschwitz we were driven out of our huts and had to assemble in a particular place . . . Then we were examined in an extraordinary way by SS doctors and put into a railway car . . . We were forced into cattle trucks and then the train set off. We were in the trucks for days. Where I was in the truck there was a fellow prisoner who tried to commit suicide in a grotesque way.'[31]

In each of these cattle trucks there was an iron stove watched over by an SS guard. 'The man sat his naked bottom onto to the red-hot stove. The SS man was so shocked that when the train stopped he went out and fetched us water to drink. Then he told us: "I was in a fighting unit of the SS and then I was wounded. As a reward I was sent here to Auschwitz, but the job is so horrible that I have asked to return to the front of my own accord. Here in Auschwitz living children are being burned in the crematorium." '[32]

The Sparkler: Op. 10 No. 8 in F major

The Eighth Étude in F major is classic Chopin – gay, colourful, sublime. With the exception of one single bar the melodic structure is played entirely in the left hand. The melody is not only joyful, but has a heroic character, while the strong rhythm makes it almost march-like. The terseness of the melody is amazing: 'over and over again it seems to be forced into the same rhythmic forms, each offering more and more glimpses of harmony.'[33]

One critic has described the Eighth Étude as being like a 'wondrous poet standing in fantastically coloured sparkling rain. In the reprise the listener is surprised by new developments in the melody in the left hand as well as by harmonic changes which introduce a peaceful mood and bring on a tender smile. In the next moment this is swept away by humorous figures and joyful passages in the coda.'[34] The unbounded vitality, the insuperable power and eagerness so typical of this piece, were also true of Alice's personality.

The Demonic: Op. 10 No. 9 in F minor

Nervous agitation, suppressed passion and a demonic drama mark the mood of the ninth study in F minor. 'The melody is morbid, almost irritating, and yet not without certain accents of grandeur. There is a persistency in repetition that foreshadows the Chopin of the later, sadder years.'[35]

The musicians incarcerated in Theresienstadt knew all about suppressed passion, but after the first secret performance of an orchestral work on 16 September 1942 this passion found an outlet. It took great daring and a measure of moral courage that is hard to imagine today. The concert was given in the prayer room of the Magdeburg Barracks at a time when public performances were still strictly forbidden. It consisted of Carlo Taube's Theresienstadt Symphony based on his experiences of the ghetto.[36] The little room was completely full. There was a string orchestra on the podium and as there were no brass or woodwind instruments, they substituted an accordion. The first two movements were dominated by Jewish and Slavic themes. The third movement particularly stirred the listeners: the composer's wife Erika sang a song the lyrics of which she had written herself, a lullaby for a Jewish child 'Ein jüdisches Kind', the only part of the symphony which has survived.

In the intense finale the first four bars of 'Deutschland, Deutschland über alles' were repeated over and over again. With each repetition, the anthem became angrier and more violent in the hands of the musicians until 'Deutschland, Deutschland' was no longer followed by 'über alles' but petered out in a horrible dissonance. Everybody knew what was meant, and a thunderous ovation greeted Carlo and Erika Taube at the end.[37]

That same kind of ritualistic repetition, in which the tension in the music mounts until you want to cry out, is also characteristic of the Ninth Étude. The message becomes ever more painful and pessimistic; then comes a dramatic explosion that dies down in the soft, delicate figures in both hands. Everything is peaceful and quiet again, like the rushing of a stream.

The Melodic: Op. 10 No. 10 in A flat major

The pianist and conductor Hans von Bülow used to say 'that anyone who is able to play the tenth study in A flat in a truly accomplished way can congratulate themselves that they have reached the pianists' Parnassus.'[38] Both hands have to perform enormous technical feats, but even more difficult is the necessity of coordinating the opposing rhythms and shifting accents.

The physician and musician Dr Kurt Singer faced an equally difficult task when he became the driving force behind the Jewish Cultural Union in 1933. The Union was established to maintain Jewish cultural life in Germany in the face of the increasing threat from National Socialism. Singer was among those responsible for four Jewish theatre companies, four symphony orchestras, several choirs and two opera companies at a time when Jewish musicians were being dismissed from musical ensembles elsewhere. Singer led over 70,000 members of the Cultural Union for five years, before handing the reins over to a new pair of hands. In 1943 this distinguished man was deported to Theresienstadt. All his musical colleagues prized and respected Singer for his towering achievements as a former director of the Berlin Opera, as the leader of the Cultural Union and as a gifted choirmaster and music critic.[39]

Singer played an important role in the musical life of the camp. He attended many of Alice's concerts and they developed a close friendship. Alice valued Singer's critical analysis, and she felt particular empathy and pity for the eminent musician, who seemed lonely and lost. Soon after his arrival, he found himself in conflict with his colleague and friend Rafael Schächter as Schächter had decided that he wanted to stage Verdi's *Requiem* in the ghetto.[40]

Singer thought it inappropriate that in a place like Theresienstadt Jewish artists should perform a Christian-Catholic work, rather than an oratorio inspired by the Old Testament. The library had copies of oratorios with Jewish themes, such as Handel's *Solomon*, *Israel in Egypt* or *Judas Maccabaeus*. Schächter, on the other hand, saw Verdi's *Requiem* as a testament to human ideals. His enthusiasm knew no bounds, and soon everything else had to play second fiddle to his performance. In the end, even Singer began to smile:

> The performance was certainly the greatest artistic event conceived or offered in Theresienstadt to date and an achievement in its punctilious preparation. It was an artistic event for certain, but sadly a long way from the concerns of the Jews as long as they were locked up in Theresienstadt . . . It was a magisterial achievement for Rafael Schächter, who studied the work over the course of the year to the degree that the choir sang without scores; and they sang cleanly, with rhythm and dynamism, heeding every gesture they received from the conductor Schächter. The love that the conductor carried in his heart for the work was clearly transmitted to every one of these fresh girls and young lads . . . It was a triumphant success . . . As a former choirmaster I was pleased to be able to say such things in public and with no envy.[41]

Not long after, Singer became extremely ill. Käthe Starke, an actress who worked as one of the camp's peripatetic cleaners, came across him in House Q 410. Quietly and unemotionally he was reciting *Faust*, complaining to the setting sun:

> *That nothing seeks to lift me from this earth,*
> *And make me strive and strive to find her!*
> *I'd see the eternal twilight*
> *The silent world 'neath the ether,*
> *Inflame the hillsides and put every dale at peace,*
> *While the silver stream mixes gold with water.*

(Part 1 1075–9)

A few days later he was bought to the sick bay, dying. Alice visited him there many times and thanked him for all he had done. She was holding his hands when he died.

The Dreamer: Op. 10 No. 11 in E flat major

The delicate arabesques in the eleventh E flat Étude are like soulful strummings of the guitar: gliding, airy and trembling. This study is actually a nocturne, which begins in a happy mood but is very soon wrapped in a veil of melancholy grace; and the dreamy melody is transformed into pain and accusation.

Chopin's contemporaries were shocked by this piece, because it is based on a provocative and novel idea: the single notes of the chord are temporarily transposed and played as so-called arpeggios. Each of the highest notes in the chord was played louder to matchless effect, described in James Huneker's 1921 critique of the Études as 'this exquisite flight into the blue'. Huneker continued, 'this nocturne which should be played before sundown, excited the astonishment of Mendelssohn, the perplexed wrath of Moscheles and the contempt of Rellstab, editor of the *Iris*, who wrote in that journal in 1834 of the studies in Op. 10, "Those who have distorted fingers may put them right by practising these studies; but those who have not, should not play them, at least not without having a surgeon at hand." '

Incandescent at Rellstab's mockery, Huneker stoutly defended Chopin. 'What surgical wizardry might have been required to hammer into the skull of this narrow-minded critic an inkling of the beauty of this composition. In future years the Chopin Études will be played for their music without reflection on the technical problems they exhibit.'[42]

As she sat rapt and spellbound listening to Alice, fifteen-year-old Zuzana Růžičková certainly had no idea of the extraordinary technical difficulties Alice had to overcome. To Zuzana, who had been deported to Theresienstadt with her parents in January 1942, the Étude seemed strikingly to embody her own life. She had had a wonderful childhood in Pilsen, growing up with her twin sister and a a cousin of her own age.

Zuzana had begun learning the piano at eight. It was soon clear that she had great talent and it was decided that at the end of her schooling she would go to Paris to study with the famous harpsichordist Wanda Landowska. But after the German occupation of Czechoslovakia no Jewish child could continue at school or take piano lessons. The eleven-year-old's dream of Paris and a career in music had been shattered.

Her piano teacher Marie Pravaznikova was kind enough to give her secret piano lessons despite the ban, even though she risked putting herself in danger. When she visited, young Zuzana hid her yellow Star of David in her pocket.[43] Just before her deportation Zuzana secretly visited her beloved piano teacher

Marie Pravaznikova for the last time and played the Dvořák Serenade in A major duet with her.

In the Theresienstadt ghetto Zuzana sang in the legendary performance of Smetana's *Bartered Bride*. She heard the pianists Gideon Klein, Bernard Kaff and later Alice, too, and her desire never to abandon her musical vocation was strengthened by their inspiring concerts.

At the time the Sarabande from Johann Sebastian Bach's *French Suite* in E major was her favourite piece of music; so much so that she copied down the score on a slip of paper and carried it with her wherever she went. It probably saved her mother's life. In December 1943 they were sent to Auschwitz: 'Zuzana's wagon was already full and her mother was pushed into another. Zuzana tried frantically to hang on to the sheet music at the very least, but with the wind, the pushing and the shoving it was blown out of her hand. Her mother ran after the paper, as she knew how important it was for Zuzana. When she came to hand the score back to Zuzana someone pulled her into the truck.'⁴⁴

They were spared the gas chambers and when the Germans desperately needed labour after the bombing of Hamburg, they quickly sent 1,500 Jewish women to Hamburg-Neuengamme. Zuzanna and her mother were among them. Without protection from the cold and working with their bare hands, the women had to clear the streets of rubble, repair damaged pipelines and fill in ditches. In February 1945 Hamburg-Neuengamme was 'evacuated' and the death march to Bergen-Belsen began.

When British troops liberated Bergen-Belsen on 15 April 1945, Zuzana and her mother were among the 56,000 starving, thirsty people living in unimaginable squalor in the throes of death.

After they returned to Pilsen in August 1945, Suzana, now eighteen, immediately went to visit her piano teacher. The joy at their meeting was tremendous, but when the old lady saw Zuzana's worn-out, virtually crippled hands she burst into tears. However, Zuzana refused to accept her fate. She managed to acquire a piano from the national collection and started again at the beginning, note by note. With a supreme effort of will she began her finger exercises once more, practising for up to twelve hours a day. Her diligence and strength of will bore fruit. She began to study in Prague and she won first prize at the ARD Music Competition in 1956 and became an internationally renowned harpsichordist. To her lasting pride, she made a recording of Bach's complete harpsichord works, including – of course – the Sarabande from the *French Suite* in E major.

The Revolutionary Study: Op. 10 No. 12 in C minor

The twelfth study in C minor, famously dubbed the 'Revolutionary Study', is like a musical hurricane. Like the best of Chopin's works, it evokes despair, pain and anger. From the first shrill dissonances to the last rousing chord it fascinates the listener by its sheer scope, its emotional power and breathtaking speed. It could almost be the musical biography of Leo Baeck, the undisputed moral authority in Theresienstadt.

Baeck had been the last public representative of the Jewish community in Germany, and the spiritual leader of the German Jews during the Nazi period. Decent, humane and utterly fearless, Baeck was seventy when he was deported to Theresienstadt. Born in 1873, he had studied at the Jewish Theological Seminary in Breslau (Wrocław) and the Institute for Jewish Studies in Berlin and was ordained in 1897.

In 1905 he published a response to the Protestant theologian

Adolf von Harnack's *The Essence of Christianity* published five years previously. *The Essence of Judaism* brought Baeck international recognition. He served as a chaplain in the German army during the First World War, but after the Nazis seized power in 1933 he became President of the *Reichsvertretung*, which represented Jewish interests at national level. He arrived in Theresienstadt on 28 January 1943 on transport 1/87 receiving the number 187 984. He soon reached the conclusion that he could 'not be a simple number', and that one should 'always maintain respect for your self'.[45] In Theresienstadt he was elected honorary president of the Council of Elders and with his sermons, speeches and lectures he was able to support and encourage his fellow prisoners, strengthening their resolve to survive.

In August 1943, a year before the Études Concert, the engineer Grünberg, a friend, went to see him during the night. It was only after the war that Baeck revealed the secret Grünberg told him:

I was woken by my best friend during the night. I had not seen him for a long time. I had no idea he had been sent to Theresienstadt, and for that reason I asked him how he had got there. He told me to stop talking and to listen carefully. He had something to tell me, something I had to know. First, however, I had to promise to tell no one. He [Grünberg] is a half-Jew and was shipped off to the east. He was sent to the big camp at Auschwitz. Like everyone else he was subjected to selection and it was decided he would be sent off to do slave labour. The others were sent away to be gassed. He knew that for a fact; everyone in Auschwitz knew it. He was sent to a work-camp, from which he escaped and made his way to Prague. I asked him how he had got in to Theresienstadt? He told me that he had bribed a Czech gendarme outside ... I had to battle with myself whether I should insist that it was my duty to convince Grünberg to appear before the Council of Elders, of which I was an honorary member, and repeat what he had heard. In the end

I decided that no one should know. If I told the Council of Elders, within minutes the story would be around the entire camp. To live in the expectation of death by gas would make life only more difficult; and there was no certainty of this death. There was also the chance that you would be selected as a slave and perhaps not all the transports ended up in Auschwitz. So I came to the difficult conclusion to say nothing to anyone about it. Rumours of all sorts were constantly circulating around the ghetto, and recently there had also been stories about Auschwitz; but at least no one knew anything for sure.[46]

As the last notes of the 'Revolutionary Study' died out and the exhausted, smiling pianist turned to face her enthusiastically clapping audience, they rose to give her a standing ovation. Although everybody needed time to recover from the intensity and passion of the music, neither the pianist nor the audience wanted the applause to end. It had been an exemplary performance. After the interval, Alice would perform the second cycle of the Études – Opus 25 – another twelve studies.

'I shall never, ever forget it!' Zdenka Fantlová wrote decades later about the concert. 'I listened as if I was in a trance.'[47] During the applause, Leo Baeck, who was sitting in the front row, rose and went over to Alice. He held her protectively in his arms and said 'Our great little artist'.

TEN

Inferno

'Never of your own free will! It doesn't matter what they promise!'

ON THE EVENING OF 20 August 1944, Stephan greeted his father with great excitement: 'I played in a film today. There were spotlights and big cameras.'

'And was the director happy with you?'

'He was very strict,' Stephan answered, 'but he said, the little sparrow is doing very well.'

At 1 p.m. the Brundibár Ensemble had gathered in the hall of the Sokolovna, the largest and most modern building in the ghetto. It had been constructed a long time before the occupation as a club house for the Sokol Gymnastics Club. It was now the cultural headquarters of the Free Time Organization. It was a splendid place, and not just by Theresienstadt standards. With its flower beds and birch trees in the front garden, broad steps leading up to the entrance and an elegant auditorium it might have been a theatre in any major city in the world. It was here that the ensemble had to give its performance for a Czech film team. In the audience that day sat not only the prisoners but also – in the best seats in the gallery – SS officers' wives and children.[1]

For the young actors the performance was particularly exciting, if tiring, and it was the first time they had played on this stage. Most of the fifty plus performances to date had taken place in the Magdeburg Barracks – a considerably smaller space – and the new venue caused additional problems for the young performers. They had to repeat scenes for the cameras again and again, until the director expressed his satisfaction. 'Paul', Stephan burst out, 'played the trumpet louder than ever. I had to put my hands over my ears.'

For days the film had been the chief topic of conversation in Theresienstadt. It was a propoganda film, made to delude audiences around the world into thinking that Jews in Greater Germany were living a good life under the protection of the Third Reich; and that they were looking after their own affairs in their own town and away from the horrors of war while Europe's civilian population were making ever greater sacrifices. This macabre confidence trick was commissioned by the SS. The film was made by the Czech production company Aktualita and filming started on 16 August and ended on 11 September.[2]

The first thing to be filmed was the Jews apparently going about their banking business. A sign had been painted on the facade of the Bank of the Jewish Autonomous Administration bearing the legend 'Savings Deposits, Paying In and Withdrawals' – a cruel mockery of the truth.

Next was the Autonomous Jewish Administration's post office. The prisoners were required to stand at the counter and take in parcels, parcels which had to be handed back straight after the filming. Film was shot of a meeting of the Council of Elders of the Autonomous Jewish Administration. For the purposes of the film the meeting was transferred from the gloom of the Magdeburg Barracks to a specially redecorated room in the Sokolovna.

In order to convince the world that the ghetto had its own beach, a bathing establishment was quickly built on the banks of the Eger. Swings were put up on which the children could amuse themselves during the filming. The Czech high-diving champion had to demonstrate his ability together with a number of other sportsmen who had to perform in front of the camera. One female athlete was banned from performing, however, because she was

blonde, and did not conform to National Socialist Jewish stereo-
types.

The film was also intended as a record of all the autonomous
businesses: the locksmiths' and the plumbers' workshops, the car-
penters, the laundry, the cobblers and the tailors. Above all an
effort was made to aggravate the anti-Semitic feelings of the public
by capturing how 'idyllic was the life of the celebrities in the Jewish
colony of Theresienstadt'. Inmates were shown under parasols,
holding champagne glasses, wearing evening gowns, promenading
in the garden or dancing on the terrace at the Sokolovna.

The very height of cynicism came with the funding of the film.
Not only were the prisoners expected to act in a film designed to
distract the public from the mass-murder being committed elsewhere, but they had to finance it themselves. The production costs
– amounting to some 350,000 crowns – were met by the sums
appropriated from the Jews.[3]

The services of Kurt Gerron, the director, were also free.
Gerron, an actor, cabaret artist and director from Berlin had fled
to France in 1933, then to Austria. At the end of 1935 he went to
Holland, where he lived until the German army occupied the
country. In the autumn of 1943 he was deported from the transit
camp at Westerbork and in February 1944 he arrived at Theresienstadt. Soon he had put together 'Carousel': an attractive programme of operetta arias, chansons and lieder from among others
The Threepenny Opera by Bertolt Brecht and Kurt Weill,[4] in which
he had played Police Chief Brown in the original Berlin production.
He had also had a successful career in films and had acted, among
others, in *The Blue Angel* with Marlene Dietrich and with Heinz
Rühmann in *Die drei von der Tankstelle*.

The SS, and particularly the 'Central Office for the Settlement
of the Jewish Question in Bohemia and Moravia', had forced
Gerron to write the script for their propaganda film, to plan the
various scenes, to hire the extras required and finally to produce
daily progress reports. None of this did him any good in the long

run: like most of those who laboured at his side, he was executed in the gas chambers of Auschwitz three months later.

The film caused strife among the prisoners. Members of the crew wore white armbands marked 'film'. As soon as one of them appeared, the majority of the ghetto inmates vanished, fearing that they might be used as extras – their protest against this farce. Others, although they were a minority, were prepared to cooperate, chiefly because they saw the project as evidence of German weakness. The Allies had landed in Normandy at the beginning of June, giving new hope that Western Europe would soon be liberated from the Nazis.

That afternoon Stephan had peered behind the scenes of the film for the first time. He saw a recording van and a lighting van, lighting engineers, cameramen and assistant directors. He liked the hustle and bustle. There was even a hairdresser to make the children look their best before they went on. When his father wanted to know precisely why this film was being made, the child naturally could find no answers to give him.

Only a few short fragments of the film have survived. One of them shows the final scene of *Brundibár*. There are more than twenty-five children on stage, but one of them is particularly noticeable: it is Stephan Sommer, the smallest of them all, standing on a box. He looks proud and upright in his white shirt, his manner revealing the fun he had appearing in every one of the fifty-five performances. Stephan only realized much later that the SS used the opera to manipulate and mislead the public. For him and others like him, together with thousands of prisoners, the opera was a source of strength, and above all a symbol of resistance, resistance against his own downfall.[5]

*

ABOUT A WEEK after the *Brundibár* performance Leopold came to call, only to find his wife alone. Just before he arrived, Stephan had been asked to turn the pages for a pianist performing in a chamber music concert. Normally Alice and Leopold used the rare hours they had together to talk about their son, about how they could protect him from unpleasant experiences and how they could arrange better schooling for him. This time, however, Leopold was so angry about what he had heard about the progress of the 'film' that he wanted to talk to Alice about that.

For some months Leopold had been friends with a former orchestral musician, whom the conductor Karel Ančerl wanted to recruit for his symphony orchestra, which had been founded with the approval of the SS. In a few weeks Ančerl had assembled twelve first violins, ten second violins, eight violas, eight cellos and a single double bass, all of them provided for by the repository of confiscated instruments.[6] In order to balance the sound in the orchestra he strengthened the double bass with two cellos. It was pure accident that the orchestra was with one exception composed only of men. A professional female musician played the biggest instrument with the deepest voice – the double bass.

The enthusiasm of the players encouraged all those concerned to put together a weighty programme of rehearsals: Handel's *Concerto Grosso* in F major, Mozart's *Kleine Nachtmusik* and Bach's Violin Concerto in E minor. After a prolonged search in the ghetto library, scores were located, paper procured and the copying organized. Night after night members of the orchestra worked, drawing staves and writing out the parts. The first concert was a sensation. Leopold was in the audience and the hall was so full that many people had to sit on the floor in the aisles.[7]

At the end of July and the beginning of August 1944 Ančerl and his orchestra began to rehearse a new programme, which was to be exclusively dedicated to Czech music. They were to play Dvořák's *Serenade for Strings*, Josef Suk's *St Wenceslaus' Chorale* and a new study for strings written specially for the concert by Pavel Haas, the Brno-born composer and pupil of Janáček, who had been in the ghetto since the end of 1941.

This evening Leopold, who attended rehearsals whenever he

could, reported that the SS had suddenly given the order that the orchestra would have to play the concert that night for the SS guards in the so-called coffee-house. Ančerl's suspicions were justified when he arrived to find an almost empty concert hall, fastidiously decorated with flowers.[8] The SS handed out black suits to the musicians. The conductor's podium was arrayed with vases of flowers to hide Ančerl's wooden clogs.

The door opened and a high-ranking official visitor in SS uniform stepped in to inspect the hall, followed by the film crew. Ančerl was ordered to conduct to camera. Then, after the first performance of Pavel Haas's work the conductor had to enthusiastically introduce the composer. The cheering audience was to be added to the film later.

Leopold and Alice commiserated with Karel Ančerl, but when Stephan returned to the room bright eyed shortly after half past seven and told the story of the concert, Leopold's pleasure at seeing his son's enthusiasm for the music took precedence over his anger and distress. At six, Stephan was the most popular page-turner among Theresienstadt's musicians and Alice and Leopold were proud of the fact.

'Did it go well?' he asked the boy.

'He played two wrong notes, but it wasn't my fault.'

*

THERE WERE HOPES and false hopes. Every day fresh rumours about the Allied advance did the rounds. From September 1944 Allied aircraft frequently appeared in the skies above Theresienstadt. The Theresienstadt chronicler Eva Roubičková noted in her diary: 'Events such as these have a monstrous effect on the ghetto: people are happy – you see joyful faces. Every day there is at least one if not two air-raid warnings.'[9]

In addition there were euphoric accounts of a planned Czech uprising in the Bohemian and Moravian Protectorate. Because of this, when the Jewish elder Paul Eppstein made a speech to welcome in the Jewish New Year 5705 on 16 September 1944, he considered it necessary to warn the prisoners: 'In the interests of us all you must maintain calm at this time, for it is a false form of heroism when irresponsible people believe that they must do something to liberate themselves. It is wholly false to believe, too, that every little thing is another nail in the coffin of Theresienstadt.'[10] He likened Theresienstadt to a ship nearing harbour. 'This harbour, however, is surrounded by mines, and the captain alone knows the way, it is a long way round but it will take us safely home. The crew can hear voices in the harbour that are calling out encouraging words to them and the crew is already impatient and can't wait to reach port, but the only right and proper thing to do is to wait.'[11]

Eppstein's warning was right. Another rumour was circulating in the camp: after the film was finished 7,000 prisoners were to be deported – and only young men who were able to work.[12] For three months there had been no such transport and cultural life had blossomed. It was an illusory peace. The majority of the prisoners responded to the many cultural offerings with gratitude but there were also those who saw such cultural activities as dancing on the edge of the volcano, believing that they only served to mask what the camp was really about.[13]

The news of the forthcoming deportation had been brought by the civilian worker Ludwig August Bartels. Since November 1942 he had been head of the economic division of the SS Camp Command.[14] If he was right, then Leopold would be deported too: he was young, strong and able to work. Suspicions quickly arose that in doing this the SS were planning to remove all the men who might be capable of staging an uprising against the heavily beleaguered German army. It was possible that the SS were frightened of the many former officers among the prisoners, who had been looking since the summer 1944 to organize themselves into groups. It was also possibly the case – as the camp leaders thought – that the authorities simply wanted all the labour they could find for the arms industry.

When Leopold had worked for the Jewish Community in

Prague, he learned how the SS thought and acted, and he was in close contact with various members of the Autonomous Authority. Even though he was in the locksmith's workshop every day, he used every opportunity to collect information and evaluate it in order to see how much truth it contained.

In the last two weeks of September 1944, the rumour became reality: the SS was planning to deport 5,000 or even 6,000 prisoners, all men under the age of fifty-five. Leopold heard that they were to be taken to the fortress of Königstein near Dresden to construct a work camp there. Some thought that talk of a work camp was a red herring, a smoke-screen that would enable the SS to drag off all the men capable of bearing arms to an ominous camp in Poland without any resistance.

In the end it was suggested that this deportation was just the first of a series that would include the women and the children in the wake of their men, possibly on a voluntary basis. Leopold was suspicious. Why wouldn't they transfer the families to the newly created work camp at the same time? What ruse lay behind this apparently tempting offer to the women, that they might themselves decide where they wanted to live in the future? Leopold was now fully convinced it was all an evil trick on the part of the SS.

*

ON 23 SEPTEMBER the leaders of the Autonomous Jewish Authority – Paul Eppstein, Otto Zucker and Benjamin Murmelstein – were summoned to appear at SS Command. SS-Sturmbannführer Hans Günther, SS-Hauptsturmführer Ernst Möhs (who had travelled up from Prague) and SS-Obersturmführer Karl Rahm now officially informed the leaders of the Authority that the war situation demanded new sacrifices and the Reich's economic capacities had to be strengthened.[15] A thorough inspection of the workshops in Theresienstadt had shown that the ghetto was not suitable for the required war production and for that reason they would shortly need to send 5,000 men away on labour duty.

The next day, the 'Autonomous Jewish Authority News'

announced that a new transport was planned. Leopold read the announcement that evening in his barracks:

> With regard to the total use of all forces at our disposal and following discussions within the department on how to considerably expand current requirements for work possibilities within Theresienstadt. As a result of the technical problems and the shortage of space this has not proved possible to a satisfactory extent and it has been decreed thereby that men capable of work will have to perform their urgent functions outside Theresienstadt in the same manner as the hut-building work detail. To this end the Department informs that on both Tuesday 26 September and Wednesday 27 September there will be work details formed consisting of two batches of men from the Reich settlement aged between sixteen and fifty-five. It has been decided that the engineer Otto Zucker will take over the leadership of the transport. As in the hut-building detail, the members of this new force will receive assurance that they are exempted from transport. For the time being postal connections are assured. For this transport all men born between 1889 and 1928 are liable. All these men are thereby required forthwith to prepare themselves immediately and assume that they will be called. There are no exemptions foreseen. Decisions relative to persons unfit for transport will be made in the lock on the basis of medical certificates. There will be no complaints or appeals; all but essential luggage is to be left behind in the settlement.[16]

The deportations began in the early morning of 26 September 1944. There was a deathly silence as the house elder came into the dormitory where Leopold was lodged and read out the names of those affected in alphabetical order. Leopold was certain that as a fit man of not yet forty his number would come up. The letter S got nearer and nearer. One after the other, his fellow prisoners heard their names; then 'Sommer, Leopold' fell from the lips of the elder like the blade of an axe.

Leopold mechanically collected his slip of paper. 'We have to inform you,' he calmly read, 'that you have been included in the transport. You will have to present yourself punctually according to the instructions of the building or house elder at the assembly point at Lange Strasse 5 (3).'[17] All those affected had to pack at once. 'Luggage can only be accepted appropriate to the work and then in as small a form as possible. It may only be composed of hand luggage containing working clothes, linen, blankets, etc. The luggage has to be brought by you personally to the lock. To avoid official measures you are required to appear punctually.'[18] Leopold had just twenty-four hours left.

The SS sought to dissipate the fury of the inmates by telling them that the assistant head of the Council of Elders and the head of the central secretariat, Otto Zucker, who was actually indispensable for the smooth running of Theresienstadt, would lead the new 'construction staff'. On top of this, Schliesser, the head of the economic division, one of the most influential men in the Autonomous Jewish Authority, would 'accompany' the transport. In the short term this move inspired trust and some people even reported for deportation voluntarily. Leopold, on the other hand, remained sceptical.

Late that afternoon he learned that the elder Paul Eppstein had been arrested, which only strengthened his view that the SS was organizing a large scale deception. Years after the war it transpired that Eppstein was taken to the Little Fortress in Theresienstadt on the same day as his arrest and shot.

*

ALICE HAD HEARD the news about the transport even before Leopold came for his daily visit. One after another the husbands of the other women in the block had brought the news to their wives: 'We have to go, tomorrow morning.'

When Leopold finally stepped into the room, he did not have to utter a word. Alice looked at him and realized the moment had come.

Leopold embraced his son. Stephan had had an idea for some time of what was happening. He held himself close to his father.

'Alice, this is just the beginning: transport will follow transport, and they will try to send the women and children, too.' Leopold spoke with an emphasis she had never heard him use before. 'If they offer you and Stephan the chance to come to me, refuse. Do you hear?! Leave Theresienstadt under no circumstances, it doesn't matter what they assure you! As long as you are at liberty to choose, you must never be tempted by the offers of the SS. Promise me that!'[19]

Alice could not answer. She looked at her husband and nodded silently, choking back her tears. You cannot make it harder for him, went through her head.

Without speaking another word the three sat silently next to one another, Stephan between Alice and Leopold. They paid no attention to the tumult around them. When Leopold rose, Stephan energetically grabbed his father's hand with his own left hand, and then with his right hand he took his mother's. He wanted to say that he was not going to let them go, neither of them. I need you both.

In silence they walked to the blockhouse door. Leopold embraced his son and Alice at the same time. He said just one single word: 'Promise?'

It was a while before Alice's reply: 'Promise!'

It happened just as Leopold predicted. The second transport had only just left Theresienstadt on 29 September when the SS let it be known that there was to be a third transport and 500 wives or fiancées would be allowed to follow their husbands. They were to assemble at the designated place to be reunited with their husbands.

The take-up among the women was, as expected, greater than the number of available places. Within a few hours all the seats had been disposed of. One mother even gave her five-year-old son to someone else to care for in order to join her husband.[20]

When Alice's friend Edith Kraus saw the chance of being able to be with her husband again she ran to Moritz Henschel, the head of the Free Time Organization, whose kindness had earned him the name of 'Papa Henschel'. He was over sixty and he was like a father to Edith. Henschel strongly advised against going with a single, unambiguous phrase: 'You will not see him again.'[21]

Otto Zucker's wife also volunteered for the transport. As a privileged prisoner and the wife of the assistant chief of the elders, they allowed her to take eight suitcases with her. When she boarded the train the SS camp commandant Rahm told the German transport leader: 'This is Frau Zucker. It is your responsibility that she lies in her husband's arms tonight.'[22] Rahm knew that Zucker had been sent to the gas chamber as soon as he had arrived in Auschwitz.

The train left Theresienstadt with 1,000 men and 500 trusting women on 1 October 1944. Only the next day an announcement blasted round the ghetto: the families of all the 5,000 deportees could follow, as long as they had not passed the age of sixty-five.[23]

In the meantime the wives had received postcards which testified to their men having arrived safely, telling them about their new work and above all of the better food.[24] Those who wanted to go were overjoyed. It was not until years later that people learned that during the journey, even before the train had reached Dresden, the deportees had been forced to write to their wives of their successful arrival at the chosen place and to tell the women to join them as quickly as they could. Three of the six mothers in Alice's billet received cards like this.

*

THE FOURTH TRANSPORT followed on 5 October, then came the next and soon after that, the next.[25] With every train that left Theresienstadt not only did mistrust grow among the remaining prisoners but greater interest was shown by the SS in keeping the daily cultural activities going strong. They did not want anyone to get the impression that the camp was about to be completely evacuated. The inmates needed to be distracted by music, theatre and lectures.

As before, officials from the Free Time Organization planned concerts and events a week in advance. There were more than 200 artists still in the camp. Some, like the conductor Carlo Taube, Harry Cohn, the second violinist of the legendary Theresienstadt Ledeč Quartet, or the singer Machiel Gobets, had already been deported.[26] New rumours pointed to the officials of the Free Time Organization. It would be their turn next, but for the time being they had to keep up appearances.

Alice continued to give concerts, this time returning to her fourth programme, which included Beethoven's Sonata in D major, Op. 10 No. 3. The famous second movement is an expression of despair. It begins darkly and the music builds until it seems to cry for help before ending with quiet resignation. Many of the listeners, by now only too aware of what the transports meant, began to weep.

Alice often sat for a while in the town hall auditorium after the audience had gone, alone with her reflections. On this occasion she left the building about half past seven, but there was still time before the curfew and she headed slowly towards Seestrasse. An SS officer standing outside the concert hall suddenly came up to her 'Are you Alice Herz-Sommer?'

Alice was terrified. 'My God' she asked herself, 'If he shoots me, what will happen to my son?'[27]

She was struck by the man's face, which did not seem to fit the uniform. Then he began to speak in a gentle, cultivated accent.[28] For months he had listened to all her concerts from outside the building. He loved the music, and the way she played it. The adagio in the Beethoven Sonata moved him the most deeply. At such moments he could forget the lunacy of the war and the conditions in the ghetto.

Alice listened silently, but fear surged through her. How would her fellow prisoners react if they saw her talking to an SS man?

She abruptly tried to tell the man that she needed to get back to her billet quickly. It was nearby and her son was waiting for her.

She had only walked a few paces when the officer called after her: 'I wanted to add, you and your son will not be on the list for the transport.'

Agitated, Alice hurried on, before what he had said caused her to lose control and break down altogether.

'And who is going to take my place on the list?' she shouted back, as she ran home. Behind her she heard the voice of the SS man saying: 'Look after your little son.'[29]

*

ON SUNDAY, 15 OCTOBER 1944, the officials of the Free Time Organization received their call-up papers. They were to be sent on a work detail and were to leave the very next morning.

'Names and transport numbers had been written down on little strips of coloured paper. It was very short, simple and final,' wrote Zdenka Fantlová, who was by then nineteen and an actress with the Free Time Organization.[30] 'Theresienstadt shook. All the actors, directors, musicians and conductors had been selected for deportation. To name but a few: Gustav Schorsch, František Zelenka, Hans Krása, Viktor Ullmann, Pavel Haas, Gideon Klein, Rafael Schächter and Karel Ančerl. The shipment was to be made up of 1,500 people . . .'[31]

Alice's friend Edith Kraus had also received a slip with her name and number on it. Her only hope was her friend Moritz Henschel, who was running the Free Time Organization. Through the intervention of an influential representative of the Autonomous Authority it was still possible to have someone's name struck off the transport list. In 1942, Edith had been spared by just such intervention.[32]

This time Henschel gave her no hope. The SS had decreed that only one pianist should be left in the camp, and as Alice Herz-Sommer had a seven-year-old son the decision had already been made in her favour.[33] Edith accepted her fate, but miraculously her name was once again crossed off the transport list – she never discovered why or who had saved her.

On 16 October 1944 276 artists and members of the Free Time Organization had to leave Theresienstadt. 'The benches provided proved insufficient and they were all squashed together on the floor of the small space. They were soon short of air, and people found it hard to breathe, 'For their bodily needs every wagon was provided with buckets. No one could give any thought to prudery, manners or consideration towards the others. At these moments we were most painfully conscious of our condemnation as sub-humans . . . The little children cried from hunger and thirst. Many sought consolation from prayer, but most had already abandoned hope,'[34] Zdenka Fantlová later wrote. She was one of the few on the transport to survive Auschwitz.

*

ALICE AND STEPHAN were now alone in the twelve-square-metre room, which until the October transport had housed ten others. It was quiet, as quiet as the grave. In this already depressing situation Alice received orders to report to the laundry at five the following morning. How would her son react when he woke up in the morning to find his mother already gone?

Stephan sensed the menace in the air. He had never seen his mother so despairing and began to panic that his mother, like his father, would disappear for ever. He cried bitterly and developed a high fever. Alice took her feverish child by the hand and went from door to door. Many of the neighbouring houses were now empty; all the inhabitants had already been deported. Finally she found an old lady and asked her to look after Stephan the following morning.

She was terribly worried when she left the house the next day at half past four and went to the laundry. Stephan had not accepted her assurances that she would be back again that evening. 'Now I am all alone in this world,' he complained through his tears, his words digging deep into Alice's soul where they remain to this day.[35]

Alice had no problem with the exhausting work. Indeed she took on a lot from her friend Edith Kraus who was working in the laundry with her, as Edith was not as strong as her friend. But as she worked she thought of nothing else except how she could care for her son and, without Edith's friendship, she would never have got through those anxious days. As they went over and over what to do, Alice suddenly thought of a solution: 'Leo Baeck!'

Ever since Alice's first concert, Rabbi Leo Baeck had always sat in the front row to hear her play. After her performance of the Études he had invited her to his Friday discussion group, held every week for a small, select group to talk of things which distracted them from the daily grind of the ghetto. Alice had accepted gladly. Baeck's voice counted for something in the Autonomous Administration and she hoped he would be able to help her now.

When she finished work she went to see him straightaway to tell him of her worries. He immediately arranged for her to move in with another prisoner, Klara Hutter, coincidentally the mother of Alice's friend, Trude.

That night, by moonlight, Alice pushed a cart carrying all her worldly goods to her new billet. As well as their scanty possessions, she and Stephan were taking their mattresses and the remains of the wood that Alice had found in their old room; it was bitterly cold that autumn and the extra firewood might prove a life-saver. She passed the empty barracks and stinking heaps of rubbish that had not been cleared for days.[36] It was a miserable sight. Stephan had tied a rope onto the cart and harnessed himself to it like a horse as Alice could not push it on her own. He had developed astonishing strength for his age; he had had to. But he knew Klara Hutter and he knew now that his mother would return the following evening and the next day and the next.

*

THE NEW HOUSE looked exactly like the old one. The room was the same size, but this time they shared it not with other mothers and their children, but with Klara Hutter and with three other women over seventy. All four women took Stephan to their hearts from the moment he arrived and Alice could go off to work in the laundry without anxiety, knowing that he would be very well looked after. But while she worked she could hear the transports rumbling ceaselessly by outside.

Hitherto the Autonomous Jewish Authority had had to draw up the lists for the transports themselves. But increasingly the SS played a larger and larger role, sending word who was to be included and who was to be left out. The SS camp commandant Rahm himself took over the job of organizing the two final transports, planned for 23 and 28 October 1944. Benjamin Murmelstein, the new Jewish elder, was allowed only to assist him.[37] When the names of the last remaining members of the Free Time Organization came up – Alice Herz-Sommer, Edith Kraus, Marion Podelier, Hedda Grab-Kernmeyer, Ada Schwarz-Klein, Hilde Aronson-Lindt, Anni Frey and Gisa Wurzel – Rahm apparently said: 'You know, let's leave it. They should carry on playing and singing.'[38] Even so he ordered that the women should immediately start work in the mica-splitting workshop.

*

WITH THE ADVANCE of the Red Army the SS closed down the gas chambers at Auschwitz on 2 November 1944. For thousands of inhabitants of the Theresienstadt ghetto, it came too late. In just four weeks eleven 'autumn transports' had despatched more than 8,000 human beings to the Auschwitz gas chambers, among them 1,800 children under fifteen.[39]

The last transport left as planned on 28 October 1944. Most of the members of the council of elders were on board, together with their families. A total of seventy people travelled to their deaths in two comfortable railway carriages.

Shortly after the train left the station at Bohušovice twenty young men were taken off the train and ordered to dig up the remains of those people who had been executed and buried in the area and to destroy their remains. No trace was to remain of the massacre. After they had done this they were shot.

'There were only a few hundred healthy men in the camp now, and all work was winding down, there was no one to clear up the rubbish, there was no one to look after the old people, no one to cook.' This is how the survivor Josef Polák remembered things later. 'But the Nazis did not consider loosening their grip. As if nothing had happened they had a dining room, a kitchen and a cinema built. Everywhere women took over the men's jobs. A group of women took over transport and carried heavy burdens. The camp began slowly to work again . . .'[40]

Life in Theresienstadt carried on. On 31 October 1944 there were still 11,068 registered prisoners and new transports were due to arrive any day.[41]

ELEVEN

After the Inferno

'We will laugh on the ruins of the ghetto ...'

THE MARCH FROM THE GHETTO to the mica-processing huts took three-quarters of an hour. There was only the most rudimentary form of heating in the workshops and the women froze. For hours at a stretch they sat at a long table and split the mica in time with one another. It was considered important war work, especially for the aviation industry; the material the women chiselled out was used to insulate electrical appliances.[1]

The artists of the Free Time Organization sat together at one table. Next to Alice and Edith Kraus were six German-speaking and two Danish women. Three days a week they had to perform the early shift, from 6 a.m. to 2 p.m., and for three days they did the late shift, from 2 p.m. to 10 p.m.

At the beginning of the shift everyone received a packet of mica pieces. These had to be accurately weighed and then split with a special tool. This was a small and dangerously sharp knife with which the exhausted women often cut themselves badly. When they were ready, the transparent leaves were sorted out for size and strength, and at the end of the shift a minimum of fifty grams had to be returned to the packet. The SS overseer threatened the women all the time with the 'transport' should they fail to reach their daily target. Many of them were so worried by this that they stole in order to have enough to hand in.

Alice hated the work. The numbing monotony upset her more active nature. The cramped positions hurt her delicate fingers, there was far too much time to think and there was the constant threat that she might be consigned to a 'transport'. Still, she had a roof over her head and could sit down while she worked; and after a few hours it even became a little warmer in the hut and the time could be used to talk quietly to her neighbours. Even so, Alice found the perpetual jabbering an additional trial. In desperation one day Alice suddenly dropped her tool, jumped up and ran out of the hut. Once outside she paced back and forth like a caged panther. There was no way out! In this moment of deepest despair, however, her iron discipline reimposed itself and an inner voice reminded her of her innate power: 'Persevere!'

It seemed more of a revelation than a warning and she returned to the work bench actually strengthened. From then on, hour by hour, day after day she and Edith talked of the past and dreamed of the future; they planned concerts for when they were free and delighted in the thought of the music they would play. Later, Alice realized that in those twelve weeks of splitting mica, she exchanged more words with her friend than she ever had with Leopold during the twelve years of happy marriage.[2]

*

AFTER THE AUTUMN transports it took a long time for things to get back to normal in the camp.[3] The utilities had collapsed. There wasn't the labour any more. The kitchens no longer functioned and there were no nurses in the sickbays. Anyone who collapsed just lay helpless on the ground. There were thousands of positions vacant in health and administration and women had to perform the men's roles, even those which were physically demanding. On 13 December 1944 the authorities announced a new Autonomous Jewish Administration[4] and with this there came, too, a new incarnation of the Free Time Organization, although its only remaining members were the women consigned to the mica-processing works. Nevertheless, by the end of December 1944 there were concerts in Theresienstadt once more.[5]

The artists received the news as a gift from heaven. Anyone performing that evening could leave the late shift as early as 5 p.m. Despite the joyful anticipation of her performance, Alice always left the hut with an uneasy, tormented feeling. Seeing the envious eyes of a hundred or so exhausted, hard-working women did not make her happy.

*

ON CHRISTMAS EVE 1944, Alice was working the late shift and, as usual, she and her fellow workers left at around ten. The way back to the camp through the darkness led them over a hill past the barracks of the Czech gendarmes, who guarded the huts. However, that night the men were nowhere to be seen. They had already retired to their guardroom to put up a small Christmas tree and cover it with festive decorations. The lights shining through the window struck the women like symbols of hope. 'The little tree not only lit up our way, but it gave us warmth. Something of the love felt by those who set it up rubbed off on us, and we carry that with us still,' Gerty Spiess wrote in her autobiography. Gerty, a German Jew, sat at a neighbouring table to Alice in the mica-splitting workshop.[6]

Alice was still bathing in that light when she returned to her billet, but she was glad that Stephan was already asleep and she did not have to try to explain that Christmas tree. The boy would have simply asked too many questions. 'What is Christmas? Why do Christians celebrate it and why is it that we Jews do not?' After the terrible weeks they had endured, she no longer had the strength to answer him.

Nonetheless, Alice enjoyed the holiday on the first day of Christmas. At last she could spend a whole day with Stephan. Pavel Fuchs paid a call, as he did virtually every day. The two friends played together in a carefree way and Alice listened to them laughing heartily as if they were living in freedom.

*

THE NEW YEAR seemed full of promise. People said that the German Reich was on the brink of collapse: 'retreat on all fronts, it can't last much longer.' The camp concerts now became symbols of the coming liberation.[7]

In the middle of January 1945, however, Alice and her musical colleagues faced a new setback. The SS ordered a final, collective punishment for the inmates of the camp. The activities of the Free Time Organization were banned forthwith. Forbidden cigarettes had been smuggled into the camp,[8] but by the beginning of February the ban was lifted. Soon there were more concerts than ever and the inmates fought over the tickets.

On 7 February 1945 Alice played the Chopin Études again. The auditorium of the town hall was completely packed and a five-page handwritten review survives, although the author is still unknown. 'Yesterday evening, 7 February 1945, the artistic world of Theresienstadt was highlighted by the great Chopin evening given by Frau Sommer-Herz ... I have heard Rubinstein's pupil, Raoul von Koczalski, play, and Rubinstein was a pupil of Chopin himself . . .' In this, though it scarcely matters in the context, the anonymous author is incorrect: Koczalski's teacher was not Rubinstein, but Carl Mikuli – one of Chopin's most important pupils What is much more significant is the fact that the reviewer was more moved by Alice's playing than by a pianist who was so close to the Chopin tradition. The reviewer continued in a euphoric vein, describing the extraordinary effect Alice had had on the audience:

> If France referred to its great tragedian Sarah Bernhardt as the 'divine Sarah' why should we not call our great Chopin inter-preter Frau Sommer-Herz the divine mirror of Chopin . . . Her superb playing ranged from melancholy, passion, the endear-ing amiability of the French temperament; just the qualities that the composer, sick with consumption, incorporated in his own idiosyncratic way. Whenever the artist, with her magical variations of tempo, released real storms of mood the natures of two nations came to the fore – the Slavic and the French

– emerging like a sculpture in sound. It was clear that the
Genius of the Muses had found a patron, and the listeners
knelt before her concert, as if in prayer.[9]

The Harp Study: Op. 25 No 1 in A flat major

'Magical! A spellbinding study, quite unique in its beauty.' Even
now, when she is over 100 years old, Alice Herz-Sommer speaks
of the Harp Study, Op. 25 No. 1 with girlish infatuation. 'It seizes
the listener from the very first note.' As Robert Schumann wrote
in 1837 after Frédéric Chopin played it to him himself: 'After the
study I saw one lovely picture after another as if in a dream, that
one has when only half-awake, and wants to dream all over
again . . .'[10] It is full of security, warmth and hope.

And, at last, the prisoners who listened rapt to Alice's playing
cherished the very real hope that they might soon be liberated. On
3 February the SS had announced that two days later 1,200 people
would be released and allowed to travel to Switzerland.[11] Hardly
anyone believed it. Even the criteria for choosing who should go
made people ill at ease: only those in good health could travel, and
no relations of prisoners who had been deported to Poland. Also
excluded were important prisoners or intellectuals.[12]

But the events on the day itself silenced the sceptics. On 5
February an express train with well-upholstered compartments
chugged into the station and every one of the 1,200 passengers had
a seat to themselves. Their original transport numbers had to be
removed from their suitcases. Rahm took it upon himself to make

sure that only respectable items of luggage were included and that all the passengers were issued with sufficient food for the journey. The SS helped the elderly to get onto the train and carried their luggage onto the wagons. During the journey the passengers had to remove their Stars of David. A few days later the first letters arrived from Switzerland.

The rescue operation had been planned many months before. In August 1944 a group of eminent Swiss figures had made contact with Heinrich Himmler through his personal physician, Felix Kersten, asking for 20,000 Jews to be released into Switzerland.[13] Initially Himmler refused, but on 8 December Kersten managed to wring a partial agreement out of Himmler, who – by then – was only interested in trying to save his own skin.

The Tender: Op. 25 No. 2 in F minor

After the promise of hope and happiness in the First Étude of the second cycle, the charming F minor study sounds tender, 'deliciously dreamy and gentle, a little like a child singing in its sleep.'[14]

Alice had often played this second study to Stephan as he went to sleep and the seven-year-old knew it very well. Now, he enthusiastically followed his mother's playing, with rare concentration and devotion. The wonderfully delicate melody moves constantly between piano and pianissimo like a gentle breeze, but though it is an enchanting piece, it is written in a minor key which casts an aura of melancholy over it.[15]

Its note of mourning echoed Alice's mood, even though the prospect of liberation seemed more real. She had no idea where

Leopold was, nor if he was still alive. Was he permitted evenings like these which lifted the morale of the prisoners? Since the National Socialists had snatched Leopold from her, Alice's concerts had always been at some level a bidding prayer for her husband's life, a plea to see him again.

The Bold: Op. 25 No. 3 in F major

The third study in F is as melodic as it is aesthetic, and an example of Chopin's compositional fantasy. There is much in the first motif that is capricious, graceful and jocular, but in the second the mood changes and a sad, plaintive motif is introduced. The graceful melody could be said to mirror the life of Zdenka Fantlová, who had left Theresienstadt for Auschwitz in one of the October transports. Zdenka arrived there on 18 October 1944 after several tortuous days in a cattle truck. Finally the door was slid back and she was able to see the guards holding truncheons and their dogs on the ramp. She breathed in air filled with a 'sweet smelling smoke as if they were burning flesh somewhere'. She told herself, 'Death reigns here, and the dangers are great. It threatens you . . . if you are lucky, they will not kill you, you will have to summon up all your strengths in order to survive . . .'[16] Zdenka had always loved music and now she could conjure up memories of the concert halls of Theresienstadt and the music she had heard there, music which had given her so much strength.

Now, however, she was standing on the ramp with 1,500 other deportees and being measured up by three SS officers. Zdenka

Fantlová understood very quickly that what happened next was 'now about life or death'.

> Someone had polished their boots until they sparkled and the deaths-heads on their caps made it only too clear why they were there. All three looked into the crowd with very uncompromising expressions. The one in the middle, who was wearing gloves, was giving orders with his right hand. You could see he was sorting: 'Left! Right! Left! Left! Left! Right! . . .' Now it was the turn of us three. My mother was terribly worried and struck with foreboding. I looked the officer right in the eye. He was a good-looking man who seemed neither particularly stern nor entirely evil, only his bright blue eyes had a steely glaze to them. Without reflection he said 'left' for my mother and with the same swift certainty, 'right' for me. When it came to my sixteen-year-old sister he made no immediate comment, so I grabbed her by the arm as quick as a flash and took her with me to the right. I still had a moment to look at my mother's face. I saw her total horror and despair and thoughts of never seeing us again. Then she was quickly lost in the crowd.[17]

After the selection came the strip search. It was absolutely forbidden to keep any personal effects.

> We had to strip in a small room and stand naked next to one another. I still had Arno's ring on my finger. I did not want to be separated from it. Quite the reverse: it was my talisman, my strength and hope; it was the flame that would keep me alive. We had to goose-step through a narrow aperture behind which an SS man was waiting to check that we really had nothing more. I was already nearly at the spot when we were thrown into panic by the sound of crying, pleas and punches. What had happened? A girl had hidden her engagement ring under her tongue, but the man in uniform had found it. He beat her mercilessly and led her away

A fellow sufferer saw the ring on my finger 'For God's sake, throw the ring away! You're mad, they'll beat you to death. It is not worth it for a bit of tin: you saw what happened to the girl in front of us . . .'

Despite what had happened I decided to run the risk. I put the ring in my mouth and rendered myself up to my fate with the SS inspector.

I was aware of all the consequences but I stood by my decision and I was ready to pay any price. He began by looking through my hair and I was waiting for the order to open my lips, but at this moment a superior officer intervened in the inspections and told him to hurry up. So I was pushed on and it was the turn of the next girl. 'Quick, off!' I had kept the ring. It was the first test fate had given me, and I had passed.[18]

The Dancer: Op. 25 No. 4 in A minor

The Fourth Étude in A minor is an infectiously rhythmic study of syncopation with an impetuous dancing melody. One of the greatest pianists of the nineteenth century, the Hungarian Stephan Heller, compared it to the first bar of the Kyrie from Mozart's *Requiem*.

Thirteen-year-old Anna Flachová was leaning against the wall of the auditorium in the Town Hall and absorbing the music, entranced by it. She was one of the few remaining members of the *Brundibár* ensemble.

Flaška, as she was called, had begun to study piano in 1937

when she was seven. Two years later she had her first singing lesson. The arrival of German troops in Czechoslovakia ruptured her childhood mercilessly. When she was ten, she was seen walking down the street, obligatory yellow star on her coat, by two German soldiers. 'What a pretty girl. Pity she's a Jew.'[19] But that was harmless compared to other anti-Semitic attacks she had to endure. When her mother bought Flaška new white shoes, a woman stopped in the street and pointed at them, screaming: 'You Jewish swine, give me those shoes. One of your sort should not have shoes like that!'[20]

On 26 November 1941, her eleventh birthday, she and her family were ordered to 'fall in with the transport'. It was the first time she had ever seen her mother cry. They arrived in Theresienstadt on 2 December 1941.

The Études worked their way under Flaška's skin; so much so that she began to see a clear aim for the future: 'If I succeed in getting out of the ghetto then I shall become a pianist.' Flaška survived, going on to study piano and singing in Prague. She later became a successful performer and a professor at the conservatoire in Brno.[21]

The Sarcastic: Op. 25 No. 5 in E minor

The introduction to the E minor study is slightly mocking, a quality shared by Karel Švenk, the most popular actor in the ghetto. Before the war he had been a professional cook and only acted as an amateur member of the 'Club of Untried Talents'. According to a later account 'his comical portrayal of a ridiculous fat man, together with his dithering, made him rip-roaringly funny as Pod-kolesin in Gogol's *Marriage*.'[22]

He had arrived at Theresienstadt with the first construction detail at the end of 1941 and began his cabaret act soon after. Despite much competition it remained the best and the most popular in the camp. Though Švenk was an amazing all-round talent – author and director, lyricist and composer – he remained modest and was always convivial: 'Švenk was a great clown above all. He did not come from an intellectual milieu, he stood where you put him, clumsy, comic but good; he could disarm and unmask the wicked opponent by a simple look – that was his typecast. He had the great sad, smiling eyes of the classic rogue who was forever the victim of the unscrupulous or the cunning. Whether they suc-ceeded or not, he always survived.'[23]

However the Council of Elders found his play, *The Last*, so provocative that for the first time they felt it necessary to censor part of it. They approved the performance on condition that the last scene be cut. Švenk pretended to comply, but when the play was performed it was shown in its entirety. It was about deportation and dictator-ship and in it Švenk mocked the Nazis' anti-Jewish policies, referring to 'Jews and cyclists, who are guilty of everything'. At the end the female dictator is annihilated, the curtain falls and the audience is told to go home. The rule of the fools has come to an end. But as an actor spoke the epilogue, another interrupted him to say that 'below and outside' the rule of the fools continued. They still could not say what they really thought. The curtain rose again and the first chords of the Terezin Hymn, which Švenk had written for one of his first cabarets in 1942, were heard. The entire cast stood hand in hand on the stage and silently mouthed the words. The audience understood only too well and rewarded the performers with unstint-ing applause. Without being able to write a single note of music, Karel Švenk had the only real anthem of the ghetto. The last words were: '. . . we will laugh on the ruins of the ghetto, Hand in hand.'[24]

But Švenk did not live long enough to hear this laugh. By the time Alice played the Fifth Étude in February 1945, he had already been sent to Auschwitz on one of the autumn transports. When the camp was liberated, he was still alive but only just and he died from exhaustion as he made his way home.

The Thirds: Op. 25 No. 6 in G sharp minor

Some commentators have said that the Sixth Étude in G sharp minor with its chromatic thirds sounds like a dance of death. It is certainly one of the most difficult pieces ever written. According to the critic Thomas Pehlken: 'With its suppressed dynamics (*sotto voce*) and its darting tempo, the piece is reminiscent of those beloved works of the romantics: the Sabbath dance scene by Berlioz and Mendelssohn's Scherzo, Op. 20.'[25]

The mysterious mood of the piece seemed to encapsulate the rumours that had been haunting Theresienstadt for days. At the beginning of February 1945 the SS issued two orders to the Autonomous Jewish Authority. The first was to construct a series of gastight rooms, the second was to fence in a large area near the perimeter walls to secure them against attempts at escape. By this stage, rumours of the gassings in Auschwitz had reached the ghetto and the prisoners were suspicious, fearing that the orders were the harbingers of death.

The camp commandant Karl Rahm sought to appease the inmates: 'How could you think such a thing – we'll have no gas chambers in Theresienstadt!'[26] He told the Jewish elder Benjamin Murmelstein that they wanted to build a bomb-proof food store and a chicken farm that would be safe from thieves.

However, an analysis of the plans for the so-called ventilation system seemed to prove what the builders feared: they were to

construct pipes that would bring gas into the rooms. One of the
technicians, Erich Kohn, told Murmelstein of the plans, declaring
that no Jews would consent to work on the building of an instal-
lation that would be used for the gassing of Jews or anyone else
for that matter. They would rather be shot before the eyes of the
whole world than continue the work. The discussion lasted all night
and next morning Murmelstein told Rahm what had been said.

Rahm immediately summoned Kohn. He asked him if he really
believed that the project was to build a gas chamber. Kohn replied
that he did. Rahm then drew his revolver and kicked and punched
Kohn repeatedly in front of the other workers.[27]

But when, later that day, the SS reported to Berlin the resistance
in the ghetto, the building works, together with the ring-fencing of
the plateau by the perimeter walls, were discontinued.[28] Clearly the
SS leadership were already feeling sufficiently insecure that they
dared not proceed against their opponents as brutally as they had
done even quite recently. After the war, when the commandant of
the Little Fortress appeared before the courts, he admitted that
Kohn's suspicions were correct. Besides converting the building
into a gas chamber, the ring-fenced plateau would be used to fence
in thousands of prisoners before turning flame throwers on them
and burning them alive.[29] Had it not been for the courageous
resistance of the ghetto building workers the SS might have chore-
ographed a last, lethal dance of death.

The Melancholic: Op. 25 No. 7 in C sharp minor

The seventh study in C sharp minor is the only slow piece in the
cycle, a moving elegy threaded through with pain and despair.

Arnošt Weiss, who was sitting in the audience for Alice's performance, was head of the Works Department in the ghetto, a key role which had – so far – protected him from the transports.

Arnošt was a passionate chamber musician and evenings of chamber music were an essential part of his life, even after he was banished from his home town of Olmütz (Olomouc) in 1940. After he arrived in Prague, he soon struck up new friendships, with the violin teacher Erich Wachtel and with the Herz-Sommers. At the weekend they often played together in a quartet with Weiss on the viola, Alice's brother Paul Herz on first violin, Leopold Sommer on second violin and Dr Jóši Haas on the cello.[30]

Then, at Christmas 1941, the German authorities decreed that under the threat of the most severe penalties, all Jews had to hand over their musical instruments immediately. Then, a month later, on 27 January 1942 Arnošt Weiss, his wife and son had to report to the assembly point bearing the numbers 825, 826 and 827. There they spent three extremely cold nights on the floor of the unheated hall before they left for Theresienstadt. But even there he found solace in music. As a little boy he had been able to whistle almost any piece of music. In Theresienstadt he was able to bring this to true perfection:

> In the camp I often went about whistling without really being conscious of what I was doing. Once in the lavatory an old man cried out to me: 'Listen young man, do you know what you are whistling?' 'Certainly,' I replied, 'Beethoven's *Razumovsky Quartet* No. 1.' The man walked up to me with tears in his eyes and introduced himself as Freudenthal, a former member of the Berlin Philharmonic and more recently concert master of the Aussig Opera. He whistled the first violin part, and I whistled the other three instruments. That was my first experience of playing a string quartet in Theresientstadt.[31]

Arnošt Weiss survived Theresienstadt as chief of the Works Division. Decades later he wrote 'Poor children! Poor adults! There were a thousand Jews on Transport V. Only thirty-two adults and five children survived the terror regime of the Nazis.'[32]

The Gracile: Op. 25 No. 8 in D flat major

The eighth study in D flat is a short, quiet masterpiece of bewitching charm and inimitable grace. 'The work is imbued with the breath of life, which has been invested with the beauty and perfection fashioned by an artist's hand, in which a divine fluid flows.'[33] Many in the audience, listening to Alice play this extraordinary piece, must have been thinking of the bitter life of the many incarcerated in Theresienstadt. Irma Lauscherová wrote in her 1968 article 'Die Kinder von Theresienstadt' (The Children of Theresienstadt):

> No butterflies fly here, no trees grow and no flowers bloom. Children, however, must live here. Children and young people, prisoners like everyone else . . . There are terrifying hygienic conditions in the overcrowded little town . . . there is a lack of food . . . The billets are overcrowded . . . It is a human antheap . . . Filth, fleas, bugs, lice, mice, rats. Infectious diseases rage . . . More than 15,000 children passed through Theresienstadt ghetto, only about a hundred ever returned.

She continues:

I'd love to know above all else whether Frau Alice Herz-Sommer, well away in Jerusalem, where she teaches in the

conservatoire, can still remember her activity in Theresienstadt. She was an excellent music teacher who used to give
a few children lessons on the old piano in the Town Hall
auditorium after the morning shift or before the evening shift
in the mica-splitting workshop. That was not enough for her,
however, and she decided that musical education should
encompass a larger number of children. She began to give
concerts for the young. Every Saturday she would sit at the
piano surrounded by her silent listeners in the late afternoon.
She would then play a motif, explain it, and then play a few
bars more, which she would then explain again and then she
would play as a virtuoso going right to the end, treating her
young public with the perfection of a great artist.[34]

Lauscherová, who before the war was a teacher in Prague, was
at the heart of the secret school system in the ghetto, but by her
side was Alice Herz-Sommer.

The Pinnacle of Perfection: Op. 25 No. 9 in G flat major

The delicately pretty melody of the Ninth Étude in G flat is
reminiscent of the theme in the third movement of Beethoven's
Sonata in G major, Op. 79 and the formal, classical language of
the piece reveals Chopin's debt to both Beethoven and Schubert.
According to one critic, the ninth Étude reaches 'the pinnacle of
perfection and artistry.'[35]

Viktor Ullmann, the most prominent composer in Theresienstadt,
strove for perfection in his works. Alice and Ullmann knew one
another well and enjoyed mutual respect. Ullmann even dedicated

his fourth sonata to her. Between the summer of 1943 and the spring of 1944 he composed his chamber opera *The Emperor of Atlantis*,[36] with a libretto by Peter Kien. Rich in symbolism and contemporary relevance, the opera is set in the mythical city of Atlantis ruled by the Emperor Uberall who is waging war against the rest of the world. Life and Death – both characters in the opera – have become meaningless and eventually Death goes on strike and no one can die. As the Emperor's soldiers lie wounded and bleeding on the battlefield, Death offers the Emperor a bargain – he will resume his duties if the Emperor agrees to be his first victim. The Emperor agrees. The opera ends with a quartet based on Luther's stirring Reformation hymn, *Ein' Feste Burg* (A Mighty Fortress is our God), later the inspiration for one of Bach's greatest cantatas, warning *Thou shalt not take Death's great name in vain*. Finally the Emperor invites Death round and asks him for his help. At first Death refuses but later he says he is ready to go back to work, but makes it a condition that the Emperor be the first victim. Because of its defiant subject matter, the opera was never performed in Theresienstadt and, indeed, the first production was not until 1975.

In October 1944 Viktor Ullmann was murdered in Auschwitz.

The Octave Study: Op. 25 No. 10 in B minor

The Octave Étude, the tenth in the cycle, is in B minor, and it is full of drama and complaint. The piece might be compared to a typhoon, so powerful is the effect of the sinister and demonic run of octaves.

The previous year, in June 1944, Theresienstadt had been shaken by the 'Affair of the Painters'.[37] A number of artists among the prisoners had been secretly sketching life in the ghetto and had hidden their drawings throughout the camp. When the International Red Cross visited the camp and one of the delegates demanded to see behind the newly restored facades of the houses, it became clear to the SS that some of these drawings had been smuggled out of the camp and into Switzerland.

As a result of this, the artists Bedřich Fritta, Otto Ungar, Felix Bloch and Leo Haas were interrogated, by none other than Adolf Eichmann. The SS produced their proof: drawings that had been unearthed from their hiding places of famished prisoners scavenging for potato peelings.

'How can you think of painting such a thing; how can you make such a mockery of the truth?' Leo Haas was asked. 'Are you trying to imply that people are hungry in the ghetto? The Red Cross has found absolutely no evidence of that.'[38] Eventually the Gestapo in Prague brought charges for 'the dissemination of atrocity propaganda abroad'.

Felix Bloch was beaten to death in Theresienstadt's Little Fortress. The others were transported east – Bedřich Fritta died in Auschwitz and Otto Ungar in Buchenwald. Only Leo Haas survived his incarceration in Sachsenhausen.[39]

The Eroica: Op. 25, No. 11 in A minor

The Eleventh Étude is without question the most passionate piece of the second cycle and in some ways it resembles the Revolutionary

Étude. The passion in Chopin's music was echoed in the life of
Rafael Schächter, one of the the most important figures in Theresienstadt's musical circle. Schächter had arrived in the ghetto as
early as November 1941 and within a year had put together a choir
of sixty male and female singers. By 28 November 1942 he was able
to put on a performance of Smetana's *Bartered Bride*. Many pro-
ductions followed, but the high point came when Schächter contro-
versially decided to represent the suffering of the Jews of Auschwitz
in a performance of a Catholic mass for the dead. His enthusiasm
for Verdi's great Requiem, however, bordered on the fanatical. At
a time when every prisoner feared for his life, Schächter worked like
a man possessed, preparing a requiem for all the victims of Nazi crimes.

Fortune did not smile on the project. The premiere took place
on 6 September 1943, but immediately afterwards a transport left
Theresienstadt for Auschwitz with almost the entire choir on
board. Even after this fearful blow, Schächter would not give up;
on the contrary he set out to find new singers and on 2 January
1944 a second performance was given, in the presence of the
president of the council of elders. All too soon, the hundred and
fifty members of the new choir were themselves packed into cattle
trucks bound for Auschwitz. Schächter assembled a third choir and
the Requiem was performed again, but with the autumn transports
of 1944 the fate of the choir and its director were sealed.

The Divine: Op. 25 No. 12 in C minor

The Twelfth and final Étude is in C minor, often called the Ocean
Étude, because its intense, dramatic melody evokes a stormy sea,

but Alice calls it 'the divine'.[40] An eyewitness who attended her concert in February 1945 wrote this about her performance: 'This inspiration filled with melancholy sweetness by the youthful Chopin can only be brought to its natural perfection by an interpreter who reads its message of rebirth and revival, and that is the God-given artist, Frau Sommer-Herz.'

TWELVE

Liberation

'As fast as my legs can carry me'

'Paul? . . . Paul!'

Paul Herz did not have the strength to turn round when he heard the voice behind him. Since early that morning he and three other prisoners had been harnessed to a cart, like dray horses, dragging it back and forth from the connecting platform outside the Hamburg Barracks to the building site on the old town walls. On the way out the cart was loaded with timber, and on the way back with earth and rubble.

Paul had arrived in Theresienstadt on 11 February 1945 and was immediately assigned to a special construction unit.[1] Several hundred prisoners had been ordered to construct a square from parts of the parallel defensive walls. Officially this would then be transformed into an artificial lake for a projected duck farm, but it was soon rumoured in the camp that the prisoners were in fact digging their own graves. It is possible that the SS was indeed planning to lure the prisoners into the square by telling them there was to be a new headcount and then flood the area. They had estimated that they could drown up to 15,000 men at a stroke in that way. The few who managed to flee, they concluded, could be finished off with a single machine gun salvo.[2]

When Paul heard someone whistle a few bars from Beethoven's

Razumovsky Quartet No. 1, his face lit up and, turning, he saw his friend Arnošt Weiss.

'Paul the violinist! . . . Can it really be you!' Arnošt Weiss, with whom Paul had secretly played in a string quartet, was the head of the Building Works in the Autonomous Jewish Authority.

'When did you get here?'

'It's my fourth day,' Paul laconically replied. As a Jew related to an Aryan he had been placed under house arrest in Prague and recruited into the labour service. Up until the last moment he had hoped to be spared from deportation but at the end of January 1945 the Germans had begun to send previously 'protected' Jews off to Theresienstadt. More than 3,500 men from so-called mixed marriages were brought to Theresienstadt from all over the Protectorate.[3]

'Can you tell me what happened to my sister?' he asked. He had had no news of Alice since July 1943.

'On Saturday night she is giving another concert,' Arnošt Weiss told him, 'for children and adolescents.' Paul's weary eyes lit up. 'Try to get through the next few days. I will look after you . . .'

Late that afternoon Paul dragged himself off to his billet and fell exhausted on to his mattress, unable to eat or wash let alone search for Alice and her family. He took refuge in sleep until the siren wailed at six the next morning. At the roll-call he heard his name read out: 'Paul Herz to report immediately to chief engineer Weiss in the Works Department.'

'I call that luck,' said Arnošt Weiss when his old friend came in, 'I need a worker and you pitch up. You will be assigned to the task at once. Come on Paul.' As they left the office Weiss added quietly, 'and besides I need someone to play with me in the evenings.'

'It can't go on much longer, do you think?' Paul whispered. Hitler's armies were on the verge of collapse on all fronts. It could only be a matter of days until the war was over and they could all go home. But Arnošt warned his friend, 'The Germans will capitulate, but they might try to get rid of us first.'

On that first day Paul was allowed to finish early, as it was Saturday. 'Alice is playing at five in the town hall,' said Arnošt Weiss, 'now be off with you.'

*

IN THE FRONT half of the town hall auditorium around a hundred children and teenagers were crowded together, with dozens of adults seated behind them. Paul Herz sat in the back row and watched his sister, delighted by her lively appearance. Alice was standing at the piano and talking to one of her confidantes. Later Paul learned that it was Irma Lauscherová, Theresienstadt's secret 'headmistress'. Paul saw his nephew Stephan in the front row, looking content and well-cared for.

Every Saturday Alice introduced her young audience to a new composer. Today she was playing the works of the Czech composer Vítěslav Novák and she began by telling the story of the artist's life.[4]

With typical skill, engaging naturalness and an unfailing ability to inspire her audience, she took them on a journey through Moravia at the turn of the century, the landscape and folklore of which had profoundly coloured Novák's music. Unlike his more famous contemporary Leoš Janáček, Novák was no modernist, but a representative of Czech late romanticism.

'In the end, with him it is always about the beauty and sublimity of nature and its meaning,' Alice enthused. Then she went over to the piano and demonstrated with what simple means Dvořák's pupil, who lived out his seventy-five years in the little east Bohemian town of Skuteč, had conjured up the song of the cuckoo so perfectly in his compositions. Alice had all the children cry out 'cuckoo' and then she replied with the sequence of notes in which Novák imitated the bird, at which they all erupted into cheerful laughter.

'Novák can also invoke the blossom on the tree and a bright blue sky in music,' Alice went on, 'listen carefully!' The melody announced the spring, which sooner or later follows every winter, and the light, which at some stage will always dissipate the darkness . . .

Alice's message was unmistakable: children, place your faith in the coming spring. Men and women, your liberation is just around the corner. But to maintain the light-hearted tone, Alice swiftly moved on to stories that her teacher Václav Štěpán had told her about Novák, a close friend, and their shared love of nature. To finish she played another one of Novák's works.

When the audience left, Paul got up and walked towards Alice. She was still deeply immersed in her work and hadn't noticed that her brother was there.

'Uncle Pavel!' Stephan cried, 'Maminko, Pavel is here, just look,' and excitedly he turned back and forth between his uncle and his mother before throwing himself into the arms of his favourite uncle. In Prague they had lived less than ten minutes away from one another and Paul had visited them at least once a week, to play music with Alice or his brother-in-law.

Paul gave himself time to cuddle Stephan and then turned to his sister.

'We had hoped you had been spared,' Alice said, looking her well-fed brother up and down with astonishment.

'Mary has her virtues, she can get hold of anything,' he responded, sounding almost as if he thought he had been caught out in some way before continuing, 'I have brought my violin with me.'

*

EARLY IN 1945 negotiations were taking place between the SS and the International Committee of the Red Cross, which had expressed a desire to send another delegation to Theresienstadt. At first the SS had predictably refused the request from the Red Cross: concentration camp prisoners were not prisoners of war and the Red Cross's responsibilities did not extend to them. Eventually, however, Heinrich Himmler overruled those who opposed the idea and decreed that in the case of Theresienstadt an exception would be made. His eagerness to please the Red Cross was clearly part of his plan to negotiate a peace settlement behind Hitler's back.

On 3 March 1945 Adolf Eichmann was – some say against his will – directed by Himmler to inspect the camp and to report back on whether the camp was presentable.[5] 'In its present state Theresienstadt will make everyone happy,' Eichmann maintained after his tour of inspection. Nothing needed to be changed. Himmler was not satisfied, however, and next day Eichmann ordered a new 'beautification' of Theresienstadt.

Ernst Kaltenbrunner, the head of the RSHA, also had to be persuaded that the Red Cross's request should be approved. In the second week of March 1945 he received Carl Jacob Burckhardt, the President of the International Red Cross, and agreed to let a member of the organization visit the the camp in order to start immediate relief work whilst at the same time postponing the date of the visit until 6 April.

Before the visit, on Eichmann's expressed orders, the walls of the prisoners' quarters were freshly whitewashed, the facades of the barracks and houses were painted, the parks cleaned up and hygiene in the kitchens improved.[6] A synagogue was set up as well and the Council of Elders was given a new office in a well-maintained house on the main square complete with carpets and telephones. The most cynical part of the refurbishment was the provision of a Jewish cemetery. The dead were no longer going to be burned but buried, according to Jewish law. Above all, cultural life was to be promoted at the highest level – after all, that had deceived the Red Cross the last time, in July 1944.

*

A FEW DAYS after Eichmann's visit the camp commandant Karl Rahm ordered the prompt revival of *Brundibár*, ignoring the fact that since the last performance in September 1944 almost the entire cast – both children and adults – had been deported to Auschwitz and murdered. Of the children, just the seven-year-old Stephan Sommer and a few girls from the Theresienstadt choir remained.

When this was pointed out to Rahm he was pragmatic. A new cast would have to be found, and immediately. Nothing impressed the Red Cross so much as children singing and dancing.

Hanuš Thein, a Prague opera director, who had also been blessed with a magnificent bass voice, was ordered to mount the production. As someone 'related' to Aryans he, like Paul Herz, had only arrived in Theresienstadt at the beginning of 1945. 'Thein, I need a children's opera!' However peculiar Rahm's order may sound in retrospect Hanuš Thein saw the potential. He could bring a lot of the new arrivals into the production and, after years of being banned from working, he could resume his profession once more.

Thein could not possibly put together a performance of *Brundibár* in the time available before the arrival of the Red Cross delegate. Humperdinck's lavish *Hansel and Gretel* was also unthinkable. As an alternative Thein suggested the Czech children's classic *The Little Glow-Worm* which the actress Vlasta Schoenová had already staged as a 'dance poem' with the choreographer Kamilla Rosenblum at the beginning of 1943. Schoenová had recited short extracts from the book and the readings had been punctuated by singing and dancing from thirty of the youngest children from Theresienstadt's Czech community. The audience loved it so much that by October 1944 there had been twenty-eight performances.

Like Alice, Vlasta Schoenová was one of the few members of the Free Time Organization who had been spared from deportation to the east. She was reluctant, however, to put on *The Little Glow-Worm* again, convinced that it was just a strategy on the part of the SS to cover up what really went on in the ghetto. Hanuš Thein eventually convinced her, arguing that traditional songs in their mother tongue would appeal to the Czech audience's patriotism and give them heart in what might prove to be the last weeks of the war.

*

ON 7 MARCH 1945 an SS inspector came to the mica-splitting hut and went over to the table of the Free Time Organization. This was to be their last day in the workshop, he told them. From now on the women had concerts to give and needed to spend their days rehearsing.[7]

With the Dutch violin virtuoso Herman Leydensdorff, Alice prepared two new programmes: one was to be an evening of Beethoven at which the singer Ada Schwarz-Klein would also perform and which would prove extremely popular.[8] Edith Kraus put together a programme of Bach, and also organized two evenings of concerts for two pianos with Beatrice Pimentel who had just arrived in the camp.

Paul Herz volunteered for the chamber orchestra. Now, instead of going to the construction site, he went to the Sokolovna, the former gymnasium, which since the 'beautification drive' of July 1944 had been turned into a community centre complete with stage, prayer room and the Free Time Organization's library. Like Paul, a few members of the orchestra had brought their instruments into the camp; others could help themselves from the confiscated instruments. A whole collection of string instruments from Karel Ančerl's now legendary orchestra were lying in an attic.

Robert Brock, an experienced musician who had often conducted in Russia and in Czechoslovakia, was appointed conductor. In addition to his daily rehearsals he had to compose an overture for *The Little Glow-Worm* and – more importantly – had to keep the commanding SS officers involved. Their attitude to the musicians was often unpredictable – as indeed it was to everybody.

While Alice felt relaxed in her musical world, Paul was troubled and asked himself what exactly lay behind the privileges they were granted by the SS. He wanted to know why his sister, for example, should be given special treatment: 'They want to save your skin, Alice, to show the world how nice they have been to the Jews in the camp.' Nonetheless, the two of them decided to take advantage of the freedom Rahm had given them and they began rehearsing a programme of Beethoven sonatas. Paul had smuggled the scores into the camp, and there was one sonata he had never played with Alice.

Stephan attended the rehearsals in the tiny room in the Magdeburg Barracks. 'I have heard that you are the best page-turner here,' Paul said to his nephew. 'Can we employ you?' Stephan was thrilled and from then on never missed 'Pavel and Maminka's' rehearsals. Even when he did not have to turn the pages he sat in a corner and watched. He remembered the next few weeks particularly well. At nine he began the day with an hour's piano lesson, after which he could – as much as was possible in a concentration camp – opt to do whatever he liked. He could listen to his mother rehearsing or go to his uncle's orchestra rehearsals. He liked these so much that he decided he wanted to become a conductor.

One day, as they rehearsed, Paul turned to Alice and asked, 'Do you still know the D major Adagio from the sixth Beethoven Sonata?'

It was a foolish question – Alice knew that the Adagio was Paul's favourite piece of music, which, when they were children of ten and eleven, they had played to their mother. Sofie Herz requested the piece almost as often as she did the splendidly melodic Dvořák Sonatina, which she liked best of all. 'We're going to do it like the old days,' said Paul, 'first the Adagio and then the Sonatina.' They had known both pieces by heart for three decades.

Alice, seated at the piano, waited for her cue. She loved these moments. Paul concentrated deeply before beginning each piece, until a slight but unmistakable shudder showed that that he was ready. Raising his left shoulder, he would give a forceful nod and begin to play. Alice studied Paul closely, so that she could come in at the precise moment. And as she did so, unhappy thoughts flooded through her. Why was she the only one of the three sisters who felt close to Paul? Was it because of their common love of music? It pained Alice that Mizzi and Irma thought their brother was a good-for-nothing, idle gambler; they had even written him off as a drunken adventurer and shunned his company. Both sisters had grounds for their opinion, but what criteria were they applying? Was it really so bad that Paul had never held down a proper job? He had never done anyone any harm. He was a bohemian, certainly, but he was also open and happy, ready to help others and took life as it came. Was that not enough? Alice had always wanted Paul to make more out of his above-average musical talent, but no one could seriously contend that he would be a better person as an orchestral performer or a violin virtuoso. Paul was amiable and warm-hearted, he was at peace with himself and in love with life; and above all he was her brother.

Paul used to visit Alice and Stephan almost daily, frequently telling Stephan his bedtime story. 'Do you actually know the story of the little glow-worm?' Stephan asked his uncle one day. He had not seen the piece performed, as it had been written for 'little ones'. Stephan had been six when he arrived in Theresienstadt and was already considered to be a 'big boy'.

'Of course,' Paul said. 'When I was a child, your grandmother often used to read it to your maminka and me. In those days every child in Czechoslovakia knew the story. It had been written by a Czech minister. He was called Jan Karafiát, and if my memory serves me well he called his book a "story for big and small children". Shall I tell you the story?' Stephan smiled. 'Then lie down and close your eyes, you big child . . .'

Paul waited for Stephan to find a comfortable spot on the mattress and then he began speaking softly: 'Once upon a time there was a mummy glow-worm and her glow-worm son. They lived in a glow-worm house in a wonderfully beautiful flower. They inhabited a lovely meadow full of blooms. One day the child was big enough to learn to fly, and from then on he practised daily, and every day he went a little further. Then he had a terrible accident. There were some children playing in the meadow and they trod on the baby glow worm . . .'

'Was he dead?' Stephan quickly opened his eyes and grabbed his mother's hand.

'No, fortunately not, but he was badly injured; the little glow-worm's mother nursed her son and nourished him with good food until he grew up to be a strong young man, found himself a nice lady glow-worm and finally the glow-worms had a wedding to celebrate.'

'What then?'

'They lived happily ever . . .'

'Oh, really.'

Now Paul had to smile. 'On the stage the piece is particularly beautiful because the children sing all the best-known popular songs.'

Stephan had picked up a little of the arguments about the production and wanted to know what they were about.

'Why does your conductor have to write an overture to it?'

'It needs to be a particularly festive production . . . and therefore it needs a festive overture. And because there isn't one yet, Robert Brock has to invent one. We have promised him that we will write out his score as soon as he has finished composing it. Every member of the orchestra has to have a score and the sooner they are written the sooner the rehearsals can begin. From tomorrow I should have my part and, if you come along too and help me, we will get it done quicker.'

Stephan's eyes lit up. 'Do you know that everyone who helps gets two tickets to the premiere?' Paul told him. 'The performance is on 20 March in the Sokolovna; that is in two weeks. Now, sleep well.'

For the next three days Paul came to fetch Stephan every morning and take him round to the Magdeburg Barracks. They sat next to one another for hours on end and while Paul copied out the score with a well-trained hand, Stephan painted illustrations to the story with great concentration. On the evening of

the third day he was rewarded with two tickets. He proudly
brought the tickets home to his mother and on 20 March the two
of them were present at an unusual premiere. Brock had chosen
the loveliest Czech folk songs and made a sort of orchestral med-
ley out of them.

'It was a polished production. Every detail had been thought
out. The children were not required to do any acting, just to
be themselves,' wrote Vlasta Schoenová about the production
later.

> The choir of glow-worms for the marriage was performed by
> Slovak children who sang Slovak songs and danced Slovak
> dances with naturalness and great ability. As many as 700
> prisoners filled the auditorium while the SS was upstairs in the
> gallery; but after the first few bars the audience had forgotten
> they were there. Songs like 'Your Green Grove' and 'Spring is
> Coming' rang out and there was not a dry eye in the house
> and the words 'And it was spring and everything was out in
> bloom . . .' brought the house down.[9]

The audience had not failed to notice that Robert Brock had
quoted the Czech national anthem in the overture and the performance, which was supposed to create a smokescreen, was instead a
demonstration of hope in the coming liberation. At the second
performance, the demand was so great that many who were not
among the 700 lucky enough to receive tickets tried to climb in
through the windows. In the next four weeks, until 20 April, *The
Little Glow-Worm* was performed thirteen times. Every time, the
theatre was sold out and every time the audience took the moving
Czech melodies to be a manifesto: we will survive, our suffering
will soon be over.

*

ON 6 APRIL 1945, as planned, a member of the International Red
Cross was given a tour of Theresienstadt. Paul Dunant, a Swiss,
was accompanied by Adolf Eichmann and Rudolf Weinmann.

Instead of the ailing camp commandant Karl Rahm, it was his assistant Hans Günther who received the delegate.[10]

Alice was concentrating on her work at the piano – practice by day, concerts in the evening – a mental as much as a physical challenge. She did not learn of the visit until after it had happened. Paul, on the other hand, was part of the SS masquerade: the chamber orchestra, with him as one of the violinists, had to play the Dvořák Serenade for Dunant and an audience of SS officers.

Dunant kept his distance during his short visit – both from the SS and the Jewish prisoners – and even today it is not entirely clear why. Was he taken in by the false beauty of Theresienstadt so that he did not believe the prisoners to be in any immediate danger? Was he anxious to prevent any further problems for the inmates because he knew that he would be coming back with other people? With the collapse of the National Socialist rule of terror just around the corner, the concert and theatrical performances must have looked like macabre nonsense. Nevertheless, he left the same day, leaving the prisoners in a state of great uncertainty.

Four days later, on 10 April 1945, Alice and Paul gave their first joint performance in Theresienstadt. Because they had many other commitments, and they lacked time to rehearse, Paul had suggested delaying the performance of the Beethoven Sonata and giving a smaller concert instead, a sort of personal gift to their many friends and relations in the camp.

Alice wanted to thank Arnošt Weiss and therefore opened the concert with the Smetana Dances, which Weiss had learned and grown to love when they all played together at the Sommers' house before their deportation. Now he sat in the front row of the Sokolovna and fought back his tears. The main work – a tribute to their vanished mother – was the Dvořák Sonatina, but because Alice had played them in her despair after her mother's deportation, and because Chopin simply could not be omitted from a concert of thanks and reminiscence, she chose the first twelve Études. These – and indeed all the music they played – gave the audience who came that night hope.

As liberation approached, the more expansive the daily cultural menu became. In the last days of the war, between 7 and 13 April 1945, the weekly programme of the Free Time Organization was crammed full of cabarets, concerts, evenings of Lieder and myriad other musical events.

On Saturday 7 April alone there was a choice of four concerts. At seven there was a performance of *The Little Glow-Worm* in the Stage Room of the Sokolovna. A quarter of an hour later Alice and Professor Herman Leydensdorff's Beethoven concert began in the Terrace Room. A few blocks away, at 14 Parkstrasse, Marion Podelier was singing Schubert, Brahms and Dvořák lieder to Edith Kraus's accompaniment; while at 2 Hauptstrasse Frank Wedekind's satire *Der Kammersänger* (The Tenor) was performed at the same time.

The next day there was a matinee of *The Little Glow-Worm*, while in the evening there was a choice of a jazz quintet and a variety show by the two cabaret artists Anni Frey and Gisa Wurzel, whose witty banter had helped their fellow women to withstand the long months of splitting mica. At the same time Hedda Grab-Kernmayer and Marion Podelier were giving a concert of opera arias. At 2 Hauptstrasse Edith Kraus was playing Bach. And so it went on. Monday's high point was scenes from Offenbach's *Tales of Hoffmann* and a recital of Schubert's *Winterreise*.

These performances were a refuge for the prisoners, a wonderful distraction. In the long term they could not alter the mood, which still wavered between fear and hope. Theresienstadt was constantly shaken by new rumours: was the SS planning fresh deportations? Or were they to be murdered here and now? Would the liberators force the Germans to capitulate in time and then release the prisoners?

*

ALICE GAVE HER final concert on 25 April 1945 and at the end of that month, the music in the ghetto fell silent for ever. On their way to his daily piano lesson, Alice and Stephan had to cross the square in front of Theresienstadt's new station. Stephan noticed the chilling-looking cattle trucks even before his mother. Hundreds of people were climbing down from them, or falling out more dead than alive. Alice had never seen people in such a pitiful condition – their heads shaven, their bodies just skin and bone, their clothing – almost exclusively striped prison uniforms – was shabby and smelled foul.

Alice held on to Stephan tightly. Together they watched the people (or those who still could) descend on a tub of soup that had been set up in the square. It was clear that these creatures had had nothing to eat or drink for days.

Hitherto, Alice had always tried to protect Stephan from seeing anything that might unsettle him. Now they were standing face to face with the truth of what had happened to those people who had been deported to the east, which had been concealed from them for so long. The prisoners came from Auschwitz and Buchenwald. Every day more and more arrived. In Theresienstadt they called the newcomers 'pyjamas' because of their striped suits. They did not just come in cattle trucks, they also came on lorries or on foot; there were hundreds and thousands of them; 5,000 by the end and with them they brought disease into the camp.

Stephan was now nearly eight and big enough to understand that the people were coming from precisely the same place that his father had been sent to. He wanted to help.

'The people need water,' he told his mother, 'and sugar.' He had picked this up from a doctor as feeding a starved body too quickly causes more damage than it cures; sugar brought immediate solace. He wanted his Uncle Paul to get hold of as much sugar as he could.

Every day Stephan urged his mother to accompany him to the new prisoners and to help them. There was no question about it: he was waiting for the return of his father. 'My daddy is somewhere in the world and if there is no one there to bring him some water and a spoonful of sugar then perhaps he won't be able to come back to us.'

Alice knew Stephan's hopes that his father was going to come back and sweep him up in his arms were fading day by day. Then, one morning a woman rushed into the room crying, 'Sommer is here, Sommer has arrived!' Stephan was ecstatic.

Alice took him by the hand and together they ran to the station as fast as their legs could carry them. With great excitement they spoke to one group after another asking about Leopold Sommer, to be rewarded with nothing more than shakes of the head; then Alice saw her brother-in-law Hans Sommer, his face fallen in and his body no more than bones. Their joy at the unexpected sighting was short-lived, followed by a more chilling realization: Leopold Sommer had not come back.

And although she continued to exude confidence to Stephan, Alice knew deep down that the hope of seeing her husband again was disappearing.

*

ON 2 MAY 1945 Paul Dunant and the rest of the Red Cross delegation returned to Theresienstadt. Hitler had committed suicide on 30 April. On 6 May the Council of Elders announced:

> Men and women of Theresienstadt, the International Committee of the Red Cross has taken Theresienstadt under its protection[11] ... The representative of the Committee, Mr Dunant, is now responsible for the running of the camp. He has confirmed the following members of the Council of Elders in their positions as leaders of the Autonomous Jewish Administration. You are safe in Theresienstadt. The war is not yet over. Anyone who leaves Theresienstadt exposes himself to all the dangers of war ... Keep calm and maintain order, help us with your labours which will render your journey home possible. Signed Dr Leo Baeck, Dr Alfred Meissner, Dr Heinrich Klang and Dr Eduard Meier.

Early in May Stephan fell gravely ill. The doctor diagnosed a rare form of measles, which, above all, causes terrible stomach pains. During the night he was in agony and could not sleep. Alice held her son in her arms night and day, trying to comfort him.

On the evening of 8 May, the day after Germany surrendered, a strange noise echoed around the camp. At first it was faint and far off but became louder and louder. Eventually Alice heard a loud cry spreading through the entire camp: 'Freedom!' Everyone was shouting the word, over and over again. Alice wrapped Stephan up, ill though he was, and ran out into the street. Russian tanks were coming down the street and heading in the direction of Prague. The headlights of the tanks and the military lorries lit up the night.[12] All Theresienstadt was on its feet. In their enthusiasm the people sang the Internationale in German, Czech, Dutch, Polish and Hungarian.[13] The next day the Czech gendarmerie arrived with their national flags flying and drove triumphantly through the streets.

Freedom was still not much more than a promise. Alice was desperately worried about Stephan, who was too exhausted to stand up; and she was missing Paul, whom she had not seen for two days. Someone now told her that he had taken a gamble with the Russian forces and that, the day before Germany's official surrender, Paul had gone with them to Prague. Long before, Alice and he had agreed that she and Stephan would come to him and Mary there, as soon as they left Theresienstadt.

But there were still difficult days ahead. The attempt to keep the newcomers away from the long-term residents had been a failure and typhus had spread like wildfire. In order to avoid infection, Alice and the other women she lived with left their room only when it was absolutely essential. Hundreds of people died every day. On 12 May a Russian medical unit arrived in Theresienstadt – it took weeks before the camp was rid of typhus.[14]

Finally they were free to go, and in the middle of June Alice and Stephan at last returned to Prague together with Alice's close friend Edith Kraus. Though Alice was physically much stronger, she grew weaker mentally. With every passing day she heard more horror stories of the SS murder squads and of the extermination camps in Auschwitz, Sobibór, Treblinka and elsewhere. At last she understood exactly what she had been saved from by her music and where she had really been for the past few years. 'If they can organize concerts there it can't be such a terrible place.' This thought had comforted Alice from her first day in Theresienstadt. That she had been playing incidental music for the transports leading straight to the gas chambers now threatened to drive her insane. And as she and Stephan returned to their home town, they had no idea whom they might see again.

THIRTEEN

Homecoming

'Perhaps there are too many of us Jews in the world?'

ALICE'S EYES FELL on the delicately embroidered letters on the cushions: SH – Sophie Herz. It had been a blessed childhood. Every evening her mother had sat on the bench before the bright blue stove listening to her playing the piano and deftly sewing or embroidering.

After two years in Theresienstadt Alice was once again lying in a properly made bed, without lice or bugs and breathing in the comforting smell of the bed linen; but her physical well-being could not dissipate her anguish: as soon as she closed her eyes she saw a sequence of nightmare images drawn from her memory which robbed her of her sleep.

Alice was on stage. She was playing the Beethoven *Appassionata*. Suddenly she heard her mother crying out for help. She leapt to her feet and to the alarm of the audience she ran out of the room, but her mother was nowhere to be seen. Her thoughts cut to the scene in the cemetery. She was walking arm-in-arm with her mother, following her father's coffin. There was another scene-change: Leopold was looking Alice in the eye and saying nothing. His look said it all: he knew what would happen to him. Then came another sequence of images: 'Now I am all alone in this world'. It was Stephan with a raging fever, crying bitter tears. He would not be comforted. The sequence came to an end.

Alice gasped for breath and reached for Stephan's hand. Although Mary had provided Stephan with his own bed he had crept into hers; in Theresienstadt he had got used to getting under her blankets and going to sleep at once.

She had to stay strong for her son's sake; she needed to put these thoughts out of her mind and look forward. For him she needed to conceal her mental torture. He had come through nearly two years incarcerated in a concentration camp virtually undamaged. The truth would destroy his childish soul. Later, perhaps, when he was bigger, she might tell him if he asked; but now there was no question of it.

The day before, Alice and Stephan had arrived on a train with hundreds of other survivors from Theresienstadt. Paul and Mary had fetched them from the station and taken them to their flat in Ververka Street. 'You must think of this as your home,' Mary told them. She meant well: she served up the kind of meal that Alice had not seen since before the war, let alone eaten. She had put one of her three rooms at her disposal, saying 'as long as you want to live here you are welcome'. She had no idea what people had had to suffer in the concentration camp, but that did not bother Alice. She herself was only just beginning to realize the extent of Nazi crimes against the Jews. And, at the same time, she suppressed her worries about her own family.

What had happened to Leopold? Where had they taken her mother? What had happened to her mother-in-law? Where were they all, her relatives, acquaintances and friends? How many of them would make it home? As soon as they had arrived at the station in Prague she had pestered her brother with questions. At first Paul had simply shaken his head in silence and then he explained that the Prague Jewish Community office was collecting reports on the fate of the Jews who had been deported.

Alice decided to go there the next day, but before that she had to fulfil the promise she had made to Stephan on their way to Prague and show him all the places of his earliest childhood. She was pleased when dawn came. She listened with gratitude to the morning noises coming from the neighbouring rooms: the clattering of cups and saucers, the whistling of the kettle, Paul's cough and her sister-in-law's laugh. Stephan was just stretching awake when Mary called them to breakfast.

Paul had got bread and rolls, and Mary brought in a soft-boiled egg for everyone: there was jam, cheese, butter and milk. Mary had a remarkable talent for organization and the best of relations with the black market. Stephan helped himself to a slice of fresh dark bread and made Alice butter it for him. He was as little interested in the rolls as he was in the egg or the jam.

*

ALICE AND STEPHAN set off immediately after breakfast. Hand in hand they made their way to the house at One Sternberg Street, which had been their home until their deportation. Not much seemed to have changed in Prague's Seventh District. Alice was clinging to the thought that she might find news of Leopold.

She summoned her courage and rang the bell. It seemed an eternity before a Czech woman opened the door. She came out onto the landing and closed the door behind her. She didn't want Alice and Stephan to see inside. She was not only brusque, but cold. There was no news, she told them, adding that although she was sorry for Alice she was not prepared to move out under any circumstances; she and her family had had a bad time of it themselves.

'Maminka, why won't she let us into our flat?' whispered Stephan, as he walked downstairs holding his mother's hand. He sounded sad and anxious, but Alice was not listening. She was tortured by the thought that she had lived from concert to concert in Theresienstadt while thousands of men were being taken to extermination camps and murdered.

Had she worn blinkers? Hadn't her music given her strength, and not just her but her fellow prisoners too, even if only for a minute? Since the liberation of the camp, she and Edith had reflected over and over again on what might have happened if they had refused the commandant's orders to play, whether it would have made any sense at all. They came to the conclusion that it would not.

'Maminka, why can't we go into our flat?' Stephan repeated, a little louder this time. In the past two years he had asked so many questions like this. What could she tell him to stop him from losing his faith in mankind? How could she stop him learning to hate? Although her heart was not in it, she tried to explain what had happened to them.

'Stepanku, when we had to go to Theresienstadt we had to leave our flat to some Czechs who were also having a bad time. We can't simply drive them away. That would simply mean matching one injustice with another. I am sure they will soon be given another flat.'

Stephan understood what his mother had told him, but despite that his childish sense of justice spurred him to say: 'I'd be happier if we could go back to our old flat . . .'

'Me, too, Stepanku: this afternoon I am going to go to the Jewish Community with Uncle Paul. They will help us out,' Alice told him on the way to the Baumgarten. Stephan wanted to see his favourite playground, but Alice could not bring herself just to sit on a bench and watch the child on the swings. She was anxious to press on to Bĕlsky Street to her parents' house. The nameplates on the door revealed only Czech names. Alice rang what had been her parents' bell. There was no answer and none from the floor above either, only a chilling silence.

Alice tried not to let her disappointment show. 'Do you see,' she said in a weak voice, 'your grandfather had this house built. I was born in this house, and Uncle Paul too. It was here that we gave our first concerts.' She laughed at the memory. 'Now come on. Let's go to the centre of town before we go home.'

As they crossed the river, Alice told Stephan stories of the bridge-keeper that she had known when she was his age. They walked down the former Elisabeth Street and along the Graben, wandered over to the New Town and crossed Wenceslaus Square.

At last they stood in Havlíček Square, near the former German Theatre, in front of the house which had been her parents-in-law's home.

Her father-in-law had died before the German occupation. Alice was grateful for that. She had not heard any news of her mother-in-law since the beginning of July 1942. But soon after, Alice learned that Helene Sommer, after three months in Theresienstadt, had been sent on to Treblinka on 15 October 1942 together with her sister Anna Holitscher.

Saturday after Saturday she had joined the extended family up there in the drawing room: Leopold's brother Hans, and his wife Zdenka and their children Eva and Otto; Leopold's sister Edith, and her husband Felix Mautner and their children Ilse and Thomas. So far only Hans Sommer had come back.

Alice looked at the row of bells and then at the letter boxes. There was no mention of the name Sommer. Her hopes faded, but she still went up the stairs pulling Stephan up behind her. When she knocked on the door her hands were shaking, but no one answered. The only thing that kept her standing were thoughts of Stephan. 'Before lunch I'll show you the view of the city from the Belvedere Park. It's lovely.'

In the park Stephan found a stick and, squatting at Alice's feet, drew a road in the gravel and vroomed as he drove his wooden car along it. Alice sat on a bench and looked into the distance. She was a stranger in the city. The war had taken her home away from her.

*

IMMEDIATELY AFTER LUNCH Paul and Alice made their way to the Jewish Community office. The administrative buildings of the Jews were situated in the former Jewish quarter of the old city, right next to the old Prague synagogue. The tiny waiting room had room for around twenty people. It was hopelessly crowded. Alice could hardly breathe, she found the atmosphere so depressing. Her gaze wandered from face to face, each and every one of them marked by the sufferings of the last few years. Most of them waited silently, a few of them muttered to one another. They were all preoccupied by the same question: which of their friends and relations had survived? And here they hoped to find answers.

Paul tried to cheer his sister up. The Jewish Community was performing real wonders. It was helping survivors to find their feet in Prague again, finding them accommodation, furniture and money. The official made it clear to Alice that only very few people had returned from Treblinka, where her mother had been taken on 19 October 1942. He still knew nothing about Leopold and her many friends and relations among the deportees, but he encouraged her, however, to come to the office every day and to ask if there was any news. Information was coming in all the time. Finally, he took a note of Alice's details and asked her to be patient for three or four weeks: 'There are few flats, but families with children have priority; that means you. And when that happens you will have your own upright or grand piano and you will be able to teach again.' Encouraged, Alice turned to go.

'How old did you say your son was?' the man called out to her as she left. 'In a few days we are going to celebrate his eighth birthday,' Alice answered deliberately. 'That's perfect,' the man said. He told her that the community was going to invite a group of children for a fortnight's stay in a castle near Prague. Irma Lauscherová was running a holiday home there. Stephan would remember her from Theresienstadt and he would have a really wonderful birthday. 'And take some clothing away for your son. The woman outside will help you. We have a depot.'

The only way Alice could persuade Stephan to go on the holiday was by promising him that she would send him a birthday surprise. It was only then that he agreed to the adventure, albeit with mixed feelings, as for the past two years he had not spent a single night away from his mother.

Alice found it even more difficult to part with her son but it seemed the sensible thing to do. She had endless meetings with officials and she didn't want to impose these on Stephan. More than anything she needed to establish her rights as a citizen of liberated Czechoslovakia. Under clause eleven of the Reichs Citizenship Law of 25 November 1941, deprivation of citizenship, dispossession and deportation of Jews had been legalized throughout the Reich. Alice was stateless, she had no rights, she was an outlaw.

At first it was easy to believe that the issue of re-granting citizenship to concentration camp survivors would simply be a formality, but the Czech authorities showed little interest in what had happened to the Jews at the behest of the Germans after 1939. They decided the matter of citizenship solely on the grounds of whether the petitioner had belonged to a Czech or a German cultural circle before the occupation.

From June 1945 the new president of the republic, Edvard Beneš issued a total of 143 decrees based on his desire to outlaw, dispossess and expel the German population of Czechoslovakia. Sudeten Germans, Hungarians, all so-called ethnic Germans, South Tyroleans who had moved with the promise of new 'living space' in the east, and even Jews whose mother tongue was German, all had to be transferred to German territory. For the surviving German-speaking Jews, this meant sending them off into the arms of their murderers.

Paul had warned his sister when she arrived that she was only to speak Czech in public from now on. He had returned to Prague five weeks before Alice, and this time had been sufficient to convince him that, even if the country was freed from fascism, the position of the Jews had not fundamentally improved. The rights of Jewish citizens to remain in Czechoslovakia after 1945 hinged on what nationality they had given in the last census, which had taken place in 1930: German, Czech, Hungarian or Jewish.

'We talked it over with Felix,' Alice remembered. At first they had thought about ticking the German box, but her brother-in-law had convinced them to claim Jewish nationality.

'I always voted for the Jewish Party,' Paul told her, but he had put down 'Czech' in 1930, because he suspected that if there were to be any problems in the future this would be the best thing to do.

'They will ask you if your friends were Czechs or Germans, what papers you read and what music you listened to and what theatre you went to. Do you understand that? The Czechs are screaming for revenge, Alice,' Paul continued, 'the Germans brought their people terror and death. Today they will not acknowledge any difference between one German and another.'

Reuven Assor, from Dux in the Sudetenland, who had emigrated to Palestine before the war and then fought in the British Army, described how threatening the situation was for German-speaking Jews in the new Czechoslovakia (or those few who had survived the concentration camps). In 1942 his parents were deported to Theresienstadt and had died there. In 1945 Reuven Assor returned to Czechoslovakia as a member of the Jewish Brigade. He set himself a target of two years to get as many survivors as possible to Palestine.

A few weeks after the end of the war Assor was travelling in civilian clothes on a train from Pilsen to Prague. There were two Czechs in his compartment who evidently saw him as one of their own and were generous enough to offer him some of their food. Assor spoke little as he did not want to be questioned. He was increasingly shocked by the conversation between the two: 'So many Jews have come back to us,' one of them said with a tone of regret.

'There were probably too many holes in the gas chambers,' his companion replied.[1]

The anti-Semitic propaganda of the past six years had had its effect. The survivors were a thorn in the side of everyone who had collaborated with the Germans and who had profited from their dispossession; and there were a good many of them.

*

CIRCUMSTANCE NOW FORCED Alice to abandon one of the most important principles in her life: honesty. The cause was the 'discussion' over her resumption of citizenship in the 'interrogation room' of the appropriate committee. The civil servant had all the time in the world to talk to Alice about things that seemed, superficially at least, irrelevant. Alice bravely clung to Paul's instructions: her piano teacher was Czech, and the music she played at her concerts had always had a strong element of Czech music in it. So far, what she said was true. Then came the lie: at home they had chiefly spoken Czech and their circle of friends was overwhelmingly Czech-speaking.

'What newspaper did you read?' droned the official. So far he had not looked up once from his notebook.

'*Bohemia* – above all for its concert reviews.'

'And how did you vote in the 1935 general elections?'

'I voted for the Jewish Party.'

'Why?'

'Because they best represented the interests of the Jewish population, or that was what I believed.'

Alice passed the test. From now on she was classified as 'Czech-speaking' and felt miserable about it. She was incensed that, just after being released from a concentration camp, she was forced to fight for her life all over again. Unhappy at having to compromise herself in this way and missing Stephan desperately, she decided to visit her son in the holiday home. She went with another mother, who was suffering as much from being separated from her son as she was, and together the two women travelled to the castle.

The two boys were overjoyed and their mothers then spent the whole day with them. At the end Stephan had tears in his eyes – he wanted to go home with his maminka. Alice sadly took her leave, without him. What happened next she only heard about days later.

After their mothers' visit Stephan and the other boy failed to turn up for dinner. A search was organized in the castle but they were nowhere to be found. The park was searched, as was the area around the castle pond and the playground, but to no avail. In the end Irma Lauscherová informed the police who sent out a formal search party. Hours later, in the middle of the night, a policeman found the two children walking down an unlit street. They were on their way to Prague, they told the man, going home to their mothers. Even years later Alice reproached herself for being irresponsible.

*

ALICE'S ONE SURVIVING friend in Prague was Edith Kraus and she often went to see her. She was also Edith's most vital support. At first, they went to the Jewish Community office almost every morning, and then later once a week. More and more reports of deaths were coming in, and mourning for lost relatives, friends and acquaintances brought the two women even closer. With every piece of bad news their hopes of seeing their husbands alive again faded: they were now officially 'missing'.

The monstrous extent of the crimes committed against the Jews in the Protectorate beggared belief: in the spring of 1939 the German authorities had counted 118,000 'racial' Jews. Between 33,000 and 35,000 managed to emigrate. In 1946 there were around 22,000 Jews in Czechoslovakia: a few who had managed to remain in hiding, survivors from the camps and others who had returned from exile. Around 2,000 of them had fought in Czech brigades in foreign armies and a further 7,000 had survived in Carpato-Russia.[2] Only a few hundred of the so-called 'German Jews' ever returned. They particularly felt the chill wind from the Czechs.

Václav Kopecký, the Communist minister of information in the post-war Czech government, indicated what little future there was there for Alice and her kind. In exile in Moscow in July 1944 Kopecký had already announced 'that the German-speaking Jews would be seen in the same light as the Germans.'[3] It was a question of not weakening the Slavic national character, not anti-Semitism Kopecký argued.

Alice wanted to give concerts again but given the climate this might prove not only unwise but possibly life-threatening, and she even wondered whether it was possible for a Jew to lead a 'normal' life in Prague. Alice discussed her concerns with Edith but not with her brother. She was close to Paul, but she had the impression that he and his wife lived by a different set of rules, rules they had laid down for themselves.

Alice was more and more astonished by Mary's extravagance. Paul had no work and Mary herself earned only a modest wage as caretaker of the building they lived in; yet neither of them seemed concerned about money. Nor was Alice happy that the drawing room was transformed into a pub every Friday night, with Mary, chain-smoking and pouring out endless glasses of wine and pilsner. Her guests smoked as well, and shouted, which prevented Alice from getting to sleep. Against her better judgement, and keeping her distance, Alice went to the party the following Friday and discovered exactly what was going on. Once a week Paul and Mary were running an illegal gambling den.

Alice knew that Paul played poker with a passion, but Mary's enthusiasm seemed to exceed even his and they also appeared to have luck on their side: they were taking big risks and winning. Alice was horrified to see the way in which Mary behaved with her principally male guests, and how she flirted with them. Paul noticed Alice's irritation and came to his wife's defence: 'You should not take that seriously, it is her Hungarian temperament. That's what she is like.'

Despite the deep gratitude she owed her sister-in-law for taking them in, and Mary's remarkable generosity, Alice withdrew further and further into herself and longed for a home of her own.

One evening there was a gentle knocking at the front door. At first Paul took no notice as visitors generally rang the bell. But the knocking grew louder until at last Paul finally paid attention and opened the door. Standing before him was Alice's former caretaker from the Sternberggasse – he recognized her immediately – and the tall haggard man standing next to her she introduced as her husband. She had something urgent to say to Frau Sommer.

Alice had told Paul how shamelessly this woman had behaved on the night before their deportation, when she had plundered their flat. What could have brought her here now? Paul hesitated, before calling out to Alice: 'You have a visitor.'

Alice was astonished how much the woman's manner had changed. She had been so off-hand towards Alice that night, and now she seemed so uncertain and willing to please. Had she come to apologize, Alice asked herself, or come to offer me back the things she stole?

'Frau Sommer, they were difficult times, not just for you but for all of us,' the woman blurted out. 'You will recall that I always found food for you.' Alice did indeed remember, but she also remembered that she had had to pay many times the market price for it. She looked at the husband, who nodded mechanically at everything his wife said; Alice almost felt sorry for him. On the night their flat was plundered he had not been there.

'You see' – the caretaker had started up again – 'if you were to put in writing that at the time of the German occupation I had always been helpful and had behaved decently, that could be helpful.' She was under pressure because people in the neighbourhood had denounced her for systematically enriching herself with Jewish possessions from 1940 to 1945.

The audacity of the woman took Alice's breath away. Her generally talkative brother was also lost for words. It took him a while before he could respond. 'What are you after? You are quite aware how shabbily you behaved towards my sister. Please, there is the door.' As he said this he pushed the woman out of the flat while Alice looked on angrily. The caretaker's husband just trotted along silently behind her.

Alice had another sleepless night. The meeting with the caretaker was the last straw. While Stephan slept happily at her side she went over and over what she had been through in the past few weeks: the humiliating interrogation over her citizenship; the discouraging reports from the Jewish Community; worry about Leopold; Stephan's nagging questions about when his father would come home.

Alice no longer felt capable of dealing with her worries all alone. She desperately needed to confide in someone. The obvious person was Edith, her best friend, but there could be no question of troubling her now: she had recently received the news of her husband's death.

As dawn broke, Alice remembered Leo Baeck. 'Our great artist!' he had called her. Alice was certain that he would be willing to help and she resolved to go to Theresienstadt that day, where she knew Baeck was still living. Paul gave her the money for the ticket and Stephan stayed with his aunt and uncle. Happily, his best friend from Theresienstadt, Pavel Fuchs, was living in the house next door.

*

THE TRAIN JOURNEY to Theresienstadt lasted just two hours. Alice had sworn to herself that she would never set foot in the ghetto again. Now she was standing in the room where Leo Baeck's Friday evening discussions had taken place and for the first time became aware of how gloomy and unfriendly the room actually was. There were a few bits of furniture confiscated, like everything in Theresienstadt, from somewhere else, but when Baeck walked in it was as if the sun had come out. As ever, he exuded strength and security.

He took Alice's hands to greet her, which immediately put her at ease. She was aware how rarely he showed any emotion. Breaking her usual custom she opened her heart and spoke of her suspicion that neither Leopold nor her mother would return; of the hateful comments made by so many of her clearly hostile Czech fellow citizens; of the cruel coldness of the Czech bureaucrats; and her worries about the future.

The rabbi was visibly moved and Alice waited for him to give her some words of consolation and encouragement. He was silent, however, and he remained so; and then, as if speaking more to himself than to Alice, he murmured: 'Maybe there are too many Jews in this world . . .'

This unexpected and baffling response pierced Alice like an arrow. She did not feel able to ask him what he could possibly mean, and did not understand it either then or years later. Seized by panic, she leaped to her feet and got ready to leave. Leo Baeck tried to stop her from going so that he might explain, but it was no use. She was too distraught to listen to another word. In her despair she ran from the room and along the chillingly familiar streets towards the station.

The encounter had really upset her but – for Stephan's sake – Alice now forced herself to take heart and accept life for what it was. In fact, there would soon be a glimmer of hope. By good fortune, Alice was given a new flat more quickly than she had ever dared to hope. An added attraction was that it was in the house next door to Paul's flat, and right next to the Fuchses. Now Stephan could knock on his friend Pavel's door whenever he chose and that suited both of them.

The house had belonged to the Fuchs family before the war but it had been appropriated by the authorities. Their legal case was clear cut and the restitution a mere formality, which nobody doubted, but it took a long time to resolve because of interminable Czech bureaucracy. The house had been inhabited by five German officers and their families, so now five of a total of fifteen flats were empty. The Fuchses occupied one immediately after they returned from Theresienstadt. The others were waiting for new tenants. Armed with this information, Frau Fuchs sent Alice to the Jewish Community office and she was granted a small flat. Because Alice had no income, they also agreed to pay the rent for the time being.

There was a room for Stephan and another for Alice; a tiny kitchen and a little lavatory with a window. The house had only been constructed in the 1930s and it was astonishingly modern. There was even a lift in which Stephan loved to go up and down. Here, Alice and Stephan found a substitute family. Apart from their landlords the Fuchses, they had Leopold's brother Hans two floors down, as well as Trude Hutter's mother, who had survived Theresienstadt.

The Jewish Community helped to decorate the flat. In a furniture store Alice and Stephan found a sofa, two chairs, a small table and a folding bed for Stephan. By 1943 the SS had fifty-four stores

At last, their own piano again.
Alice giving Stephan a lesson in 1945.

Alice and Stephan treasured
Leopold's spoon, brought to
them by a fellow prisoner
from Auschwitz.
It was all they had to
remember him by.

Alice, in 1947, with her friend
Robert Sachsel

Reunited in Prague,
Alice and Mizzi in 1947

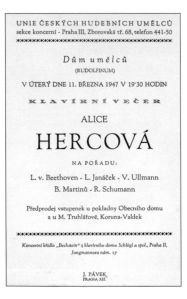

UNIE ČESKÝCH HUDEBNÍCH UMĚLCŮ
sekce koncertní - Praha III, Zborovská tř. 68, telefon 441-50

Dům umělců
(RUDOLFINUM)

V ÚTERÝ DNE 11. BŘEZNA 1947 V 19·30 HODIN

KLAVÍRNÍ VEČER

ALICE

HERCOVÁ

NA POŘADU:

L. v. Beethoven - L. Janáček - V. Ullmann
B. Martinů - R. Schumann

Předprodej vstupenek u pokladny Obecního domu
a u M. Truhlářové, Koruna-Valdek

Koncertní křídlo „Bechstein" z klavírního domu Schlögl a spol., Praha II,
Jungmannovo nám. 17

J. PÁVEK
PRAHA XII.

A publicity photo and the poster
for Alice's first pre-war concert

The family reunited in Israel in 1949: back row, left to right, Irma
Weltsch and her daughter Ruth, Emil Adler and his son Heinz (Chaim),
Felix Weltsch; front row, Stephan (Raphael), Alice and Mizzi

Raphael with his mother
on the balcony of the
Adlers' flat in Jerusalem

Raphael around 1956.
During his national service,
Raphael was a saxophonist
in the Israeli Army's
military band

Max Brod with Ruth Weltsch and her husband
Benjamin Gorenstein in 1966

Jerusalem in the 1960s. From left: Alice's best friend,
the pianist Edith Kraus, with her second husband, Mizzi Adler,
Alice, Alice's niece Ruth, with her husband Benny Gorenstein
(behind Alice), and Edith Kraus's daughter with her husband

Alice and Mizzi, with Mizzi's
daughter-in-law, Bath-Sheva Adler

Raphael Sommer, cello virtuoso

Emil Adler, Alice and Mizzi in Braunwald, in Switzerland, in 1966

Alice at her
son's grave

Alice's 100th birthday

Alice, aged 102, listening to music at home in Hampstead, in 2005

in Prague filled with confiscated Jewish property set up in the community's synagogues, prayer-rooms and community halls. The documents pertaining to the stolen goods displayed the legendary German sense of order, as evidenced by statistics drawn up on 16 March 1943. At this point only half the empty Jewish homes had been cleared of their furniture, but already the following objects of value had been 'secured': 603 upright or grand pianos, 9,973 objets d'art, 13,207 complete kitchen or drawing-room suites, 21,008 carpets, 55,454 pictures, 621,909 glasses and pieces of porcelain, 778,195 books, 1,264,999 textiles and 1,321,741 pieces of household or kitchen equipment.[4]

Alice veered between enormous gratitude and deepest mourning as she walked round the depot seeing piano upon piano. Naturally she looked first for her own Förster grand, but she could not find it among the hundreds of instruments. Every one of the pianos had a story to tell. How many of their owners had died?

Without Stephan at her side Alice would not have been able to bear the atmosphere in the storehouse. But, in a delightful way, he distracted her from her sad thoughts. Every piano that Alice tried elicited a comment from Stephan on the quality of the sound. Alice was astonished at how precise his judgments were. They finally opted for a black, middle-sized Steinway grand with a crystal-clear tone. With a piano, Alice could be properly happy for the first time in ages.

Two days later the delivery lorry was parked outside the door. With great effort men dragged the grand up the three flights to the flat. When it was finally in place, Alice had to laugh. The piano virtually took over the entire room. There was just enough space for the sofa bed, the little table and two chairs plus the narrow bookshelf.

After what had seemed an eternity, but was in fact just eight weeks since she had left Theresienstadt, she was sitting at a grand piano once again. A piano tuner had been round and she had been able to postpone paying him for the immediate future. Alice sat down and played the Schumann *Abegg Variations*. Why did she choose them? Was it because they brought back memories of happier days? Or was it because she had played them in the first Masterclass concert? She still remembered *Prager Tagblatt* writing the next day: 'the prize for the evening goes to Alice Herz.' Or was it simply because the work exuded such a light, airy, even gay mood, which meant that, while she played it, at least she could forget her unhappiness?

FOURTEEN

Prague

'A thousand times worse than under the Nazis.'

LEOPOLD SOMMER HAD BEEN part of a column of thousands who were driven from Auschwitz in Poland towards the west. Together with other prisoners he was being moved to Dachau. An Auschwitz survivor had brought the news to the Prague Jewish Community office. Alice had been consoled by the fact that Dachau was not an extermination camp like Treblinka or Auschwitz. If Leopold had survived the death march, he must have been liberated in Dachau, and he might come home any moment. Whenever she heard a knock at the door now, her heart began to pound.

It was already the middle of August 1945, and Alice was seated at the piano one morning when she was distracted from her playing by an unexpected ring on the bell. Irritated, she answered the door. The man there was wearing the kaftan of an Orthodox Jew. His eyes seemed ready to sink into their sockets. Alice noticed his unkempt beard and a hat that had once been respectable; under the shadow cast by the brim his face looked even more emaciated. The man held out his hand. His skin was like blue-grey paper.

He told her that the Jewish Community had given her address to him. He spoke Yiddish and his voice was apologetic. All at once Alice recognized him as the father of the eight children who had lived next door to Stephan and her in Theresienstadt. Like Leopold he had visited his family almost every night.

A few days after Leopold was deported to Auschwitz, the Orthodox Jew and his four sons had also left Theresienstadt. The girls stayed behind with their mother. Alice had been unable to come to terms with the apparent indifference with which the woman had submitted to her destiny: 'What God permits must God approve' she repeatedly told Alice, 'and then it will be all right'. Whenever Alice had cause to quarrel with the strange twists of fate that had occurred in her life, she thought of this woman and her unlimited faith in God.

Alice invited the man in. She wanted to ask him what had become of his family, but she could not find the words. 'All four sons fell in Auschwitz,' said the man, as if he could read her thoughts. 'The ramp – they did not even allow us enough time to say goodbye to one another.' He was disturbingly calm as he spoke. His wife, too, and their four daughters had not returned either.

There were a few minutes of silence, which to Alice seemed like hours. She searched in vain for words of condolence, but the one word screaming in her head was 'Leopold'. Instinctively she closed her eyes, as if the darkness could protect her from the truth. 'L-e-o-p-o-l-d' continued to echo. When she opened her eyes and drew breath, the visitor began to talk slowly again. It had been a good thirty-five years since her grandmother had taught her the language of her forefathers, and Alice had lost interest in it soon afterwards. But, although Yiddish was foreign to her, she understood the man. It seemed to her as if no other language expressed sadness and mourning more starkly.

In Dachau he had shared a bunk with Leopold Sommer. They were all suffering from typhus. When Leopold realized he was losing his strength he asked the man to go to Alice and Stephan.

Silence fell again. Finally the man fumbled in his pocket and drew out a packet rolled in newspaper and handed it to Alice. She nodded to him as if to say that he should unwrap it. It was a battered tin spoon: Leopold's spoon, which he had taken from Prague to Theresienstadt, and on to Auschwitz, Flossenbürg and Dachau.

'Did he have to suffer much?' Alice asked, looking through the man into nothingness.

At the end Leopold was scarcely conscious. In his bouts of fever he had often whispered Alice and Stephan's names; and he had smiled.

*

'MAMINKO, ARE WE going to take the tram today?'

Alice had no idea how long she had been sitting there already, staring at the tin spoon, when Stephan came running though the door: 'Didn't you promise me?'

Alice clutched the table and forced herself to smile as she rose to greet her son. She stroked his head gently, first with her right hand and then with her left, and then with her right again. Breathing deeply and slowly she brought herself back to here and now. Stephan was what it was all about.

Although she had to concentrate as hard as if she were playing a piano concert before a full house, she managed to say in a manner that was as warm as it was spirited: 'Yes, let's go my love.' It was yet another 'yes' to life.

As they were going out Stephan's gaze fell on the spoon without taking it in. Alice followed him. 'It is just a spoon,' she thought. 'The memory of our time together no one can take away from me. And Stephan? He is Leopold's legacy. He must not suffer.' But Alice still has the spoon.

The tram stop was about 200 metres from their door. Whenever he was allowed to go out onto the street alone, Stephan watched the tram coming and the passengers getting in and out, and heard the driver ring his bell to announce the fact they were heading off. Stephan was firmly convinced that he had never travelled on a tram in his life. He was only four when the Jews were banned from using public transport

When Alice and Stephan turned into Bělsky Street, the next tram was drawing up to the stop. 'Maminko,' Stephan urged. Alice didn't let him see that it was only with supreme effort that she was able to put one foot in front of the other. 'We are going to go from here to the last stop on the line,' she said, 'and then we'll come home.' Stephan was as pleased as punch and pulled on his mother's hand. They rushed to reach the rails and got into the front carriage. Stephan had his heart set on standing at the front by the driver.

Alice bought two tickets: 'To the last stop and back again.' The driver waved at her as if to say 'I have already got that.' And then he turned to Stephan: 'And you my little friend, what's your name?'

'Stephan, but everyone calls me Stepanku.'

'Would you like to become a tram driver one day?'

'No, I am going to conduct an orchestra.'

The driver was amazed, but he was quick to find a fitting reply: 'Do you know Stepanku, a tram driver and a conductor, there is no difference in the end. The conductor decides when to start, and so do I. The conductor decides whether to go faster or slower, and I do that too.'

Stephan's face registered disbelief.

'All right then, come here. I'll show you how a tram driver conducts.' The tram driver laughed and helped the boy into his compartment. They held onto the wheel together, they braked together, they rang the bell together. At the last stop, together they negotiated the loop. Stephan was ecstatic.

'You are welcome to drive with me whenever you feel like it,' the driver told him as he said goodbye. 'I can always use a good tram conductor like you.'

In the next few weeks before school began there was hardly a day when Stephan did not wait at the tram-stop until Josef, 'his driver', came by. Then, after school, he spent most of the afternoon with him trundling around the north of Prague.

*

'I don't think Josef has any idea about music.' At dinner that evening Stephan tried to come to terms with what driving a tram and conducting an orchestra had in common, and the similarities between applying the emergency brakes and a string orchestra that is playing out of time. 'Both of them sound frightful', he said in satisfaction. 'Daddy needs to play for Josef one day.'

'Stepanku', Alice launched in. She had been looking for her chance all evening. 'Stepanku, your father is not coming back. This afternoon a man came here. He told me what happened to Daddy . . .'

Stephan climbed without a word onto his mother's lap. Instinctively he took on the role of the comforter. 'But Maminko, you always said that Daddy's soul could not die.'

'You are right, my love, of course Daddy will always be with us. We can't see him, but when we are as quiet as mice and we open our hearts as wide as this, then we can feel him there. He will protect us, always.'

Stephan slept comfortably that night. Alice sat up thinking for a long time and eventually made a decision that she kept to for many years: she would utter not a word about Theresienstadt, and not a word about Leopold's death.

*

Look ahead, resume life; for Alice that also meant giving concerts again as soon as possible. Before the war she had played regularly on the wireless, both on the German station and the Czech. Paul Nettl, the husband of her friend Trude, had been in charge of the German station before fleeing to the United States with his family in 1939.

The German station had been taken over by the Nazis and at the end of the war it had been shut down by the Czechs; but Alice found people with whom she had worked well before the war still working at the Czech station. A leading producer offered Alice the chance to resume her concerts. From time to time she could appear on the short-wave programme and he even suggested a date. The concert would be broadcast live, would be heard worldwide and would be very popular.

'I must try and tell Mizzi and Irma about this,' Alice thought. 'But at least if they hear me on the wireless they'll know I am still alive.'

In the months before the war began, the sisters had exchanged a few letters, but since then they had had no news of one another. Alice did not even have an address for them, and there were no telephone connections with Palestine. Not even the Jewish Community could help with this one: contacts with Palestine were only slowly being established.

On the off-chance, Alice went to the post office to try to send a telegram to Jerusalem: 'Coming Thursday, midnight concert from Radio Prague on the Short Wave. Stop. Alice.'

The post office clerk was unable to help. Alice needed to come back the next day, and in the meantime he would make enquiries as to whether he could send the message to Palestine. Eventually she was able to send it, but without a proper address all she could do was hope that a telegram sent to 'Prof Emil Adler, doctor, Jerusalem' would arrive. She had originally intended to send the message to her brother-in-law Felix Weltsch as well, but she abandoned that idea when she heard how expensive sending a telegram would be. She assumed that, as a physician in the public service in Jerusalem, Emil Adler would be better known than the university librarian Felix Weltsch and therefore the telegram would be more likely to reach him.

The days sped by as she prepared for the concert. On the Thursday in question Alice sat down shortly before midnight at the concert grand in the studio of Czech Radio. Her neighbour, Valery Fuchs, had just woken Pavel and Stephan so that they could listen to the concert, but had her message reached Jerusalem?

It was not until weeks later that Alice learned what excitement the telegram had caused in the family. It had arrived promptly in Emil Adler's office at the Hadassah Hospital. Since 1940 he had been running the rehabilitation clinic there. Generally a calm man, his hands shook when he opened the telegram and he immediately dropped everything and rushed home: Alice was alive. When Mizzi read the telegram it was as if a dam had burst, she cried so much.

On the evening of the concert the relatives gathered around the Adlers' wireless set: besides Mizzi and Emil, there was Felix and Irma and their daughter Ruth. It was midnight, but Palestine was an hour ahead of Prague and they had to be patient for another hour. On the dot of one came the announcement in Czech: 'We will now hear Beethoven's *Appassionata* played by Alice Herzova in Prague.' By the end of the first few bars even the men had hidden their faces in their handkerchiefs. Alice was alive, but what of Leopold and Stephan? Within a few weeks, Alice was in regular correspondence with her relatives again.

Alice's live broadcast had made others aware that she was still alive, too, among them, the Czech journalist and writer Michael Mareš. Mareš had met Alice at a private concert in 1943, not long before she was deported. She had played the *Appassionata* then, too, and he had always felt the sonata was like the voice of an unavoidable catastrophe. From their very first meeting, Alice felt a kind of community of souls with Mareš, despite their age difference; she was twenty years his junior. Although his rough and ready wit and his particular brand of repartee were strange to her, they fascinated her nonetheless. He was like an uncle to her, but there were frequent moments, however, when his extravagant compliments revealed that he was in love with her.

The day after the broadcast, Michael Mareš went to the Jewish Community to find out Alice's address. On his way to her flat he picked a beautiful bunch of flowers in the Belvedere Park, but they did not seem sufficient to express his joy at her survival and his admiration and love for her. Mareš was a passionate collector of modern art, and, knowing how open Alice had always been to the avant garde, he decided that he should give her the most valuable picture in his collection. When, with great excitement, Mareš rang the doorbell of Alice's flat, it was opened by Stephan who looked at him curiously.

'Stepanku, don't you remember? We went to the cinema together two years ago, a bag of ice fell on your trousers . . . I am Michael.' They both laughed.

'If you like, we could go to the cinema again tomorrow.' The ice was well and truly broken.

Alice's face lit up when she came to the door. It was not really her style to hug guests when she greeted them, but in Michael Mareš's case, she made an exception and gave him a kiss.

'We have so much to tell one another,' he said joyfully, 'but first of all I have a request: play me the first movement of the *Appassionata*.'

Alice looked for an appropriate jar for the flowers, put them on the Steinway and began to play. After this private concert, Mareš handed her his present: a portrait of a young Parisian woman by Toulouse-Lautrec.

From now on there was not a week that passed without a visit from Mareš, who would be a trusted support in the post-war years. Over the next few years Mareš was like a father to Stephan, always listening to what he was saying, and Alice could talk to him not only about everyday worries but also the difficult political situation. Mareš was a convinced communist and dreamed of a just society, but became increasingly angry with the way in which his Party friends dealt with their political opponents.

*

Now that they had a flat, Alice had to find a school for Stephan. She and Valery Fuchs had become close friends and together they went to talk to the local school committee, but they were unlucky enough to come up against an incompetent official. Stephan and Pavel, both born in 1937, should have been starting their third year at school, but the official wanted to put them in a class with six-year-olds in the first year.

Since the war ended, children who had survived the war in

hiding-places or camps and who had never had any formal instruction, had to be interviewed by the committee. The committee decided that the boys would have to sit an entrance test to decide if they were fit to go into the higher class, and they were astounded at Stephan and Pavel's performance in the exam. Both spoke perfect Czech, both could read and write without a problem, both knew their tables. From September 1945 they entered the third class and the primary school was just a few doors from their home. They had of course been well taught by Irma Lauscherová in her clandestine lessons in the camp.

Stephan and Pavel loved going to school. What for most children was a duty was for them a privilege, at least at the outset. As Irma Lauscherová later wrote,

> They would then go to school in September. They were going to receive books, exercise books, pencil cases, pens, a sketch book, a pencil, crayons and a satchel! Maybe even a rubber! What joy! For those people who have never had the experience of being deprived of a sheet of paper where they could write on one side at least. For someone who did not live through it, it is hard to make them imagine what it is like to lack a pencil. No one knew what our children had to do without.[1]

Stephan in particular excelled in all subjects. Over and over again he challenged the teacher, which made the other children laugh. No one took offence at this apparent cheekiness, for they could see there was no ill-will behind it.[2]

When he came home from school at midday, Stephan did his homework first. In the cold winter months he kept his coat and hat on as the flat was badly heated. Although there was an incredible rapport between mother and son, Alice sometimes found it difficult to discipline Stephan. The day began at quarter to six with the morning wash and breakfast. From seven on the dot to quarter to eight, Alice taught her son the piano. Sometimes Stephan made an attempt to rebel: he could not see why he had to practise so much every day. Alice insisted on it, however, not only because

he had such a prodigious talent, but because discipline and aware-
ness of goals needed to become part of his life. The conflict did not
begin in earnest, however, until Ilonka Štěpánova began to teach
him.

Václav and Ilonka Štěpán were the first friends Alice visited
after her return from Theresienstadt. She had a terrible shock when
she heard that her former teacher had been suffering from a
malignant brain tumour and had died in terrible pain in 1944.
Ilonka nonetheless offered her services as Stephan's teacher and
Alice, thinking that it was sensible for the boy to have another
teacher as well as his mother, had accepted. Despite this their
morning classes continued as usual.

Stephan was making enormous progress. At nine he played
Debussy, at ten the first Beethoven sonatas. However great his
interest in new works and composers, he always started the day
with Bach. Alice left him to choose the piece.

*

AS SOON AS STEPHAN left the house in the morning Alice sat
down at the keyboard and practised for four hours, just as she had
done in the years before her deportation. While the boy was doing
his homework or playing with his friends, she taught. She kept the
evenings for going to concerts and little by little she found a new
circle of friends. But horrible news continued to arrive. Leopold's
brother Hans was mourning his wife Zdenka, his ten-year-old
daughter Eva and seven-year-old son Otto. All three were gassed
in Auschwitz. Alice already knew that her mother-in-law Helene
Sommer, together with her sister Anna Holitscher, had been killed
in the gas chambers at Treblinka. For her sister-in-law Edith
Mautner and her husband Felix there was clearly no hope left.
Since their deportation to the Litzmannstadt Ghetto in Łódź in
October 1941 there had been no trace of them. Their children Ilse
and Thomas were still waiting for their parents in Sweden.

Joseph Reinhold, the former head of the Priessnitz sanatorium
in Gräfenberg, survived the war in hiding in Russia in dramatic

circumstances and with the help of his Christian wife. He returned to Prague a physical and mental wreck. On one occasion Alice took him along to one of her concerts. At the first Beethoven sonata he collapsed in tears and had to leave the auditorium before the end. A few months later he died.

In Alice's immediate circle twenty people had been killed by the Nazis, only she and Stephan had survived. Two survivors and twenty dead. The ratio directly mirrored the broader scale of the tragedy. On 15 March 1939 there were 118,310 Jews in the Bohemian lands. Of these 14,045 survived: about 8 per cent.[3]

When Alice and Stephan received a letter from Robert Sachsel, Leopold's oldest friend, they were delighted. Sachsel and Leopold had been to kindergarten together, trained together, moved to Hamburg together and returned to Prague together at the beginning of the 1930s. Only the war had separated them.

Alice now learned that Robert had survived, but in dangerous circumstances. In the winter of 1941 he was very ill with rheumatism and should have been in a wheelchair, but he still had to shovel snow on the streets of Prague. As Robert's father could see that his son would not survive this physical torture, he bought a small house in the Slovakian spa of Piešt'any in the name of Robert's nurse Anita, and concealed sufficient money there for Robert to survive on.

The Sachsels were one of the best-known and richest Jewish families in Prague. Since the 1790s their forefathers had lived a deeply religious life in the orthodox community in Neubydzow (Nový Bydžov) about ninety kilometres north-east of Prague. They started a linseed oil factory which soon became a huge business with outlets all over Europe. In the nineteenth century Robert's grandfather became one of Bohemia's leading businessmen. He had seven sons and was able to pay for their training.[4] Robert's father, too, was a successful entrepreneur before he was deported to Theresienstadt with his wife; neither came back.

*

IN THE AUTUMN of 1945, Alice and Stephan took their first holiday together. They travelled to Zwickau in the north Bohemian Sudetenland – a long and wearisome journey – where Robert Sachsel was living in the farmhouse of his nurse Anita's parents. Alice was shocked at seeing Robert again. He seemed much older than she remembered and was wheelchair bound. Despite that Alice and Stephan spent some lovely days together, and the beauty of the surrounding countryside encouraged them to go on long walks. There were also lots of animals in the farmyard, which Stephan helped look after, and a neighbour's child taught him to ride a bicycle. There was even a piano in the parlour, which Alice and Stephan could play to their hearts' delight. For the next few years, they visited Robert annually.

After the initial joy at seeing one another again, Alice and Robert spoke chiefly of the past. Robert had a pressing need to talk about what had happened, as he had only been released from his hiding place a few weeks before, and Alice was a good listener.

When the Jewish community in Piešt'any told him that all Jews were to be rounded up the next day, Robert's nurse decided on a course to save him. She pushed his bed into a little bay window in the drawing room, placed a sofa next to it and then put a large bookcase in front of the bay. Robert's Jewish doctor, whom Alice also cared for, was hidden in the cellar of the house. In order not to arouse suspicion she took a job locally. For months no one knew anything about the hidden men except for a handful of loyal and fearless friends, and it was rare for anyone to pay them a call.

Shortly before the end of the war, somebody told the local German army administration about the hiding place. With no prior warning three Nazis searched the house and stayed there, and Anita was interrogated day and night without a break. Robert Sachsel must have been able to hear every word from his hiding place. One problem was that when he slept he snored loudly, so Anita had to turn the radio up or put on the vacuum cleaner.

After a few days two of the Nazi officers left while the third continued his search. By the sixth day Anita was in such utter despair that she broke down under interrogation and pushed the bookshelf to one side. Robert had neither eaten nor drunk for six days, and he was lying in his own excrement. The German was lost as what to do at the sight of this dishevelled creature and suddenly he seemed to become conscious that Robert's state of health was his responsibility. He helped Anita to clean him up and take him down to the Jewish doctor in the cellar, who was able to provide him with the care he needed. Robert and the German remained friends for the rest of their lives.

*

EVERY DAY IN PRAGUE had its bittersweet moments. One day when Stephan came home from school there was a little dog running up and down in front of the door to the block of flats; Stephan put down his satchel and let the dog lick his hand. It did not take long for them to become the best of friends, but it was not to last long.

A middle-aged woman suddenly stormed out of the house next door. She was shaking with rage and proceeded to reprimand Stephan. How did he have the cheek to play with strange dogs: he should leave it alone immediately. Her furious outburst had already made Stephan uncomfortable, but then she stood right in front of him, gesticulating wildly. Before he could say anything, her voice took on a sinister tone. 'Are you one of those people who have come from Theresienstadt and who have taken away our homes?'

'We haven't taken anyone's flat away. Someone took our flat away.'

'It has all got to stop!' the woman screamed. 'A Jewish brat and cheeky as well.'

Stephan stared incredulously at her angry face, as she renewed the attack 'They should have gassed you and your mother. Then we would finally have been left in peace.' For the first time in his life someone had wanted Stephan dead. He ran home horrified, straight into his mother's arms. She could see that something terrible had happened and gave him the time to have a proper cry.

So was this everyday life in Prague? Events like this led Alice to doubt whether the new republic was really the place for her. She was shaken when in 1946 she read the newspaper reports of the Polish pogrom in Kielce on 4 July. Thousands of Polish Jews then fled to Czechoslovakia in fear of their lives.[5] Although they received aid from the American Jewish Joint Distribution Committee ('the Joint') and were visited by emissaries from Palestine, the Czech authorities insisted that the homeless Jews should leave the country again as quickly as possible. 'To accept Jews is like accepting lice, they are both God's creatures after all.' That line surfaced in an anonymous letter which was actually printed in the newspaper *Dnešek*.[6]

About 7,500 German-speaking Jews had survived the final solution and had returned to Czechoslovakia. They had little hope of being accepted as equal partners in the republic and by 1946 roughly 3,000 of them had already decided to leave their home a second time. When on 10 September 1946 the Ministry of the Interior issued a directive that 'all persons of Jewish origin' were to be excluded from the 'normal transports' and therefore were not to be seen as part of the German population that was being expelled, many of them were given fresh hope. Three days later, however, a decree stressed the 'non-Slavic' origins of the Jews. Citizenship and repropriation of property would only be granted if these persons had, in the past, pursued no active 'Germanization'. All those Jews who had been at German schools, had read German newspapers or belonged to German associations, or if they had spread German culture, were affected. As, of course, was Alice.

*

ALICE, HOWEVER, WAS defiant. She was not going to let them make her abandon hope. At the beginning of 1947 she received a surprise invitation to perform in a concert in Stockholm as part of the Czech–Swedish exchange programme. Czech works were to take pride of place. Alice's mind jumped to the days of the First

Czech Republic, to President Masaryk and his policy of tolerance, equal rights and freedom. Perhaps this offer was a sign that a new democracy was being created in which she and other Jews would have the right to express their opinions freely, and that they could travel where and when they wanted?

Michael Mareš provided her with a book to read on the journey, which would take more than two days. Stefan Zweig's memoirs *Die Welt von Gestern* (The World of Yesterday) had first been published in Stockholm by Bermann-Fischer, a German publishing company that was now based in Sweden. Alice was gripped from the first line: it was the story of her own generation.

The idea that she might be heading for Stockholm as a representative of the 'old order' did not appeal to her. She saw herself as an ambassador for a republic that was rebuilding itself and which, if it was to appeal to her, would be founded on the traditions established by Masaryk.

On the day of the performance she tried out the Bechstein grand in the Stockholm concert hall and decided that its tonal colour was eminently suitable for Schubert's Sonata in B major, with which she was to open the programme.

The concert was completely sold out. Before she went on stage she looked through the crack in the dark red curtain. All these expectant faces: none of them knew anything of what had been her fate. The applause was restrained when she went on stage, but Alice was certain that she would reach the hearts of the audience with the great Schubert sonata. She particularly loved the piece, which she had studied with Ansorge at the masterclass. Whenever she began to play the slow movement it was as if her heart stood still. After the first applause Alice noticed that the Schubert had indeed excited the audience. Her interpretation of Robert Schumann's Symphonic Study, Op. 13 with its ideal, romantic colouration enthralled the audience so much that there were cries of 'bravo'. Alice left the stage at the interval content with her performance thus far.

In the second half she played a selection of Czech compositions, works by Bedřich Smetana, Alois Hába and Bohuslav Martinů. Smetana's *Czech Dances* had always been well received at her concerts up to now and Stockholm was no exception. The three piano pieces by Hába were just as well received as was the Martinů dance. She ended with the Chopin Études. It seemed particularly appropriate that she should play the Études in the first concert she had given abroad since the war, convinced as she was that they had saved her life.

One member of the audience, however, had already heard Alice play all twenty-four Études. Zdenka Fantlová, now twenty-two, had survived Theresienstadt, Auschwitz and Bergen-Belsen. 'No one in the audience knew what binds me to that pianist. No one knew what it meant to live through a concert of the twenty-four Chopin Études in a concentration camp.'⁷ Zdenka had been freed from Belsen more dead than alive and in July 1945 she had been sent to Sweden by the Red Cross to convalesce. It was there that she learned that she was the only member of her family to survive: mother, father, sister, all of them had been murdered.

Zdenka had made up her mind that she would thank Alice personally after the concert and tell her what strength she had given her in Theresienstadt. The door to the performers' dressing rooms was half open and through it Zdenka could see that Alice already had a visitor, a woman she clearly knew well. Both women were in such an emotional state that Zdenka did not want to disturb them. She withdrew from the room unnoticed and it was to be another four decades before Alice Herz and Zdenka Fantlová met and became friends.

Alice's visitor was her childhood friend, Helene Weiskopf. It had been eight years since their last meeting just before Helene's emigration to Sweden. They arranged to have dinner in the restaurant of the hotel where Alice was staying. The colourful memories of their childhood and the terrible experiences of the past eight years made for a moving evening. Alice could not help but notice, however, that Helene had lost her positive outlook. Her third marriage had just failed and it was also possible that Helene was already suffering from the cancer that would cause her such distress that she committed suicide in 1950.

*

THE TRIP TO STOCKHOLM provided Alice with an opportunity to enquire after Leopold's nephew and niece. In 1939 seven-year-old Ilse and her four-year-old brother Thomas had left on a *Kindertransport* for the theoretically safe haven of Norway. As a doctor, their father Felix Mautner had accompanied the transport and personally delivered the children to their foster-family. His plan to save himself and his wife by going abroad came to nothing. They were both deported to the ghetto in Łódź before Theresienstadt had even been opened.

The German march into Norway was the beginning of an odyssey for Ilse and Thomas, an odyssey which took them from Norway to Sweden and from foster-parents to foster-parents, from camp to camp. Now they were fifteen and twelve and were living with a foster-family in Stockholm.

Alice had announced her arrival in a letter to the foster-parents. They were simple, uncomplicated people; at least that was Alice's first impression. The flat was small, modest and tidy, and the children greeted their aunt stiffly by shaking her hand. Embarrassment and insecurity was written all over their faces. Alice was a stranger to them. Ilse seemed particularly shy and insecure: most of the time she answered only with a nod, and avoided eye-contact with her aunt. On the other hand Thomas soon recovered his composure. In the middle of the conversation about school, Alice was hit by the inevitable question about Felix and Edith Mautner.

'Perhaps you know something new about my mummy and daddy?'

Alice shook her head.

Thomas chose this moment to ask Alice almost to beg her to tell his foster-parents that neither he nor his sister in any way wanted to be adopted. The foster-mother, who was obviously very strict and insensitive, had been pressurizing the children to adopt her surname.

'I want to have the same name as my parents,' Thomas said. 'If they are alive . . . and even more so if they are dead.' Thomas had made his point, although he had received no support from Ilse. As a result, the children's relationship with the foster-parents got even worse.

Alice was very sad to leave them. Her brother-in-law had looked after her both emotionally and physically when Stephan was born and she had liked him very much. Now she felt responsible for his children.

On the day she left Sweden she received a telephone call in her hotel room: it was the foster-mother, agitated about the whereabouts of Ilse. The girl had disappeared immediately after Alice's visit and had not reappeared since. Alice had travelled to Sweden full of hope, she returned to Prague racked by worry. Two days later she received a telegram to say the police had found Ilse. Fearing that Alice would have her put in a new children's camp, the girl had gone into hiding.

While the relationship between Alice and Thomas grew closer over the years, Ilse always kept a distance from her aunt. At every meeting she revealed the scars of what the National Socialists had done to her and her family. For Ilse, like so many other survivors, living seemed to be a heavy, if not unbearable, burden.

*

ALICE WAS DEEPLY grateful for the fact that Stephan seemed to have come through the years of oppression and imprisonment relatively unscathed and that he, like his mother, had the capacity to enjoy life to the full.

There was scarcely a week that passed when Alice and Stephan did not go to a concert together, but the boy's life changed when he attended a performance given by the Yugoslav cello virtuoso Antonio Janegro. It had already struck Alice many times that Stephan was enthralled by the sound of the cello. As a boy of three and four he used to listen to records of Brahms' Double Concerto for Violin and Cello for hours on end. Janegro's playing delighted him so much that he kept jumping out of his seat.

In the break Stephan made a decision.

'I must learn the cello!' It was not a vague 'I'd like to learn the cello', but a more urgent 'I must'. It was clearly said with deep conviction and Alice believed him. The next evening Alice took him round to a former colleague, the Czech cello teacher Pravoslav Sádlo. Before the war he had played in their chamber music concerts. Sádlo had the reputation of being the best cello teacher in the city and was a man with many interests and also known as a passionate collector of historical cellos. He had already heard of Stephan's extraordinary musical abilities and was happy to start teaching him immediately.

Stephan had his first lesson on his tenth birthday – Sunday, 21 June 1947. Sádlo lived on the fourth floor of a majestic building in the old city. Stephan was beside himself with admiration when he saw a glass cabinet, almost as high as the room itself and stretching from wall to wall, filled with cello upon cello. He was fascinated by their beauty and variety and he busily counted them up: twenty-one instruments in all sizes and shades of wood. In the middle of the room there was a sort of podium on which the pupil had to sit during his lessons. There was a piano right next to it and Sádlo asked Stephan to play for him. The boy began with a series of two-part inventions by Bach; he then played the first movement of Beethoven's *Pathétique*. Finally Sádlo asked him a few questions on musical theory: Stephan passed with flying colours.

Sádlo was so impressed by the boy's abilities that he gave him a cello that very day. Stephan was over the moon when he packed up the instrument in in its cloth cover and took it home.

'Maminka, this is the loveliest birthday present I have ever had. I am so happy,' Stephan exclaimed as they left the house. 'From today I will never need a birthday present again.'

Stephan eagerly awaited every Sunday from then on and Alice was excited on his behalf. Even after three hours he had made such progress that he was able to play a small piece by Bach and his cello teacher was finally convinced that he had discovered a great talent. A few months later he accepted him as a member of his teaching seminar at the Rudolfinum, where there was a specialized children's department. Stephan was a model pupil. Soon, he would have the opportunity to show off his talent to his relations.

*

ALICE AND MIZZI had been exchanging letters for months. One happy mid-summer's day in 1947 the twins stood facing one another for the first time in eight years: they cried for joy.

Alice did not show how shocked she was by Mizzi's appearance. Pessimism and persistent worry had cut deep furrows in her sister's face. Alice thought she looked old, whereas it was hard to believe that Alice herself was forty-four. Her smile was still girlish, and her eyes were brimming with courage and inner calm.

Mizzi had come to Prague with her husband and her son. Heinz had left the city as a boy of eleven, now a man of nineteen stood before Alice. Like many young emigrants he had adopted a Hebrew name in Palestine and now even his parents called him 'Chaim' or 'life'. Alice's brother-in-law seemed to be basking in the light of professional success; he was now playing a key role in Palestine's health service while maintaining his own practice at the same time.

The sisters had six days together. The crux of all their conversations was whether and when Alice and Stephan were going to emigrate to Palestine. As a piano teacher Alice had an excellent chance of establishing herself there. The Jerusalem Conservatory would be surely proud to number her among the staff. In the meantime, however, the political situation in the 'Promised Land' had deteriorated in every way. Mizzi told Alice the story of the *Exodus* with great excitement. At the end of July, just before their departure, nearly 4,000 men, women and children – the biggest group to date of Jewish refugees from Europe – had arrived in Haifa on the vast ship. The British had refused them entry and forced them to return to France, thereby provoking terrible disturbances in Palestine.

The uncertain political situation – an economic crisis together with the British decision to terminate their mandate in Palestine – made them uncertain about making the move. Emil, Mizzi and Alice were in agreement that it would be best to wait until the New Year to see if the situation calmed down. Then Alice could start making plans. The United Nations would be taking over responsibility for Palestine from the British and the country's independence could not be far off now.

Emil and Mizzi's political *volte face* amazed Alice. She remembered Emil as an intellectual who thought about enlightenment and progress in Europe and who was a stranger to nationalism in all its forms. Before his emigration he had shown no sympathy for the Zionist movement. In the intervening years, however, he had turned into a fierce defender of Zionism. Without a country of their own, without a refuge for persecuted Jews from all over the world, without a strong defensive army, the problems of Jewry in the world could never be solved. Mizzi had also turned into a passionate Zionist, something Alice had only previously encountered in Felix Weltsch. And when Chaim Adler spoke of the pleasures of the Pathfinder Movement, he awoke longings in Stephan.

*

'MASARYK IS DEAD!' The news was given to Alice on 10 March 1948 while she was at the grocer's. The fifty-six-year-old foreign minister had, they said, been found by his staff in the courtyard of his ministry. The bathroom window to his private apartment on the second floor was open. Jan Masaryk was wearing his pyjamas.

There had been a political crisis on 20 February, and twelve ministers had resigned, members of the Czech National Socialist Party, the Catholic People's Party and the Slovak Democratic Party. In effect, it had been a communist coup. Alice knew this, but the fact that Jan Masaryk, son of the first president, had remained at his desk had comforted her.

He was the best-loved politician in the country, seen as a
guarantee of democracy and the continuation of his father's far-
sighted policies. It was easy to believe the rumours that he had
been murdered. It was said there were signs of a struggle in the
bathroom. There were razor blades on the floor and a pillow in
the bath. It was said that the Russian secret service had thrown
him out of the window. Others maintained that the so-called Czech
state security, the new communist organ of repression, was responsible for the crime. A third school asserted that he had committed
suicide to tell the world of the growing dangers of communist
dictatorship.

The newspapers were celebrating a 'victorious February', but
as far as Alice could see, it was no more than a communist
takeover; a bad omen for social progress. To her astonishment she
learned that one of the government's official policies was to fight
anti-Semitism. Alice could not believe her eyes when she read
Kopecky's statement of 12 March. He had always been a communist, but up to now he had also voiced the sharpest anti-Semitic
comments. Now he assured Prague's Jewish community once and
for all, 'that the developments which were taking place in Czechoslovakia would prove the final defeat for the fascist anti-Semites in
their midst. The new regime wants the Jews to enjoy the broadest
range of religious, social and civil rights.'[8]

When the communists seized power they stopped talking about
compensation. Any hope harboured by the surviving Jewish population that they might see their property again proved illusory. Far
from returning people's possessions, the new government went a
stage further: the state dispossessed all homeowners. The block of
flats in which Alice and Stephan had been living was appropriated
by the state. Pavel Haas's parents were robbed for the second time.

A few weeks later, Alice received a report that her friend
Michael Mareš had been arrested and charged with treason. She
immediately asked for permission to visit him, which was granted.
She tried to console her friend; his arrest must have been a
misunderstanding; he was not guilty of anything. Nonetheless, he

remained in prison for many years before being rehabilitated. He died in 1971.

*

FEAR AND DISTRUST now governed Czechoslovakia. Alice always had to ask her visitors to refrain from saying anything critical about the state in the fear that Stephan might pick something up and air it at school. She became so insecure that she hardly dared open the door, convinced the comrades would come and take the boy away from her if anyone heard of her critical opinion of the regime. 'Gigi says it is now a thousand times worse than it was under the Nazis,' Ruth Weltsch reported at the time.[9]

Although Alice found it extraordinarily difficult to work out the contradictory events and tortuous developments in the country, she had decided that she had to leave. She wanted to leave Prague as quickly as possible and go to the newly founded state of Israel; she wanted to go to Mizzi and Irma, but, according to Ruth, 'she didn't know whether she would get there.'[10]

There was a pro-Israeli faction within the Communist Party that planned (or so the rumour had it) to deliver large consignments of weapons to Israel. During the Protectorate the Germans had made Czechoslovakia their weapons store, and the factories and storehouses had been left largely intact. The stock of weaponry was in part already old and not worth that much, but even so, with access to these supplies Israel could possibly guarantee its survival. They needed to fix a price; the delivery dates needed to be settled; there were instructors to be found; there were secret transport routes to Israel to be worked out: all measures that were in clear contradiction of UN guidelines, and things that could not be undertaken if the Czech leadership had acted alone. The green light for the weapons deal came from the USSR. They were hoping that Israel would become a willing satellite of the Soviet Union. After all, there were many Soviet sympathizers in Israel, because of the Russian contribution to the victory over fascism.

The rumours were confirmed when the heads of the Prague

Jewish Community asked Alice to give a benefit concert at the Rudolfinum at the end of November. She was to play works by Beethoven and the profits were to be used for the defence of the new state. The money was earmarked to buy Czech weapons, which nobody bothered to keep secret any more.

When Alice's brother-in-law in Israel heard the news he decided to use a professional trip to Switzerland to visit the World Health Organization as a pretext to go on to Prague for the concert. It was an impressive occasion. There were more than 1,000 people sitting in the imposing concert hall of the Rudolfinum. Representatives of the Jewish Community introduced the concert, followed by speeches given by representatives from Czechoslovakia and Israel. Then Alice played her inspiring interpretation of selected Beethoven sonatas. The evening raised a sum of money far higher than that expected by the organizers. It was also a personal triumph for Alice. She had rarely played before such a large audience.

Immediately after the concert Alice and Emil talked about the steps she needed to take in order to leave the country. Her brother-in-law impressed on her the need to hurry. It had been clear to him for a long time that Israel would never develop into a satellite state of the Soviet Union. When the Russians began to understand that, Emil feared they might refuse to grant any more visas.

'Have you got our visas yet?'

All week Stephan pestered his mother with the same question, but the granting of permission to leave was a long drawn-out process. It lasted from November 1948 to January 1949. 'PS: has anyone heard anything from Gigi? The story goes that they are not letting anyone out of Czechoslovakia any more,' Alice's niece Ruth wrote to her father on 25 January 1949.[11]

It was a race against time. Many of the necessary committees were unhelpful. When it was clear that the communists had forbidden the export of valuables to Israel, Ruth had an idea: she was going to make contact with a volunteer pilot who had flown from America to Jerusalem to train the Israeli Air Force and to fight in the war against the Arabs. He readily agreed to track down Alice during a planned trip to Czechoslovakia. The young man was called David Herschl, and he was being instructed on how to fly Czech aircraft somewhere near Prague. Once he had been given a plane he could fly to Israel, taking some of Alice's valuables with him.

Herschl flew to Prague, and began his training with Czech instructors, reporting to Alice on his first free weekend. She was suspicious of him at first, but after he showed her Ruth's letter she trusted him. The pilot lived for a week with Alice and Stephan and became a friend to both of them. Alice decided to give David two rings, the Toulouse-Lautrec and two other pictures to take to Israel; because it was strictly illegal to take stamps out of the country, he took Stephan's stamp collection, which he loved above all else. It was hidden among the weapons.

Alice's wish to take her Steinway Grand to Israel looked as if it would prove impossible. The new regime had decreed that all valuables being exported were subject to a levy, so not only had she to get permission for the Steinway, which seemed less and less likely with every passing day, she also had to find the money for the substantial bribe – in effect, she had to buy her own instrument from the state. Once again, though, Alice was lucky.

Evidently informed by Ruth of Alice's difficulties, their old friend Max Brod, who was also now living in Israel, wrote to the President of the Republic, Klement Gottwald. Brod's words continued to carry weight in Prague and about two weeks later Alice was summoned to the ministry. A high-ranking, but foul-mouthed official had been told to deal with the case: 'That's what it's like with you Jews, you still want to rob us,' he blurted out in greeting, without so much as looking up from his desk.

The piano had never been the property of the Czechoslovak state, but had belonged to a Jewish family murdered by the Nazis, was Alice's reply.

'You don't want to work, but you want to suck the blood from the state.' At this Alice lost her temper. Without reflecting on the consequences she hurled these words back at him: 'Very few Jews survived the Final Solution, but despite this we are suffering as much under the communists as we did with the Nazis. It won't be like this forever, one day it is going to be just as bad for you Czechs and then you will think of me, and then you will reflect that you pitilessly slandered a survivor of the Final Solution. And you will finally see how inhuman your arguments were.'

Alice fled in tears. For a week she heard nothing. Then, to her surprise the postman handed her a letter granting her permission to export the Steinway. It was signed by President Klement Gottwald. The price was a sum that she would not have been able to save in ten years. Salvation had come from her family in Israel.

Felix Weltsch had a bank account in Prague, and Alice now had to withdraw the money. There were mind-numbing weeks negotiating the usual minefield of bureaucracy, and Alice's attempts to withdraw the money were checked at every stage. Eventually, she got it and entrusted her piano to a transport company.

A few days before her departure, Alice went across the road to the grocer to buy bread, milk and other necessities for the journey. Over the past four years the shopkeeper had always been decent towards her, but now she could feel the enmity of his customers all around her. Many Czechs resented having a Jewish survivor in their midst.

It was her last day in Prague; she had nothing to lose any more. She suddenly felt the desire to tell the antipathetic people around her in the shop what she thought of them. On her way out she made a half turn: 'I would like to say goodbye to all of you today,' she said. 'I am leaving, going to that place where you Czechs always wanted us Jews to go: Palestine.' Most of the customers looked at their feet in embarrassment. One of those present, however, surprised her by saying 'Frau Sommer, if you would allow me to hide in your suitcase, I'd gladly come with you.'

That evening Ilonka Štěpánova came round. In the years since Theresienstadt the friendship between the two women had grown by degrees; their last hours together were steeped in memories, but above all in sadness.

'Now you are going to a land where only Jews live,' Ilonka said as she left, 'What are you looking for there? But if they were all like you, however . . .'

Alice was perplexed and deeply hurt. 'That is the worst insult that you could say to me on leaving. Do you really think the Czechs, the Russians, the Hungarians or any other race is better than the Jews? Isn't it true that there are good and bad people everywhere?'

FIFTEEN

Zena

'Don't look back now, just straight ahead'

'AND WHAT HAPPENS if they take my cello away at the border?'

'No one will take your cello away,' Alice calmly told her son. 'We have it in writing. The official papers say that the cello is your property. No one is going to take that away from you!'

They were both standing at Wilson Station, the Kaiser-Franz-Joseph Station of Alice's childhood. It was 1 March 1949. Ten years before Alice had said goodbye to her sisters Irma and Mizzi at this station. Now, at long last, the time had come to be reunited with them again. There were several hundred people milling about, all beginning the journey to Israel that day. At least as many friends and relations had turned up to say goodbye, Paul and Mary among them. Alice did not refer to the fact that this was goodbye for ever.

The Jewish Community had even set up a podium on the platform and prepared a farewell programme. A representative of the community gave a speech about the Jewish dream of their own land, long desired and littered with sacrifices, which had finally become a reality with the foundation of the state of Israel. When a group of young people broke into the *Hatikva* many people burst into tears. It was the Zionist hymn which most of those present knew from their childhood and it was now the Israeli national anthem. Alice was moved and looked at Stephan, who was holding his beloved cello. He was almost twelve and still half a head shorter than her and, as he had done so often with his father, he was singing a descant.

When the train set off at around midday the anticipation of arrival began to mask the sadness of parting. The dreadful experiences of the last few years had driven a wedge between Alice and her beloved Prague. Would her heart find another home in Israel? She did not doubt it.

Mountains of luggage blocked the corridors and carriages, with some families travelling with as many as fifteen bags and suitcases. No one who found a seat was going to give it up. In a compartment for eight, at least thirteen people had to find a place. Stephan was distrustful of the situation and clung on to his cello, but in order to provide some more room Alice tried to convince him to put it in the corridor right next to the door to the compartment so that he could see it when he wanted.

'They are not going to take it away from you,' she repeated; but Stephan would not be talked round: 'They wanted to take away your grand piano.'

When Alice had come home in despair after the battles she was having over the piano, it was Stephan who distracted her and cheered her up. Since he had seen with what injustice and cruelty the Czech state had behaved towards his mother, he was understandably worried about his own instrument. In Theresienstadt Alice had tried to shelter Stephan from the harsh realities of life, but now, Alice realized, Stephan was old enough to deal with them himself. While it had taken Alice four difficult months to organize their departure from Prague, her friend Edith Kraus seemed to be losing her battle with the bureaucracy for the right to leave with her piano. Edith, too, wanted to leave for Israel in the next few weeks and was in despair about her instrument.

'Why is it that we can take our grand but Edith cannot?' Unequal treatment like this bothered Stephan all his life.

'It is probably because Max Brod interceded for us,' his mother replied.

After an hour and a half the train came to a halt at the border town of Gmünd in the Upper Waldviertel. The Austrian side of the divided town fell under the Soviet Zone of Occupation. From there the journey would take them through Vienna and occupied Austria, then over the Brenner Pass to Genoa. The passengers were in good spirits. They were comforted by the fact that the journey had been organized by the American Jewish relief organization, the Joint, which had partly funded it, as well as dealing with all the additional travelling formalities.[1] When the train was taken into a siding and kept in an open field on the Czech side of the border, the passengers were, at first, not worried.

A lot of Czech customs officers got on board, together with Russian soldiers, and began an extensive inspection. After waiting for two or three hours the travellers began to grow anxious. Suddenly one of them said there was a rumour that the train had been refused entry into Austria and that the plan was to take them back to Prague. Another suggested that there was a gang of smugglers on board, and as soon as they were arrested the train would proceed.

Many of the travellers consisted of young families with small children, most of them born after the war. It was cold and wet, the temperature in the train fell to 14°C and the water ran out after a few hours. The discomfort soon affected the adults as well as the children, many of whom were crying and screaming.

Hours elapsed and the waiting paralysed the travellers with boredom. To keep Stephan occupied Alice made up puzzles that he had to solve, giving him only the first and last letters of a word, which he had to work it out by asking the right questions. Stephan loved games like this.

The games provided a temporary distraction but as darkness fell the mood in the train also darkened. Alice covered Stephan with her scarf and laying his head in her lap she endeavoured to stroke him to sleep. He was unable to close his eyes, however, and she, too, remained wide awake thinking about the cold night, the discomfort in the packed compartment, and the dreadful anxiety that they were about to be seized and imprisoned again.

Her thoughts travelled back to Theresienstadt. How long were they going to be left without food? Their water bottles were as good as empty and she was saving the last few drops for Stephan. Alice could remember only too well that thirst was harder to bear than hunger. How often had she suffered from thirst in the camp? And where was she going to wash? Once again, mankind's most elementary needs had been disregarded. Once again they were being treated as sub-human.

When morning came and the train was still standing in the siding, she thought of a solution. She took Stephan's hand and got out of the carriage with him. It was raining heavily. 'We are going to those houses over there,' she told him and pointed to the railway workers' dwellings on the other side of the field which could be seen on the horizon. 'There we shall wash and fill our water-bottles.'

It took more than half an hour before they reached the houses and they were soaked through. Alice knocked on the first available door. The occupants were helpful, they sat them at the breakfast table and heated up a big pot of water so that they could give themselves a good wash. When Alice and Stephan returned to the train with their full water bottles, the situation was the same as when they had left. No one could say why the train was not moving.

Suddenly, after a twenty-nine hour delay a piercing whistle came from the train and it shunted forward with no more explanation than why it had stopped. Alice stared out of the window. In which direction would they go? Once she was sure that they were heading into Austria she was seized by an overwhelming feeling of happiness: after the years of privation, dictatorship and tyranny she was finally bound for freedom.

The journey through the snow-covered Brenner Pass was some compensation for the hours of anxiety, but more misfortunes

awaited them in Genoa. The ship that was due to take them to
Israel had left the port a short while before and was now only a
distant spot on the horizon. The crew had clearly decided to take
other people who wanted to get to Israel: hundreds of them were
constantly waiting there, often for days on end.

The 350 emigrants had to spend another night in the unheated
carriages. The damp and cold affected the children above all and
many of them fell ill. Stephan was also suffering from tonsillitis.
Alice asked the Polish-born Dr Ziv, the Israeli charged with accompanying the train, to stay with Stephan and the other sick children
while she went to the Jewish Community in Genoa to organize
help.

'Stephan do you hear me? Your maminka is now going into the
centre of Genoa to fetch help. Listen, I am going to be gone a few
hours, but I shall come back soon.'

Stephan nodded weakly. When his mother had left him for
work in Theresienstadt he was frightened that she had gone
forever. Now he was four years older and knew that his mother
would never leave him.

*

ALICE DID NOT speak a word of Italian and with a combination
of English and German and great effort she found her way to the
offices of the Jewish Community. There she learned that her fellow
passengers would be leaving the train to be put up in neighbouring
private houses and small hotels. Four days of uncertainty later, the
journey started again, and the train proceeded to Brindisi, where
a Greek ship had been laid on to take the emigrants to Palestine.
When the ship left the harbour it was completely full and they had
five days of stormy seas ahead of them. Alice was badly seasick,
but Stephan had recovered from his tonsillitis and spent hours
exploring the ship with some children of his own age.

After what seemed to be days and days at sea, Haifa – for
many the prettiest town in Israel – could be seen on the horizon
with the wooded slopes of Carmel in the background. Alice was

astonished at the beauty of the strange landscape and she realized just how little she knew about her new home – the promised land of Israel.

The ship dropped anchor off the coast and a small vessel took the passengers into the harbour. As the boat came close to the harbour wall Alice heard a familiar voice call out her old nickname: 'Gigi!' It was her nephew Chaim whom she had last seen two years before when he had come to Prague. Now he was twenty-one and studying sociology in Jerusalem. For two weeks he had been waiting in Haifa harbour for Alice's arrival. Arriving in a new country was not daunting for Alice now that one of her loved ones was there to greet her.

They spent their first night with Felix Weltsch's brother Willi, who practised as an architect in Haifa. The next day in Tel Aviv there was a moving reunion with Alice's niece Ruth. The girl whom Alice had fed as a baby and later taught the piano had grown into a fine, handsome woman.

The search for their cases proved unexpectedly difficult. More than a thousand cases had been unloaded from the ship and these were distributed in different places all over Tel Aviv. For three days Alice and Stephan hunted down their bits of baggage, but one little case filled with shoes remained impossible to locate, and so the two of them had to walk about Tel Aviv wearing their Prague winter shoes.

*

DON'T SPEAK ABOUT Leopold's death, about Theresienstadt or about the extermination of the Jews. Don't look back, but keep looking forward and with that live as best you can in the present. This was Alice's philosophy and she had passed it on to Stephan. In the past year neither of them had spoken about the camp. Although Alice was happy to be in Israel, she was dreading the first evening with her family as she did not know how she would react when they asked her about the occupation, Theresienstadt, Auschwitz and Dachau?

In Mizzi's small flat in Jerusalem the table had been laid for a party, and lovingly decked out with flowers and candles. There were nine seats around it as they were expecting the whole family: besides Mizzi, Emil and Chaim Adler, Alice's sister Irma was due with her husband Felix, while their daughter Ruth was coming from Tel Aviv with her second husband Benjamin Gorenstein.

Everyone greeted one another with great warmth, but after a quarter of an hour they were all talking about the political events of the last weeks and months. They spoke German among themselves, like the old days, and Alice was pained to discover that after two years of Theresienstadt and four more in post-war Prague Stephan was scarcely able to speak the language any more. What did German culture mean to him? It was still as important to her as ever, but how would she be able to teach him to appreciate it? She decided that as soon as he had learned enough Hebrew she would begin speaking to him in German again.

On 14 March 1949, a few days before her arrival, Chaim Weizmann had been elected the first president of the new state. In January a truce had been agreed with Egypt and since then the Star of David had been flying in Eilat in the Gulf of Aqaba, providing Israel with access to the Red Sea. In February the Knesset, the freely elected parliament, convened for the first time, and approved its first prime minister and cabinet under David Ben-Gurion. The talk that evening at Mizzi's was all about the new state of Israel, the victory in the war of independence and the threat from the Arabs. Alice was relieved and amazed that no one spoke about the war in Europe or of the crimes committed against the Jews. It was not just true of Alice's family, but of families throughout Israel: no one spoke of the final solution or of the dead. They all concentrated on building up the new state; everyone looked forward, as she did herself.

It was a new experience for Alice, who had always been apolitical, to find that politics was the main topic of conversation whenever the family sat down to dinner together. Current affairs were hotly debated and each person felt themselves jointly responsible for the new state, so it was inevitable that everyone would have an opinion about the government's decisions. Even Mizzi who, when she was in Prague, showed more interest in literature than in anything else, was now well versed in the political issues of the day. For Alice, though, rebuilding her life was her priority; politics could wait.

From the first day that they were reunited the twins were inseparable once more. For the next twenty-five years, until Mizzi's death, barely a day passed that Alice did not call on her sister. Apart from her mother, Mizzi said once, she loved only three people in the world with all her heart: her husband Emil, her son Chaim and her twin sister Alice. Despite their different characters, it was never a one-sided relationship; each gave the other strength and support. But close though they were, they were also quite critical of one another. Mizzi was quick to defend herself when Alice encouraged her to look at the sunny side of life. Once Mizzi cried out: 'But Alice, life has just as many dark sides! Don't delude yourself by denying it.'

*

ALICE WAS PARTICULARLY struck by two things in her new homeland. One of them was her almost childish astonishment that Jews did all the jobs in the country. Never had she seen Jewish bus drivers, dustmen or postmen in Prague. The other was how modest and cramped everyone's lives were. Even people in important positions, with high incomes, lived in what were generally small flats. The spartan lifestyle was obvious to her at every turn, and she was surprised at how difficult it was to get used to the lack of space in Mizzi and Emil's flat.

The flat was in the Rechavia district, a particularly leafy part of Jerusalem, inhabited by many European immigrants: intellectuals, artists and civil servants. The houses were usually two storeys and constructed from a local, shiny white stone and, with their occasional front gardens, they looked European. The inhabitants were careful to preserve a European way of life and in some streets the German language predominated, while in others it was mostly Czech or Russian. Many of the older inhabitants seemed to have stopped making an effort to speak Modern Hebrew. It was here that Alice would spend the next thirty-seven years of her life.

Emil had financed the purchase of their flat in 1939 with the money he brought with him, together with a generous loan from the authorities for new arrivals. It consisted of a tiny kitchen together with three little rooms. Every afternoon the biggest of the three served as a surgery. There was a massive writing desk, a bookcase and a glass cabinet filled with medical instruments. The second room was a waiting room. It was sparingly furnished with some simple chairs and a sofa, which could be folded out in the evening and became Emil and Mizzi's bed. The third room contained a huge wardrobe and a table and chairs. It was there that they ate – and where Chaim slept. During the three weeks that Alice and Stephan lived with Mizzi and Emil, Chaim stayed with friends.

Life with the relatives was not always easy. It had been clear for a long time that Mizzi needed an operation. Even when Emil assured his wife that the operation was routine Marianne was sceptical. While she was in hospital in Jerusalem Alice was supposed to run the household. Marianne explained the housekeeping and the afternoon surgeries, and the concert pianist was temporarily transformed into a charming assistant to the consultant.

Alice visited her sister at the hospital every day, even sitting beside Marianne when she came round from the anaesthetic. Alice saw that her sister wanted to say something and leant over. In a whisper Marianne confided: 'Life is terrible!'

*

IN THE MONTHS following the foundation of the state, 145,000 people arrived in Israel and were assigned to twenty-nine camps dotted about the country. More than half of them lived in tents, the rest in huts,[2] but they were all dreaming of a home of their own.

Three weeks after her arrival, Alice went flat-hunting. First she had to become a citizen, but after the humiliating treatment she had received at the hands of the Czechs she was made to feel welcome in Israel. A lovely official suggested that Stephan might want to adopt a more typically Hebrew name in the future and proposed David, Ben or Raphael. Stephan was very pleased with Raphael. Then it was time to find a flat and again Alice was lucky. They needed to live somewhere convenient for the Conservatory, her future place of work, and if possible close to Mizzi and Emil. Because she had arrived in Jerusalem without any means of her own, the Conservatory paid her an advance and Mizzi and Emil also provided her with money to get started up. She planned to work as hard as she could to provide Raphael with a decent education, and did not want to pay more rent than she had to.

With her sister's help Alice found accommodation in a four-bedroom flat which she had to share with another family. It was about ten minutes on foot from Mizzi and fifteen from Irma. Each family had two of the rooms and shared the kitchen and the lavatory.

An Arab family of six lived in the other two rooms. Two diametrically opposed life-styles came together in that small space: Alice the pianist, an example of the central European Jewish bourgeoisie, and the Arab family, illiterate, uneducated workers who had grown up in the Muslim tradition, but Alice was immediately impressed by their kindness. At the beginning they communicated only by friendly gestures, but Raphael learned Modern Hebrew remarkably quickly and, after a few weeks, he was able to interpret.

When a couple of weeks later a lorry drove up delivering beds for the two of them and the Steinway grand, Alice found that the piano took up two-thirds of the room and left her with even less space than she had had in Prague. She tenderly stroked the instrument and sat straight down at the stool to play a soft melody. It had been more than ten weeks since she had played the piano and nearly all the keys were sticking. When she opened the lid she immediately shut her eyes to banish the horror of what she saw: whole strings had rusted, the interior workings of the piano were ruined. It was clear that the piano had been kept outside for weeks on end during the rainy months of February and March. The Steinway, every pianist's dream, was unusable. There was nothing for it but to use her first earnings to purchase a second-hand piano.

Shortly after their arrival someone knocked on the door and when she opened it she saw to her great surprise an old friend from Prague, Richard Gibian. He had emigrated to the United States with his wife and four young little sons in 1939 and had come to Israel to visit his sister. When Raphael came out to say hello, Richard remembered how, even as an unborn child, he had demonstrated his musical talent at the Kolisch Quartet's concert. Mutual friends had told Richard about Leopold's death in Dachau and to spare Alice's feelings he did not raise the topic. When he asked her to play something for him Alice explained what had happened to the Steinway grand.

'We'll it fixed,' said Richard. In Prague he had been a successful businessman making typewriters. He noted the number and date of the grand piano and wrote to the firm's Hamburg depot to order a whole set of new strings, together with all the hammers. A few months later the spare parts arrived in Jerusalem and a piano maker, paid by Richard, came round to install them. At the end of 1949, even though it never achieved the quality of tone it had had before, Alice could play her Steinway once again.

*

THE DIRECTORSHIP OF the Jerusalem Conservatory had waived the usual auditions and handed Alice's contract to Irma even before she had landed in Israel. The reviews of her many concerts and the reference supplied by a fellow Czech piano teacher guaranteed her future reputation. This would have been more than enough, but Max Brod also praised Alice's talent as a pianist. His reputation as a music critic was so good that the director of the Conservatory was left in no doubt that Alice's appointment would be an honour.

It was a tradition that new members of the staff should give a concert. There was a small auditorium in the building that held about 150 people. Alice applied her usual serious approach to the first concert in her new homeland, playing Beethoven's *Appassionata* and Smetana's *Czech Dances*, which met with great success. Not only were all her colleagues sitting in the audience, but most of the students and, of course, her sisters and their husbands. Alice had not realized that there was stiff competition between the teachers for the approval of their pupils, their monthly stipends depending on the number of pupils they had on their books, so she had not prepared her concert with this in mind. Nonetheless, over the next few days many students came to her, wanting to be taught by her.

Over the next few weeks, Alice quickly established a new routine. She was particularly pleased that she had had no problems finding Raphael a place in a good local school. When he entered the class for the first time neither master nor pupil quite knew what he was doing there.[3] As he spoke no Hebrew he introduced himself in Czech, but fortunately the teacher was of Russian origin and could follow what he said. Suddenly the teacher remembered that he had been told that he was going to have a new pupil who had survived the concentration camp at Theresienstadt. There were no other boys in the class with a similar background, but he quickly told the boys what the European Jews had suffered under the Nazis and asked them to be particularly attentive to their new classmate. At first Raphael had to put up with the fact that everybody laughed at his funny accent, but after a few weeks he could easily make himself understood in Hebrew and with his good-humoured observations, and the many pranks he played, he was soon accepted by his peers.

After a few weeks the music teacher asked Raphael to give a concert for the children in his year. He began with some preludes and fugues, which Johann Sebastian Bach wrote for his son and which were later published as *The Little Clavier Book for Wilhelm Friedemann Bach*, but it was his performance of Beethoven's *Pathétique* that completely won over his audience. Here was an eleven-year-old boy playing like a concert pianist – and playing by heart. From that day onwards he was admired by every boy at the school and he went on to give a number of piano and cello concerts in his time there.

Alice still taught her son every morning, then as soon as he had left for school she began her three or four hours of practice. She didn't like to spend time cooking and so she met Raphael at noon every day at Maria Polack's house, some five minutes away, where they joined a group of six or eight other guests. Maria was originally from Vienna and, as kind as she was cultivated, she regularly cooked for professional people. It was there that Alice met her first pupil, Esther Erle, and her mother.

Maria soon took account of Alice's eating habits: little in the way of salt or spice, lots of fruit and a bit of fish or chicken from time to time. In the first few months, before Alice could make herself understood in Hebrew, she would speak in German, English or French, according to her fellow diners' origins.

At 2 o'clock Alice started work at the Conservatory, while Raphael went home and did his homework, practised the cello and had private lessons in Hebrew, English or music theory. Alice usually taught for three or four hours every afternoon, sometimes for longer. Her route home led her past Mizzi's house and she would often drop in for quarter of an hour before heading home, where she knew Raphael would already be waiting for her. Their dinner together was an important ritual, during which they recounted everything that had happened that day.

One of the advantages of Alice's modest living arrangements was that the Arab family were happy to keep an eye on Raphael when she went out in the evening; she went mostly to visit Mizzi and Emil, but only for about an hour. The disadvantages of the small flat became apparent equally quickly, however. In every free

moment Alice gave private lessons, while Raphael was often practising cello in the next room. The resulting tonal confusion was
disturbing, but Raphael found a solution. When piano students
came he would practise his cello in the lavatory.

'And what will you do when one of our neighbours needs to
use it?' Raphael beamed: 'Then I shall go into the hall and play a
little louder . . . until the smell has gone away.' And that is what
he actually did and over the next few years it proved the best
solution.

*

TOWARDS THE END of July 1949, a few weeks after his twelfth
birthday, there was a ring at the doorbell. Raphael answered and
was ecstatically happy to see David Herschl, with whom he had
spent such unexpectedly happy days in Prague. In fact a picture of
one of the aircraft David had shown him then was on the wall
above his bed. Raphael's cousin Ruth had told them what happened to David since he had left Prague:

> Herschl flew from P[rague], direct from Gigi, the aircraft was
> loaded with – among other things – Gigi's (scanty) belongings
> and the idiots [at Tel Aviv] did not recognize the Skymaster
> and started the alarm. What did that mean? That meant they
> failed to light the airport and the plane could not land. I
> should add here that the aircraft was not working [properly]
> and of the four engines it started with, only two were still
> functioning. That meant that the valuable cargo it was carry-
> ing had to be pushed overboard, that meant in other words,
> the whole consignment. With considerable effort he reached
> Erez [Israel] where they would not switch on the lights, so he
> circled T[el] A[viv] like an idiot and at very low altitude, and
> still there was no light. He could find no radio connection, he
> fired flares and made all the signals possible, but down below
> it was dark. What can you do when you have no fuel left and
> no power to climb. Herschl landed in the Jam [sea]. Some of

Gigi's things ended up in the sea. Herschl and the crew saved themselves and some of Gigi's things. So he arrived here yesterday crazily cold with some wholly sodden things of Gigi's and Steffi's stamp album which was completely sea-waterlogged. I have dried out all the stamps and put them in envelopes. They have been salvaged. I will send Gigi two golden wedding rings and (these are also here), three pictures (which are also wet through) ... It is a wonder he is still alive.[4]

Herschl then decided that he wanted to deliver the salvaged stamps in person. At the same time he finally handed Alice the Toulouse-Lautrec, which was coated with a layer of sea-salt. Years later, when she had put enough money aside, Alice had the picture restored.

*

'ZENA', OR SIMPLICITY, was one of the first Hebrew wordsthat Alice learnt. Many years after the state was founded a satirical folk song characterized the years between 1949 and 1952 as the 'Zena-regime'. It was a time of biting economic measures which affected all citizens alike, and which for the most part meant great privations. Above all, the new Israel needed money to ensure its military security as well as for the assimiliation programme for the many immigrants. Alice, too, had used the assimilation programme: her intensive course in Hebrew was paid for by the state.

Nearly everything was rationed then, and every family had to take account of their allotted 'points'. There was a shortage of milk, cheese, jam and margarine. You also needed to have 'points' for shoes, clothes, soap and many other vital ingredients of everyday life. There were queues of people outside every shop. A rumour went around that in Israel you got everything twice: once on the radio and once more in the shops. Every day, the goods that were available and where they could be obtained was announced on the wireless. Everyone who heard the news then tore round to the appropriate shop and stood in the queue.

Alice did not listen to the announcements. She was happy with fruit and vegetables and the two foods that were not rationed: bread and fish. She quickly learned the Modern Hebrew words for these, for everything else she needed much longer. Most of the time, Raphael did the shopping.

The fact that no one locked their doors in the Rechavia district was probably because no one had any more than his neighbour. There was no obvious crime among the population, who originated mostly from Europe but with a smattering of people who had emigrated from the Mediterranean and North Africa. After the depressing years of Nazi occupation and Stalinism, when any knock at the ever-bolted door could mean danger, Alice found this particularly refreshing. Mutual trust seemed to be an expression of the enthusiasm that people had for making the Jewish state work. Even Alice could play her role in the process by contributing her knowledge and ability as a piano teacher. She never lost this feeling in the thirty-seven years she spent in Israel. It was for this reason, too, that she, in contrast to many people of her age, had the ambition and strength of will to master the new language.

When Alice learned vocabulary she showed a preference for ideas rather than anything connected with everyday life. 'You make me think of an immigrant newly arrived from Germany who drowns in the sea because no one can understand his cries for help,' Marianne remarked. 'You need to learn how to say bread, milk, potatoes and common things like that, so that you can survive from day to day; rather than concerning yourself with so many abstract things the whole time.'

Alice defended herself: 'But for me, those things are more important than everyday life. In the end I want to be able to talk about things, I want to go to the theatre and read books.'

Alice had always found it easy to learn languages. Since childhood she had been able to converse fluently in German, Czech,

French and English. It surprised her therefore, how difficult she found it to learn Hebrew. Although she was fascinated by the attractive logic of the grammar, it was a long time before she could hold a proper conversation. She subscribed to two newspapers, the very serious *Ha'arez* and one aimed at new arrivals, written specially in an approachable idiom. She tried to read the newspaper every day, but for a long time it was a waste of time. The unfamiliar alphabet was hard to decipher; and she found the idea of unwritten vowels that had to be imagined extremely irritating. For weeks she could not construct a single sentence and came close to giving up. It was no consolation to her that her fellow immigrants did not find Modern Hebrew any easier.

Eventually she got hold of an exercise book, which she carried with her at all times. Whenever she came across a new word, at the grocer's, on the bus, while teaching or at concerts, she would ask about it and write down what it meant. This lonely battle continued for years, and Irma and Marianne often shook their heads about the amount of energy their sister expended on the language. After a while she could understand Hebrew reasonably well, although she went on making mistakes when she wrote or spoke it. It took decades before Alice felt that she had mastered the language. In retrospect she calls it one of her 'life's great performances'.

SIXTEEN

Jerusalem

'Only in Israel did I feel happy in my soul.'

'MAMINKO, THEY ARE ALL having their bar mitzvahs this year.'

Raphael had been curious about his fellow pupils' forthcoming bar mitzvahs since he had started at his new school. The ceremony, which takes place on their thirteenth birthday, marks the moment when Jewish boys come of age. At least as important as being able to claim the honour of being 'grown-up members' of the Jewish community were the presents the boys expected to receive at the family party afterwards. Most of them were hoping for their first bicycle.

Raphael was different. He neither knew the meaning of the words bar mitzvah, nor could he work out whether it had any significance for him. But he clearly understood, from the discussions in the school playground, how important the event was to his fellow pupils and this awoke vague longings in the boy, as well as one absolutely concrete wish: to belong.

'Am I actually going to have a bar mitzvah of my own?'

Alice was not ready for this question. Traditional religious beliefs had never played a part in her life, nor had her brothers Georg and Paul had a bar mitzvah. Although Alice knew there were three main religious groups in Israel – orthodox, conservative and reformed Jews – she did not feel she belonged to any of them. She tried to explain this to Raphael. Naturally they would have a big party for his thirteenth birthday, of course he could invite his friends and relations, and he would indeed get presents, but did he have to have a bar mitzvah?

At first that was enough to placate the boy, but as the weeks passed he became increasingly depressed. His new friends were getting ready for their parties; they were receiving religious instruction and dreaming of what they were going to eat at the celebratory feast at which they would be the chief guest. He alone was an outsider. As so often before, Alice sought the advice of her brother-in-law, Felix. In his view the Jewish religion was also important for non-religious Jews. Without a religious foundation, he argued, neither Zionism nor Israel would be possible. It was complicated and often difficult, but national and religious values, however illogical their relationship to one another might seem, were inextricably linked. He therefore thought that all thirteen-year-olds should have the opportunity to celebrate their bar mitzvahs: the stronger their consciousness of history and tradition the more it promoted the feeling of togetherness that was vital for the construction of the state of Israel.

Alice was convinced, but how was she to prepare Raphael for the celebration in the time she had left? Most of his friends had been having instruction for months. Felix suggested that she ask his friend Friedrich Thieberger, the son of a rabbi who had once been a famous religious teacher in Prague and was now living in Israel, for help. Alice had met him many times at the Weltsches, when she was a girl; he had been teaching Kafka Hebrew then. For the next four months Raphael received private instruction from Thieberger and throughout his life he never lost the enthusiasm for Jewish history that his tutor awoke in him.

In the morning of the first Sabbath after Raphael's thirteenth birthday family and friends gathered at the synagogue. Raphael was smartly dressed in a white shirt and new navy-blue trousers. He read out the text from the Torah faultlessly with a crystal clear treble voice, which was in striking contrast to the expression on his face which read: from now on I am grown up.

The Thiebergers and the director of the Conservatory were present at the family party afterwards. Raphael knew only too well how little money there was in this first year in their new country and had not dared hope for a bicycle. His pleasure was therefore all the greater when a brand new one was revealed. They had all chipped in: the Weltsches, the Adlers, and the Thiebergers.

From her first years in Jerusalem, Alice visited her sister Irma and her brother-in-law Felix every Sunday afternoon. It was the high point of the week for her. Felix was now recognized as a philosopher in Israel and his ethical writings earned him a prestigious Ruppin Prize from the city of Haifa in 1954. Alice, impressed by his wisdom and enlightenment, was always fascinated by what he had to say. Alice was also happy to see what a touching grandmother Irma had become. She spoiled both her grandchildren and Raphael too with culinary delights, often cooking several meals at once in order to give all the children their favourite dishes.

In spite of this, though, Irma's uncontrollable temper was as bad as ever. 'The fury continued unabated, and I cannot suggest anything any more. I cannot suggest any possible cure but I can see how unhappy she is,' Felix wrote to his daughter Ruth in 1958. 'She is incapable of relieving the feelings, which we are all given to, for one single moment. Nothing helps, be it religion, philosophy, art, or a proper relationship with her fellow man.'

*

ALICE HAD NEVER BEEN remotely sentimental. But at the beginning of 1953 she was on the way to her usual early morning swim when she suddenly realized that she would be fifty at the end of the year. It set her thinking. There was no question that she led an ideal life: she played her music and enjoyed culture in all its aspects; she had a circle of good friends and she enjoyed a plunge into the splendidly cool water of the swimming baths. Raphael, too, with his warm, steadfast character was at her side. What more did she need?

Should she have married again, as Mizzi had suggested? She had never given it serious consideration, despite having had some

significant admirers. Alice had no wish to impose a stepfather on Raphael, but it was not just for his sake that she had no wish to remarry. It was as much to do with her constant striving for independence. Marriage would mean too tight a bond and she could not hope for another considerate man like Leopold.

And what about the piano? Did she want to give more·concerts and teach less? In the end, she didn't think so; she was happy with the balance between them. Recently, she had given a number of concerts every year and she did not find the teaching a burden. On the contrary, it was a constant source of joy, whether her pupils played well or not. The only thing she wanted, she concluded, was to have her own separate flat again, and it didn't matter to her how big it was.

*

AT THE AGE of fifteen Raphael discovered he had a talent for acting and joined an amateur group. Through it he developed many new contacts and good friendships that would last throughout his life. One day a presenter on Radio Jerusalem launched an appeal to schools to nominate a talented schoolchild to appear on a programme for children and teenagers. Raphael was the first choice at his school and from then on reported daily to the radio station straight from school, putting together a stimulating programme which was broadcast live. During it he read aloud, played his cello or the piano, and explained different pieces of music. Not only did he gain respect from his own peer group but he was also earning his own money for the first time. The listening figures rose from programme to programme and it soon gained something like cult status.

For years Raphael had seen how hard his mother had to work to pay for everything they needed. He knew that she had been saving up for a long time for the flat she so desperately wanted. Without saying much about it, he decided that he would pay for a good many things himself. He bought not only his own clothes and shoes but also paid for his English and cello lessons. For a while Raphael was so involved in his role as radio moderator and actor that music played second fiddle.

In 1954 the seventeen-year-old heard from his cello teacher that Paul Tortelier and his wife and children had arrived at Kibbutz Maabarot to spend a year living in Israel. Tortelier was a legend. As far as Raphael was concerned there were just two towering figures in the world of the cello, Pablo Casals and Paul Tortelier. He had all their records and had read in a French review: 'If Casals is Jupiter, Tortelier is Apollo.' Raphael's teacher wrote to Tortelier on his pupil's behalf and was able to tell the boy that he had an audition the following weekend.

It was to be one of the key moments in Raphael's musical career. He was fascinated by the charismatic virtuoso and how Tortelier and his wife, the cellist Maud Martin, responded to each other. Their relationship was both a communion of talent and a great love affair. On the evening he arrived at the kibbutz, Raphael attended a concert at which they both performed. He could feel how their love and passion was reflected in the music they made.

The next day Raphael met their children, Yan Pascal and Maria de la Pau. Yan was the same age as him and an ambitious violinist while his sister Maria was an excellent pianist. It seemed to Raphael that they were the perfect happy family and, despite his remarkably close relationship with his mother, he was suddenly acutely aware of the pain of being without a father.

Tortelier auditioned Raphael and was immediately sure that he had heard a more than hopeful talent. The rough diamond, however, needed polishing. Tortelier told Raphael that he must practise more than he had up to now and invited him back to Maabarot in three weeks to work with him. There was a regular bus from Jerusalem, and Raphael could get there in two and a half hours. The months that followed laid the foundations for Raphael's future. Tortelier agreed with his teacher that as soon as Raphael had finished school he was to go to Paris as soon as possible and start studying the cello there.

*

RAPHAEL'S MANY SUCCESSES seemed to justify to him the view that he could concentrate on the things he enjoyed to the detriment of the subjects he did not. He often missed maths or physics lessons and his teachers were doubtful that he would pass his leaving certificate, but at the same time they had to acknowledge his talent as a musician. Alice tolerated Raphael's lack of interest in the natural sciences, and was overjoyed that he was going to Paris; he would get through school in his own way. Raphael's aunts Irma and Mizzi were a lot more critical. They could not understand how he could be so indifferent to the results of his final exams. Their warnings and reproaches seemed to have an effect and in his last year at school Raphael made a great effort and got his leaving certificate.

As a concentration camp survivor Raphael was exempted from national service, but nonetheless he wanted to volunteer. Alice felt that a boy like Raphael, who had grown up without the firm hand of a father, might find some positive benefits from a period of service in the army. Both Alice and Raphael agreed that in gratitude to their new country he should show his readiness to defend it.

The first six weeks of basic training were hard, but after it was over Raphael loved being a soldier. He became first cello in the Israeli Army's Symphony Orchestra, playing not just the cello but also mastering the saxophone, the trumpet, the clarinet and the oboe. He performed in concerts not only in Israel, but also in Europe – even in Germany.

During his time in the army he came home almost every weekend in a good mood. Alice knew that he had been working hard preparing for a nationwide competition, the winner of which was to receive a grant to study music abroad in an academy of his choice. When Raphael turned up unannounced in the middle of the week beaming from ear to ear, she immediately guessed that he had got the grant.

*

IN 1955 ALICE bought at last the two-bedroom flat she was longing for. It was at 5 Ben Labrat, not far from her first rented flat. The house looked much like the others in the street and in the Rechavia district in general. It was constructed from the local stone and surrounded by a little garden. It was on a raised ground floor and not only did it have a front door of its own but it was a little bigger than her previous flat. There was enough room for the grand and an upright piano and for her books too. In the second, rather smaller room there was an iron bedstead and a relatively large table at which ten people could sit. From both rooms you could step out onto the balcony, which stretched round the whole flat, offering a view over a wonderful floral courtyard.

There were around twenty houses on the street, and after a few weeks Alice knew all her neighbours quite well. At the top of the street were the Erles with their daughter Esther, Alice's first pupil, who had arrived illegally from Berlin in 1935. Next door lived the Czech writer Viktor Fischl; Fischl like Alice had arrived in 1949 and had now adopted the Hebrew version of his name – Avigdor Dagan. In the same house as the Fischls lived the family of a lawyer from Prague, Dr Schulz.

There was one shop in the street, immediately opposite Alice's front door. From this Arab grocer Alice was able to buy everything she needed: fruit, vegetables, chicken and fish. She spoke to the grocer in Hebrew, with the writer and the lawyer in Czech and with the Erles and most of the others in the street in German.

*

AT THE END OF October 1956, air-raid sirens sounded across the country. People rushed out onto the streets. There was a blackout: Israel was at war again.

The cause was Egypt's decision to nationalize the Suez Canal Company and to use its tolls to finance the construction of the new Aswan Dam. The financing had been promised to them by the USA and Britain, but they had cancelled the agreement in the summer of 1956. Britain and France, as shareholders in the Suez Canal Company, saw their economic interests in the region threatened and, with Israel, they made plans for an attack. Israel was also threatened as any blockade of the Suez Canal would put supplies to their country at risk. The Egyptians had concluded a pact with the Soviet Union but the latter was facing problems because of moves towards greater independence in Poland and Hungary. Israel seized its moment to invade the Sinai Peninsula and thereby keep the passage to the Red Sea and the Suez Canal open.

When the war broke out, Alice was worried that she might not have done the right thing in being so vociferous in her approval of Raphael's joining up, but as a member of the army's orchestra Raphael was not sent to the front. She was relieved, but her questions about the actual causes of the conflict between the Arabs and the Israelis became increasingly pressing. Was there a way out of the crisis? How could she get on so well with her Arab neighbours, yet there was war between Israel and Egypt? The dominant thinking in the country, allied to the precept that the Jews should 'never again be victims', seemed to be a source of injustice in the country's dealings with the Arabs. Her own decision not to speak about the extermination of the Jews was emblematic of the tacit agreement between the survivors and the rest of the Israelis. The result was, however, an uncomfortable black and white thinking in Israeli society: here were the new Israeli war heroes and there were the 'lambs who allowed themselves to be led to the slaughter'. Despite her doubts Alice was proud of the Israeli Army, which in the short period between 29 October and 5 November 1956, and with the support of the British and the French, was able to defeat the Egyptians and conquer the Sinai Peninsula.

*

IN THE SUMMER OF 1959, ten years after her arrival in Israel, Alice and Raphael were once again on the quay in Haifa, but this time to say goodbye. Raphael had successfully finished his national service and he was leaving for Paris to study the cello in Paul Tortelier's class at the Paris Conservatory.

Alice was thrilled, naturally, but anxious, too. She was now fifty-six and knew that her son would go his own way. The older Raphael became the more he resembled his father and, like Leopold, he didn't discuss his emotions and preferred to listen rather than talk. Mother and son stood silently together on the quay and looked at the ship that would be shortly leaving the harbour and heading for Europe. When the whistle blew for the last time to summon the passengers on board, he affectionately embraced his mother and said: 'A letter a week!' It was his goodbye present.

*

IN MAY 1960 Adolf Eichmann had been captured by the Israeli secret service in Argentina and the news was on everyone's lips. The man who had organized the final solution had been taken prisoner. Alice had not spoken to anyone about the concentration camps for more than a decade and she had put those years out of her mind. Now, however, reading the newspaper reports about Eichmann and the unimaginable slaughter of millions of Jews, much came back to her. As the Eichmann trial approached, the tacit agreement between the survivors and their fellow citizens not to discuss what happened ended. The trial began in Jerusalem on 11 April 1961, and the Israeli Attorney General, Gideon Hausner, was the chief prosecutor for the state of Israel and had written the indictment. He offered Alice the chance to attend the trial as she had known him well for years. Not only did he live in the same district, but his daughter came to Alice for piano lessons; Hausner was even a good piano player himself. In the months before the trail opened he was under enormous pressure and, as a non-religious Jew, he used to go round to see Alice on Friday nights when the others celebrated the Sabbath, and play duets with her. Alice was astonished how well Hausner could play from the sheet music, better than many professional pianists. Now, she wondered what it would be like to stand face to face with the man who had been behind Auschwitz and Theresienstadt, the man who had been the murderer of her mother and her husband.

When Alice sat in the courtroom for the first time, the sight of Eichmann upset her less than the witnesses who spoke for the prosecution. She was very shaken when she realized that she could not relate her experience with that of those who had lost everything and who had experienced the extermination camps at first hand. At least she had been able to save her boy, and she still had her sisters.

When the court met the next time she concentrated her attention on Eichmann, watching his reactions and listening to the answers he gave to the points in the indictment. She was horrified to find that she pitied him. She was, of course, aware that a mass-murderer was sitting before her, but she could clearly feel how wasted his emotional life was. How miserable people like that, who lacked human feelings, whose hearts had never learned to love, whose minds had never experienced culture, really were.

She went to the courthouse three or four times. Everything she saw and heard forced her to the conclusion that 'man is born in a storm', and that every man has the capacity either to do good as well as something abominably evil. Her overwhelming reaction was to feel that 'We must not hate! Man must not learn to hate.'

*

A YEAR BEFORE he finished his studies Raphael took part in the famous Casals Competition in Belgium, which attracted a great many young musicians from around the world. Raphael felt that the competition treated him and his fellow soloists like racehorses that had to run against one another. It promoted competitiveness and the desire for fame, which ran counter to his idea of music, but he realized, however, that without these competitions a career as a soloist was an impossibility. Over the next few years he went from competition to competition and when he won his first competition it was his mentor – Paul Tortelier – who was the happiest. A year later, in 1962, Raphael finished his studies and was awarded the Grand Prix of the Paris Conservatory. In the 1960s only three or four cellists out of thirty or more every year were awarded this highest honour. Raphael was at the beginning of what was possibly an international career.

The following year Raphael took part in the Piatigorsky Competition in Boston. Gregor Piatigorsky was a highly original American cellist of Russian origin who was almost as famous as Casals. He was a much sought-after partner for musicians of the quality of Vladimir Horowitz, Nathan Milstein, Arthur Rubinstein and Jascha Heifetz. Once again Raphael took the competition in his stride and won the first prize. Possibly even more significant was his success in the Munich International Cello Competition organized by the ARD that same year. A star-studded jury could not reach a decision between two cellists, Raphael Sommer and Sujoschi Zuzumi, and instead of awarding a first prize, they gave two seconds.

When Raphael won the Santiago de Compostela cello competition – then one of the most important in the world – in 1965, his reputation was secured not just in Europe, but also in the United States. It resulted in a highly prized invitation from Rudolf Serkin, the director of the Canadian Marlboro Festival. Like many of his more famous colleagues, the American pianist was Russian by origin. His towering fame was not only based on his Bach interpretations, but also on his magnificent interpretations of classical and romantic music. It was the highest point in Raphael's career so far.

*

TOWARDS THE END of his time at the Paris Conservatory, Raphael had become close to one of his fellow students, Sylvia Ott, a sensitive but practical young woman who was studying the piano. Their wedding was quietly celebrated in Paris in 1966, but sadly Alice was not able to attend it because of her professional commitments. Instead she invited them both to come to Jerusalem straight after the wedding. Alice was very taken with her daughter-in-law, and was particularly impressed by the serious way with which she approached Jewish history and the Jewish religion.

Meanwhile, Raphael had been offered a tempting post as a cello teacher at the conservatory in Manchester, and the young couple moved to Britain, but chose to base themselves in London. There Sylvia taught music at the French Lycée, while Raphael commuted to Manchester by train.

*

ALICE WAS SITTING at lunch with her niece Ruth during a visit to Tel Aviv when Ruth's eighteen-year-old son Mickie burst through the door and announced, 'We are at war!' It was 5 June 1967; everyone in the country knew that Israel was facing its severest test since its foundation. In 1948 the USSR and Czechoslovakia had supported Israel with arms during the war of independence. During the war against Egypt in 1956 it had been Britain and France who had been their allies. This time the Soviet Union was supporting Israel's enemies, Egypt, Jordan and Syria. And unlike the promises made and the support given in 1956, the West was extremely cautious.

Alice left for the bus station immediately. She wanted to get back to Jerusalem as quickly as possible and prevent Mizzi from worrying. The journey normally took a good two hours, but it was nearly midnight before she got home.

In crises such as these Alice had always sought to maintain her daily routine, and therefore on the first morning of the war she sat down at her piano and began to practise. The telephone rang and rang. In the hope that the caller would eventually give up she tried to ignore it and carried on playing, but the telephone would not stop ringing. She got up angrily and picked up the receiver. Before she could say a word she heard Mizzi's voice: 'Alice, have you made sure there is a curtain over your window? The blackout has been strictly imposed.'

The Israeli army showed remarkable skill in the offensive. At

5.30 on 7 June 1967 the radio news reported that they had seized Jerusalem's old city – the Arab quarter. The Israeli army's superiority was so great that Jordan agreed to a truce the next day. Syria conceded the following day and then Egypt. On 11 June the last shot was fired at the front. The 'Six Day War' was over.

A few months after the Israeli victory Emil telephoned, sounding uncharacteristically depressed 'I have cancer – glandular cancer. I give it two years at the most. Do you think I should tell my family?'

Although Alice was shaken she had an answer: 'Emil, if you are asking me, I would not tell Mizzi. It would kill her.'

It was not long before Emil had to spend weeks in hospital and, even though he never explained what was really wrong, Mizzi was inconsolable. For the next three and a half years, however, she selflessly cared for her husband with no thought for herself. The only ray of light in these difficult times was the birth of Alice's first grandchild, David, in 1969.

After months of decline, Emil died in 1971, by which time Mizzi's health was also failing. Her anguish at his death was so great that she developed angina in addition to her many other ailments, but the major blow was when she was diagnosed with lung cancer. Once again it was left to Alice to decide whether her sister should be told the truth and once again Alice suggested that she should be spared. They told her she had tuberculosis. But she had been married to a doctor and worked as his surgery assistant for many years, and remained sceptical.

Alice visited her sister more and more often, spending not only days but nights at Mizzi's bedside. Two minutes before she closed her eyes for good, Mizzi told Alice: 'That time you played the midnight concert from Prague, which we heard here in this room, it was the most moving experience of my entire life.'

*

SOON AFTER MIZZI'S death, Alice's work at the conservatory came to an end after twenty five years. She decided to leave Israel for a while, wanting to be near her son and to visit friends in Sweden. London was her first stop. Raphael's family had grown again: her grandson David had been joined by a brother on 23 May 1974. In her grief, Alice was consoled by the sight of five-year-old David helping to look after his newborn brother, Ariel. She stayed with her son's family for several weeks, during which time she realized, with increasing distress, that neither he nor his wife was happy with one another. Raphael was a reserved and rather introverted man, but he loved the company of his close friends. His idea of a perfect evening was to spend time with one of them, putting the world to rights. His wife, on the other hand, had none of his need for friends and often felt that his cherished circle was imposing on her.

Alice decided to rent a tiny flat in London at the beginning of 1975. Now, Alice thought, she could come to London when she wanted and be independent. She would not be a burden to anyone but could at the same time be close to her son and her growing grandchildren. A few months later Raphael stood outside the door to her flat with a suitcase in his hand: 'It's finished, I can't go on,' he blurted out. He wanted to live apart from his wife for a while. Alice decided to spend a few months in Sweden, leaving Raphael in her flat where he could find peace and time to reflect. In the end he decided on divorce; returning to his wife was out of the question.

*

IN THE YEARS from 1975 to 1986 Alice lived in London for two months during the summer and in November and December she travelled to Sweden to see Robert Sachsel to help him out of his winter depression. The rest of the time she remained in Israel. She could finance these trips from her Israeli pension, together with the money that she received as a 'victim' from Germany.

Whenever Alice returned to Israel from London or Sweden the news that she was back spread quickly. Every day there were calls from friends and former piano pupils, many of whom wanted private lessons from her. At seventy-two, Alice felt she was still needed in Jerusalem; she was still professionally active.

In the style of the concerts she held at home in her Prague days, she started to keep open house on Friday and Saturday afternoons. At four there was tea and coffee and her legendary apple cake, which Alice made according to an ancient Prague recipe and which she had learned from her mother. More than a dozen friends and acquaintances sat around the big table in the smaller of the two rooms. There was relaxed conversation about the situation in the country, about the latest rumours, and about new books or the concerts they had been to that past week.

One of the most loyal members of the circle was Amoz Witztum who studied economics in Jerusalem between 1976 and 1986. It was a Saturday afternoon in December 1979 when he knocked on Alice's door for the first time and he remembers these musical afternoons fondly: 'The tea and coffee party lasted about an hour before Alice invited her guests into the piano room and sat down at the Steinway grand. People sat down, not just on the chaise-longue and the one or two chairs, but also on the floor when there were insufficient places. She prepared a different programme each week which, with a short break, lasted for two hours. Alice always played from memory.'

*

FOR MORE THAN a decade Alice commuted between Israel and London, until her son asked her if it would not be better for her to make London her permanent home. The thought of spending her remaining years close to Raphael was enough for her to decide to leave Israel, though her wide circle of friends deeply regretted her decision.

She sold the Steinway grand as her savings did not quite stretch to buying a one-room flat in London, but took the upright piano with her. The other bits of furniture she gave away. In the weeks before she left, the flat was almost bare. One last time she bought a block of ice from the Arab iceman to chill her groceries. She had known him for more than thirty years, and he was still transporting his blocks of ice with a horse and cart. She had been his only customer for years – most people had a fridge by then – but now he would lose her trade, too.

Epilogue

'*Music takes us to paradise*'

'WHEN I TRY TO COUNT up how many forms I have had to fill in over the years: declarations before every journey, tax forms, declarations of currency, customs formalities, requests for entry permits, requests for exit visas, registrations and resignations; how many hours have I stood in the waiting rooms of consulates and committees; how many officials have I faced – friendly or hostile, bored or overworked; how many examinations and interrogations have I lived through at borders. When I think of these things I realize how much of our human dignity we have lost in this century when we young people had dreamed of freedom in the coming cosmopolitan world.'

Alice put down Stefan Zweig's memoirs on the tiny table next to the sofa which she used to sit on during the day and which, with a few adaptations, served as a bed by night. On her calendar she had marked the day 26 November 2003 with a small cross, and the following Saturday with a bigger one. On that day her daughter-in-law Geneviève and her two grandsons David and Ariel were going to give a party; more than a hundred friends and relations were coming. They were due to arrive from Israel, the USA, Czechoslovakia, Sweden, Australia, France, Austria and Germany. There was two hours to midnight, two hours before her hundredth birthday.

A standard lamp lit the one-room flat. Alice allowed her gaze to wander over the photographs on the wall, the oil painting of her son, the books on top of the wardrobe, the modest little piano and the radio. She had come to London from Jerusalem seventeen years before, aged eighty-three, a great age which few of us are privileged to reach. But Alice had conquered yet another world. She liked the place: it was a peaceful part of Hampstead, a few minutes walk from her son. There was a swimming pool round the corner and she liked the way the English looked after their gardens.

She enjoyed Raphael's frequent visits – he came for lunch and always brought new things to talk about – and she liked to be close to her two grandsons. At the beginning she had been lonely without her familiar Jerusalem circle of friends, and in the first years she wrote to Jerusalem daily and often called Edith or one or other of the friends or acquaintances she had left behind.

Alice was soon able to make a new circle of friends, which was almost certainly due to her remarkable talent for listening and for giving people her time. 'Isn't life wonderful?' she often asks and her answer frequently ashames people whose destinies have been kinder to them than hers has been. 'Yes, life is wonderful.' Whatever life threw at her, Alice accepted it.

Alice accepts new friendships when they are offered to her – as they often are – and is grateful. As she says, they are 'wonderful in their way'. One such friendship started in 1993 when she was ninety years old and she met the young music journalist and violinist Tony Short at a conference on the extermination of the Jews. Since then they often play together: Beethoven, Schubert, Mozart, the whole classical sonata repertory.

Even at a hundred Alice practised the piano for three hours a day, went for walks, spoke to her friends, read every night and, three times a week, went to lectures at the University of the Third Age, studying the History of Judaism, French literature and philosophy. Her thirst for knowledge remained unquenched.

As she did every evening before she went to bed, Alice listened to classical music on the radio: she wanted to be awake to hear the clock strike twelve and announce the new day. Usually, she did not miss a single note of the concert, but on this evening, as she listened, she allowed her thoughts to drift.

Every day without pain was a gift, with every morning at the piano and every afternoon visitors from all over the world filling her with happiness. Perhaps, she thought, I have been favoured and I will be able to end my days with a smile on my face, as a sign of my deepest gratitude for an intense and fulfilled life. Death did not frighten her; she had met it often enough and her bitterest experience had been only two years before.

*

IT WAS EARLY on a November morning in 2001, a few days before Alice's ninety-eighth birthday. She was just coming back from the swimming pool, where she swam two lengths every day, when she was surprised to see Ariel come towards her. He accompanied her to the door of her flat, where his brother David and one of Raphael's friends were waiting for her. Alice did not have any idea why they were there. She opened the door and asked them all to come in. They waited until Alice had sat down on the edge of her bed. Finally David said in a depressed, monotonous voice: 'Raphael died yesterday.' There was silence. Alice sat there as if she had been turned to stone, her thoughts slipped into an unpleasant nothingness. But after a minute's pause it was she who spoke first:

'Are you all OK?'

The silence returned.

'Did he have to suffer?'

Ariel shook his head. Then he finally found the strength to speak. From what he knew Raphael had not suffered. The doctors in Tel Aviv had tried to save him with an emergency operation but he did not come round from the anaesthetic. He had had a heart attack while on a successful concert tour of Israel.

Alice had been filled with joy as she followed his recent new burst of musical activity. Raphael had played as a soloist with many great European orchestras in the late sixties and early seventies, under the batons of such well-known conductors as John

Barbirolli, Antal Dorati, Lukas Foss, Charles Munch and Vladimir Ashkenazy. Over the years his solo performances had become rarer. She didn't know if that was due to his teaching schedule and his role as conductor in a string ensemble in Manchester, or whether it had more to do with the seventies when the concert platform was increasingly dominated by more extrovert people whom the media took up for a while and then, just as quickly, dropped. Alice was well aware that Raphael avoided flamboyant behaviour when he played and wanted every serious musician to play a subordinate role to the music. But at the beginning of the nineties, Raphael had become a member of world-famous Solomon Trio and was performing again.

For three weeks Alice appeared to have weathered this latest cruel blow. She did not change her daily routine and went every morning early to the swimming pool, then played the piano for three hours, received her friends in the afternoon and in the evenings sought to distract herself by reading. But then she collapsed. She was mentally and physically shattered. She was diagnosed with a blocked intestine and had to have an operation, after which she drifted between life and death. Her grandson Ariel waited at her bedside the whole time, even spending the night on the floor of the ward. Slowly, very slowly, she recovered and as she did so, she told herself that Raphael had had a rich, fulfilled life and had been spared the miseries of old age.

*

HOW ODD IT WAS, Alice thought, that in the night preceding her hundredth birthday she had had the same dream she had had many times since the end of the Second World War: arm in arm with her mother she was slowly marching behind her father's coffin. Every time she had seen these images in the last six decades, however, she felt neither fear nor consternation; merely a feeling of closeness, security and warmth.

But why always this dream? It was a long time before she realized that she was more similar in character to her father than her mother. She had inherited his way of dealing with people, his extreme strength of will, his limitless ability to work. Was the dream meant to remind her of that? Or did she feel the warmth because at such times she felt nearer to her mother than she did normally?

On the morning of her hundredth birthday, as she does every morning she cleared the kitchen table and put the cheese back in the fridge, where there was a huge pot of chicken soup. Every Monday Alice buys a chicken which the butcher has to chop into seven equal portions. She boils the chicken pieces to make soup, which is divided into seven portions – enough for her needs for an entire week. The soup derives its special flavour from the different vegetables she adds: celery, carrots, leaks, peas, onions and sometimes sweetcorn too. For more than four decades Alice has enjoyed her soup ritual, and for minimum cost she manages to prepare her main meals for the entire week. She uses the time she saves for the things that seem more important to her: music, reading and friends.

After breakfast comes the daily routine. She tidies up the flat. First of all she rolls up the cushions and bedclothes in order to make a sort of sofa where she always sits when she has visitors. Then she washes the table and the lavatory and finally she pulls both chairs up to the table so that any visitors who come that afternoon can feel comfortable.

Years ago she had read a biography of Immanuel Kant. The citizens of the city of Königsberg (Kaliningrad), so they said, used to set their watches by the philosopher's daily walk. Alice and the scholar have that in common. At half past nine on the dot she leaves her flat and walks for just enough time to be able to come in, take off her coat, change her shoes and begin practising the piano at ten.

There was no exception on her hundredth birthday. At ten she sat down at the piano and began to play Johann Sebastian Bach's twenty-four preludes. Until her ninety-second year she was able to play her entire piano repertoire, although she had not given a concert for years. Then she felt a stiffening of the index fingers of

first her left and then her right hands; both fingers became completely stiff and stuck up in the air like hooks. After that she
had to relearn a part of her repertoire according to an eight-finger
system.

The only thing that made her break her routine that day were
the calls from all over the world. The first person to congratulate
her rang before her walk at around quarter past nine. It was her
best friend Edith Kraus, calling from Jerusalem. Edith, at ninety,
was in much worse health than Alice; she had not been able to
play the piano for years. All sorts of memories of Israel arose as
they talked. The years she spent there were the most important
in her life, she thought, looking back on them. For the one time in
her life she had felt she was making a genuine contribution to the
construction of the state that would be a new home to so many
threatened and distressed Jews. Even today the thought of it fills
her with pride and satisfaction.

Since living in London Alice has become more critical of the
Israeli situation. She thinks that it was a mistake not to give the
Arabs equal rights from the beginning. Many conflicts might have
been avoided had they talked rather than reverting to arms, and
she is sure that more blood has been shed than was necessary. The
result has created unnecessary hatred, which has upset her in recent
years.

Although the telephone kept ringing, Alice found joy and peace
in her morning piano playing even on this great day. Music has
been her source of strength all her life, her religion, and her safe
haven: 'It is music', her life has taught her over and over again,
'that takes us to paradise'.

NOTES

ONE *Twins*

1 Joseph Karniel, *Die Toleranzpolitik Kaiser Josephs II*, Gerlingen 1986, 381–5.
2 Maryk Zborowski and Elisabeth Herzog, *Das Schtetl. Die untergegangene Welt der osteuropäischen Juden*, Munich 1991, 246.
3 Peter Demetz, *Prag in Schwarz und Gold*, Munich 1998, 471.

TWO *Roots*

1 Felix Weltsch, writings on the personality of his wife, Irma Weltsch, in Weltsch Papers, 94.72.8/1 (*circa 1936*), German Literature Archive, Marbach.
2 Ibid.
3 Max Brod, *Streitbares Leben: Autobiographie*, Munich 1960.
4 Felix Weltsch, *Judenfrage und Zionismus. Eine Disputation*, London 1929.
5 Brod, op. cit.
6 Quoted in Hans Tramer, 'Die Dreivölkerstadt Prag' in Heiner Lichtenstein and Kurt Löwenstein, eds, *Robert Weltsch zum siebzigsten Geburtstag*, Tel Aviv 1961.
7 Franz Kafka to Grete Bloch,

19 February 1914, in Hans-Georg Koch, ed., *Kafkas Briefe 1913–1914*, Frankfurt am Main 2001.
8 Max Brod, *Der Prager Kreis*, Frankfurt am Main 1966.
9 Gustav Janouch, *Gespräche mit Kafka: Erinnerungen und Aufzeichnungen*, Franfurt am Main 1968.

THREE *World War*

1 *Prager Tagblatt* 5 August 1914.
2 Kafka to Grete Bloch, 19 February 1914, *see* Koch, op. cit.
3 Georg Herz to Felix Weltsch, 27 November 1916, in German Literature Archive, Marbach, D: Kafka, Weltsch, Sign. 22.11.1916.
4 Felix Weltsch to Franz Kafka, 6 February 1918, in German Literature Archive, Marbach, D: Kafka, Sign. 92.5.14/7.
5 Weltsch, op. cit., 1936.
6 Ibid.
7 Franz Kafka to Irma Weltsch, 20 July 1917.
8 Ibid.
9 Franz Kafka to Felix Weltsch, 20 November 1917.

10 Franz Kafka to Felix Weltsch, postcard from Zürau, January 1918.
11 Anthony Beaumont, *Alexander Zemlinsky, Biographie*, Vienna 2005, 402.

FOUR *Music*

1 Walter Niemann, *Meister des Klaviers. Die Pianisten der Gegenwart und der letzten Vergangenheit*, Berlin 1921, 19.
2 *Prager Tagblatt* 1922, Piechocki Archive.
3 Louis Laber, 'Zemlinsky auf dem Theater', in *Der Auftakt*, 1921, 223.
4 Quoted in Beaumont, op. cit., 419.
5 Ibid., 407.
6 Niemann, op. cit., 25.
7 Niemann, *Klavierlexikon*, Leipzig 1918, 303.
8 Niemann, op. cit., 1921, 25.
9 Ibid.
10 Felix Weltsch to Friedrich and Sofie Herz, c. 1916, in Literature Archive Marbach, D: Kafka, Weltsch, Sign. D 92.5.13.
11 Ibid., 1936.
12 *Prager Abendblatt* 1924, Piechocski Archive.
13 *Česke Slova* 1924, Piechocski Archive.
14 *Prager Abendblatt* 1924, Piechocski Archive.
15 *Prager Tagblatt* 1924. Piechocski Archive.
16 *Selbstwehr*, issue 1, 1 March 1907.

FIVE *Marriage*

1 Niemann, op. cit., 1921, 259.

2 Peter Demetz, *Rainer Maria Rilke Prager Jahre*, Düsseldorf 1953.

SIX *Occupation*

1 Brod, op. cit., 1960, 276.
2 Ibid., 273.
3 Ibid., 267.
4 Ibid., 269.
5 His name figures on documents from the Jewish community from 24 April 1942.
6 Guido Fischer, 'Arthur Rubinstein – Ein Jahrhundertphänomen' in *Pianonews – Magazin für Klavier und Flügel*, 1999, 21.
7 Arthur Rubinstein, *Mein glückliches Leben*, Frankfurt am Main 1988, 630.

SEVEN *Theresienstadt*

1 Hans-Günther Adler, *Theresienstadt 1941–1945. Das Antlitz einer Zwangsgemeinschaft*, Tübingen 1955, 61.
2 Jäckel, Longerich, Schoeps, ed., *Enzyklopädie des Holocaust*, Munich and Zurich 1998, Vol. II, 1159–60.
3 Adler, op. cit., 266.
4 Ibid., 64.
5 Ibid., 63.
6 Karel Lagus, 'Vorspiel' in *Theresienstadt*, 1968, 11; Adler, op. cit., 16.
7 Adler, op. cit., 266.
8 Ibid.
9 Ibid., 691.
10 Josef Polák, 'Das Lager' in *Theresienstadt*, 1968, 56.
11 Adler, op. cit., 688.

12 Rudolf Franěk, 'Brundibár' in
   Theresienstadt, 1968, 272–81.
13 Ibid.
14 Ibid.; Hannelore Brenner-
   Wonschick, *Die Mädchen von
   Zimmer 28. Freundschaft,
   Hoffnung und Überleben in
   Theresienstadt*, 2004, 173.
15 Milan Kuna, *Musik an der Grenze
   des Lebens*, Frankfurt am Main
   1993; Brenner-Wonschick, op. cit.,
   182.
16 Adler, op. cit., 71–218; Lagus, op.
   cit., 10–21.
17 Polák, op. cit., 25.
18 Ibid., 26.
19 Ibid., 26–7.
20 Ibid., 27.
21 Adler, op. cit., 50.

EIGHT *Happiness*

1 Kuna, op. cit., 239.
2 Karas, op. cit., 47–9.
3 Kuna, op. cit., 156–9.
4 Ibid., 239.
5 Joža Karas, *Music in Terezin
   1941–1945*, New York 1985, 32,
   50; Kuna, op. cit., 238, 317.
6 Ingo Schultz, *Viktor Ullmann. 26
   Kritiken über musikalische
   Veranstaltungen in Theresienstadt*,
   with an introduction by Thomas
   Mandl, Hamburg 1993.
7 Irma Lauscherová, 'Die Kinder von
   Theresienstadt' in *Theresienstadt*,
   1968, 97.
8 Schultz, op. cit.
9 Hans Krása, Josef Stross, Gideon
   Klein, Pavel Libensky:
   'Kurzgefasster Abriss der Geschichte
   der Musik Theresienstadt, 1943', in
   Ulrike Migdal, ed., *Und die Musik*

   spielt dazu, Munich and Zurich
   1986, 164.
10 Günther Batel, *Meisterwerke der
   Klaviermusik*, Wiesbaden 1997, 85.
11 Karas, op. cit., 103–10.
12 Ibid.
13 Philipp Manes, *Als ob's ein Leben
   wär. Tatsachenbericht
   Theresienstadt 1942 bis 1944*, ed.
   Ben Barkow and Klaus Geist, Berlin
   2005, 137.
14 Erich Springer, 'Gesundheitswesen
   in Theresienstadt' in *Theresienstadt*,
   1968, 132.
15 Ibid., 126–35; Polák, 30; Adler, 151.
16 Polák, op. cit., 37.
17 Ibid.
18 Starke, 1974, 40.
19 Adler, 691.
20 Ibid.
21 Franěk, 277.
22 Ibid., 279.
23 Ibid.; Kuna, op. cit., 205.
24 Franěk, 276.

NINE *The Gates of Hell*

1 Friedrich Niecks, *Friedrich Chopin
   als Mensch und Musiker*, Leipzig
   1890, Vol. II, 274.
2 Schultz, 9–32; Verena Naegele,
   *Viktor Ullmann, Komponieren in
   verlorener Zeit*, Cologne, 2002,
   325.
3 Schultz, 61.
4 Ibid., 9.
5 Käthe Starke, *Der Führer schenkt
   den Juden eine Stadt*, Berlin 1975,
   97, 101.
6 Adler, 7–8.
7 Foreword by Thomas Mandl to
   Schultz, op. cit.
8 Ibid.

9 Schultz, 61.
10 Tadeusz A. Zielinski, *Chopin, sein Leben, sein Werk, seine Zeit,* Bergisch Gladbach 1999, 328.
11 Kuna, 238.
12 Ibid., 184.
13 Joachim Kaiser, *Große Pianisten in unserer Zeit,* Munich 1989, 217.
14 Kuna, 298.
15 Niecks, II, 275.
16 Zdenka Fantlová, *'In der Ruhe liegt die Kraft' sagte mein Vater,* Bonn 1999, 55.
17 Ibid., 68.
18 Ibid.
19 Ibid., 68–9.
20 Ibid., 171.
21 Karel Berman, 'Erinnerungen', in *Theresienstadt,* 1968, 255.
22 Ibid.
23 James Huneker, *Chopin – der Mensch, der Künstler,* Munich 1921, 130.
24 Ibid, 131.
25 Zielinski, 393.
26 Kuna, 296–300.
27 Ibid., 300.
28 Huneker, 131–2.
29 Interview with Thomas Mandl, 2 December 2003.
30 Ibid.
31 Ibid.
32 Ibid.
33 Raoul von Koczalski, *Chopin – Betrachtungen, Skizzen, Analysen,* Cologne-Bayenthal 1936, 96.
34 Zielinsky, 393.
35 Huneker, 34.
36 Kuna, 215.
37 Ibid.
38 Jim Samson, *Frédéric Chopin,* Stuttgart 1985, 100.
39 Starke, 94.

40 Kuna, 196–204.
41 Ibid., 202–3.
42 Ibid.
43 Silke Bernd, 'Zuzanna Rûžicková in *Lebenswege von Musikerinnen im 'Dritten Reich'; und im Exil,* ed. Musikwissenschaftliches Institut der Universität Hamburg, Hamburg 2000, 370.
44 Ibid.
45 Ibid., 381.
46 Adler, 153.
47 Fantlová, 109.

TEN *Inferno*

1 Brenner-Wonschick, 295.
2 Hans Hofer, 'Der Film über Theresienstadt' in *Theresienstadt,* 1968, 194–9.
3 Adler, 179–81.
4 Eva Šormová, 'Monographien über Kurt Gerron' in *Theresienstädter Studien und Dokumente,* 1995, 249–57.
5 Franek, 272–81; Kuna, 205–12.
6 Ančerl, 'Musik in Theresienstadt' in *Theresienstadt,* 1968, 260–3.
7 Ibid., 262.
8 Ibid., 263.
9 Eva Roubičková, *Theresienstädter Tagebuch,* 1944, Archives of the Theresienstadt Museum.
10 Miroslav Kárný, 'Die Theresienstädter Herbsttransporte 1944' in *Theresienstädter Studien und Dokumente,* 1995, 7.
11 Ibid., 8.
12 Ibid., 10.
13 Adler, 578–620.
14 Kárný, 7.
15 Ibid.
16 Ibid., 8.

17 Adler, 284.
18 Ibid.
19 Interview with Alice Herz-Sommer, 10 April 2003.
20 Manes, 426.
21 Interview with Edith Kraus, 19 January 2006.
22 Adler, 189.
23 Polák, 43; Manes, 428.
24 Manes, 430.
25 Karný, 24.
26 Manes, 421.
27 Interview with Alice Herz-Sommer, 24 November 2003.
28 Ibid.
29 Interview with Jürgen Stenzel, 26 November 2003.
30 Fantlová, 118.
31 Ibid.
32 Kuna, 41.
33 Interview with Edith Kraus, 19 January 2006.
34 Fantlová, 114.
35 Interview 10 April 2003.
36 Ibid.
37 Polák, 44.
38 Adler, 588.
39 Polák, 44; Karný, 21.
40 Polák, 44.
41 Ibid.

ELEVEN *After the Inferno*

1 Adler, 131–2; 403, 410, 435, 588.
2 Interview with Edith Kraus, 19 January 2006.
3 Adler, 191.
4 Ibid.
5 Ibid., 194.
6 Gerty Spiess, *Drei Jahre Theresienstadt*, Munich 1984.
7 Karas, 171.
8 Adler, 194.

9 Handwritten review in the possession of Alice Herz-Sommer.
10 Niecks, 322.
11 Adler, 196.
12 Ibid.
13 Ibid.
14 Robert Schumann, quoted by Koczalski, 95.
15 Zielinsky, 463.
16 Fantlová, 116.
17 Ibid.
18 Ibid., 119.
19 Brenner-Wonschik, 96.
20 Ibid.
21 Ibid., 369.
22 Norbert Frýd, 'Kultur im Wohnzimmer der Hölle' in *Theresienstadt*, 1968, 228.
23 Ibid.
24 Ibid.
25 Thomas Pehlken in www.magazin.klassik.com under Meisterwerke, Chopin-Etuden.
26 Adler, 198.
27 Fuchs, 329–31.
28 Ibid., 331.
29 Arnošt Weiss, 'Musikleben in Theresienstadt' in *Theresienstadt*, 333.
30 Ibid., 247.
31 Ibid.
32 Ibid., 248.
33 Koczalski, 124.
34 Lauscherová, 99 and 110.
35 Bernhard Garóty, *Chopin, Eine Biographie*, Hamburg 1990, 469.
36 Schultz, 1993.
37 Willy Haas, *Die literarische Welt. Lebenserinnerungen*, Munich 1957, 171–6.
38 Ibid., 173.
39 Ibid., 174.
40 Zielinski, 473.

TWELVE *Liberation*

1 Transport AE3 of 11 February 1945, according to the memorial book for Czech deportees, Vol. II, 1298.
2 Polák, 46: Weiss, 332.
3 Polák, 45.
4 Lauscherová, 110.
5 Adler, 198.
6 Polák, 47.
7 Adler, 588.
8 Karas, 174.
9 Kuna, 214.
10 Adler, 199.
11 Ibid., 212.
12 Ibid., 213.
13 Ibid.
14 Ibid., 214.

THIRTEEN *Homecoming*

1 Reuven Assor, 'Deutsche Juden in der Tschechoslovakei 1945–1948' in *Sudetenland* 33, 1992, 162.
2 Ibid.
3 The Czech exile newspaper *Československé Listy*. Quoted in idem, 163.
4 Karel Lagus, 'Vorspiel' in *Theresienstadt*, 1968, 20.

FOURTEEN *Prague*

1 Lauscherová, 97.

2 Interview with Pavel Fuchs, 12 March 2006.
3 Jana Svoboda, 'Erscheinungsformen des Antisemitismus in den böhmischen Ländern 1948–1992' in Hoensch, 1999, 229.
4 Beaumont, 423.
5 Assor, 162–8.
6 Ibid., 164.
7 Interview with Zdenka Fantlová, 26 November 2003.
8 Svoboda, 232–3.
9 Ruth Weltsch to Felix Weltsch, 4 January 1949 in Literature Archive Marbach: Weltsch, Sign. 94. 72. 19/2.
10 Ibid.
11 Ruth to Felix Weltsch, 25 January 1949 in Literature Archive Marbach: Weltsch, Sign. 94. 72. 19/4.

FIFTEEN *Zena*

1 Svoboda, 229–48.
2 Martin Hauser, *Wege jüdischer Selbstbehauptung*, Bonn 1992, 269.
3 Interview with Chaim Adler, 12 May 2006.
4 Ruth Weltsch to Felix Weltsch 4 January 1949 in German Literature Archive, Marbach, Weltsch, Sign. 94.72.19/2.

ACKNOWLEDGEMENTS

Many people have made generous contributions to this book. We would like to thank the following for their patience and for informative answers to our questions as well as their ability to direct us to sources and giving us a critical appraisal of various sections and chapters:

In Great Britain: Zdenka Fantlová, Anita Lasker-Walfisch, Arnold Paucker, Ariel Sommer, David Sommer, Geneviève Teulières-Sommer, Amos Witztum.

In Israel: Chaim Adler, Esther Friedmann, Mickie and Eli Gorenstein, Greta Klingsberg, Uri Weltsch.

In the Czech Republic: Vojtěch Blodig, Tomáš Federovič, Anna Flachová, Anita Franková, Jana Šplichalova from the Jewish Museum in Prague and the Theresienstadt Memorial.

In the USA and Canada: Pavel Fuchs, Joza Karas, Paul Kling, Herbert T. Mandl.

In Austria: Leopold Aschenbrenner, Nikolaus Brandstätter.

In Finland: Georg Gimpl.

In Germany: Volker Ahmels, Wieland Berg, Hartmut Binder, Peter Bohley, Renate Flachmeyer, Raphaela Haberkorn, Thomas

Klapperstück, Wolfgang Witiko Marko, Carsten Schmidt, Ingo Schultz, Jürgen Stenzel, Christa Stünkel, Brunhild Piechocki, Klaus Wagenbach, Norbert Wiersbinski and the staff of the German Literature Archive in Marbach.

In Belgium: Daniela Weingärtner.

It is not enough to thank Alice Herz-Sommer. She has inspired and followed this project with youthful curiosity and stamina, an amazing memory and a rare humour. Our conversations with her have made our lives so much the richer.

INDEX

Adler, Emil (Mizzi's husband) 85, 87–8,
    106–7, 166–7, 284
  Alice in Israel 294, 296, 297
  cancer 317
  emigration 105, 107, 280–1
  Friedrich's death 92
Adler, Hans Günther 166
Adler, Heinz 'Chaim' (Mizzi's son) 105,
    106, 280, 281, 293, 294, 296
Adler, Marianne 'Mizzi' (née Herz; Alice's
    twin sister) 74, 87–8, 106, 266,
    267, 316
  Alice in Israel 294–6, 297, 300
  Breslau 90
  and Brod 36
  business studies 57
  childhood 8–15, 17, 18, 20, 21, 22–9,
      32, 39–40
  death 317
  emigration 104–5, 108, 280–1
  Emil's illness 317
  father's death 92
  and Kafka 36–7
  marriage 85–6
  and Paul 236
  post-war meeting 280
  radio programme 267
  school 45–7
  Seder 32, 34
  swimming 35
  war declaration 40, 41
'Affair of the Painters' 225
Aktualita 191
American Jewish Joint Distribution
    Committee 274, 290
Ancerl, Karel 194–5, 203, 234
Anitschka (Alice's maid) 94, 110
Ansorge, Conrad 57, 61–2, 63, 64, 66,
    69, 70, 83, 275
Aronson-Lindt, Hilde 206

Assor, Reuven 252
Auschwitz 156, 179–80, 188–9, 201,
    241, 261, 262, 270
  Berman 176
  Fantlová 214–16
  gas chambers close 206
  liberation 219
  Meyer 178
  Růžičková 186
  Sattler 178
  Ullmann 224
Autonomous Jewish Authority 124, 147,
    156, 157, 197–8, 206, 229
  children 144
  new incarnation 209
  reviews 165–6
  SS orders 219

Bach, Johann Sebastian 1, 300
  Concerto in E minor 111–12
  Partita 56–7, 88, 146, 148, 150
  Well-tempered Clavier 168, 170
Backhaus, Wilhelm 65, 95
Baeck, Leo 187–8, 189, 205, 242, 257–8
Bartels, Ludwig August 196
The Bartered Bride 135, 158, 186, 226
Bauer, Felice 51
Baum, Oskar 35, 36
Bauschowitz Valley 159–60
Beethoven, Ludwig van
  32 Variations in C minor 89
  Sonata in A major, Opus 110 65, 82,
      95, 96
  Appassionata 85, 88, 146, 148, 245,
      267, 268, 299
  Adagio in D major 235
  Sonata in D major 161, 162, 167, 202
  Pathétique 300
  sonatas 284
Beneš, Edvard 105, 251

Ben-Gurion, David 294
Berg, Alban 84
Bergen-Belsen 186
Berman, Karel 175–6
Billroth, Theodor 54
Blech, Leo 98
Bloch, Felix 225
Boronow, Ernst 86, 88, 89–91, 96
Brahms, Johannes 54, 57
Brailowsky, Alexander 118
Brock, Robert 234, 237, 238
Brod, Max 30–1, 32, 34, 35–6, 49, 90,
    106, 285, 289, 298–9
    emigration 105, 107–8
Brundibár 134–40, 157–9, 190–1, 193,
    232–3
Buchenwald 178, 241
Bülow, Hans von 182
Burckhardt, Carl Jacob 232
Burger, SS Commandant Anton 157
Burian, Emil František 95

'Carousel' 192
Casal Competition 314
Casals, Pablo 309
census 159
Chopin, Frédéric 1
    B minor Scherzo 147
    Études 118–20, 146, 148–9, 162,
        165, 167–73, 175–7, 179,
        180–1, 182, 184–5, 187, 189,
        211–12, 213–15, 216–19, 221,
        222, 223–7, 239, 276
    Piano Concerto in E minor 72–6
    Stuttgart Sketches 120
Cohn, Harry 202
Cortot, Alfred 95
Council of Elders 156, 157, 159, 188–9,
    199
    Auschwitz 206
    The Last 218
    new offices 232
    propaganda film 191
    Red Cross protection 242
Czech Philharmonic 72–6
Czech-Swedish exchange programme
    274–5

Dachau 178, 179, 261–3
Dunant, Paul 238–9, 242

Dvořák, Antonín
    Serenade 239
    Sonatina 235, 239

Eckstein, Hannah 164
Edelstein, Jakob 159
Eichmann, Adolf 117, 158, 225, 232,
    238–9, 313–14
The Emperor of Atlantis 224
Eppstein, Paul 195–6, 197, 199
Erle, Esther 300, 311

Fantlová, Zdenka 169, 173–5, 189, 203,
    204, 214–16, 276
Fischl, Viktor 311
Flachová, Anna 'Flaška' 216–17
Forkel, Johann Nikolaus 146
Franta 1, 3–4, 6, 15, 92
Free Time Organization 134, 145–6,
    154, 157, 165–6, 179, 190, 201,
    202, 203–4, 233–4, 240
    ban 211
    mica-processing 206, 208–9, 234
    new incarnation 209
Freudenfeld, Ota 134–5
Freudenfeld, Rudolf 134–5, 136, 158
Freudenthal, 221
Frey, Anni 206, 240
Frey, Kurt 147
Fritta, Bedřich 225
Fröhlich, Karel 158
Fuchs, Pavel 145, 154, 210, 257, 258,
    266, 268–9
Fuchs, Valery 266, 268

Gärtner-Geiringer, Renée 144
German Academy for Music and Drama
    57–8, 59, 61–7, 69–70, 71–2
Gerron, Kurt 192–3
Gibian, Richard 298
Gobets, Machiel 202
Gorenstein, Benjamin (Ruth's 2nd
    husband) 294
Gorenstein, Mickie (Ruth's son) 316
Gottwald, Klement 285
Grab-Kernmayer, Hedda 206, 240
Grünberg, 188–9
Günther, SS-Sturmbannführer Hans 197,
    239
Gutmann, Adolf 162, 172

Haas, Jóši 221
Haas, Leo 225
Haas, Pavel 194, 195, 203, 282
Hába, Alois 276
Hácha, Emil 102, 103, 105, 106, 108
Hadega 111
Hamburg-Neuengamme 186
Hanusová-Flachová, Anna 169
Harnack, Adolf von 188
Hausner, Gideon 313–14
Heller, Stephan 216
Henschel, Moritz 201, 203
Herschl, David 285, 301–2
Herz Brothers 1, 5, 13
Herz, Friedrich (Alice's father) 4, 5–7, 9,
     13, 14–19, 21, 22, 55
   death 92–3
   health 91–2
   holiday 36
   marriage 1–3
   orthopaedist 50
   religion 32, 33–4
   schools 45
   telephone 77
   toll money 27
   war 40, 41, 48, 52–3
Herz, Georg (Alice's brother) 6–7, 17,
     31, 41, 56–7
   death 93
   war 48–9
Herz, Irma see Weltsch, Irma
Herz, Karl (Friedrich's brother) 4, 5
Herz, Marianne 'Mizzi' see Adler,
     Marianne 'Mizzi'
Herz, Mary (Paul's wife) 115, 246–7,
     255, 288
Herz, Paul (Alice's brother) 7, 17, 18, 31,
     39, 91, 93, 115, 246–7, 249–50,
     254–5, 288
   gambling 255
   horses 15
   The Little Glow-worm 236–8
   military academy 57
   return to Prague 243, 251–2
   Theresienstadt 228–31, 234–6,
     239
   violin 29, 37–8, 44, 54, 221, 234–6,
     239
   war 41
Herz, Sofie (Alice's mother) 1–4, 6–12,

     14, 15–19, 21–2, 26–7, 30, 32–3,
     37, 56–7, 77, 235, 245, 250
   Alice's marriage 94
   deportation 115–17, 140
   Friedrich's death 92, 93
   German occupation 104–5
   health 91
   Leopold's loan 114, 115
   pet-names 47–8
   war declaration 41
   and Weiskopfs 39
Heydrich, SS-Obergruppenführer
     Reinhard 128, 174
Himmler, Reichsführer SS Heinrich 155,
     213, 231–2
Hitler, Adolf 101, 102–3, 104, 105
   Hácha talks 108
   Poland 108
   suicide 242
Hofmeister, Greta 136
Holitscher, Anna (Leopold's aunt) 116,
     249, 270
Hötzendorf, Conrad von 41
Huneker, James 185
Hutter, Klara 205–6, 258
Hutter, Trude 44–5, 62–3, 78–81, 82,
     111, 205

International Red Cross 158, 225,
     231–3, 238–9, 242

Janácek, Leos[v] 60
Janegro, Antonio 278–9
Jerusalem Conservatory 280, 297,
     298–300, 317
Jewish Autonomous Administration,
     propaganda film 191
Jewish Community 246, 249–50, 254,
     258–9, 261, 284, 288–9, 292
Jewish Community Organization 117,
     121, 123, 124, 125, 196–7
Jewish Cultural Union 182–3
Joseph II, Emperor 4, 5, 128

Kaff, Bernhard 144, 186
Kafka, Franz 30, 32, 34–5, 36–7, 41–3,
     51–2
Kaiser, Joachim 171
Kalicz, Jenö 63–4, 66–7, 69–70, 73
Kaltenbrunner, Ernst 232

Kant, Immanuel 325
Karafiát, Jan 236
Kersten, Felix 213
Kettner, Gisela 69
Kielce 274
Kien, Peter 224
Klang, Heinrich 242
Klein, Gideon 143, 158, 172, 186, 203
Klemperer, Daisy 45, 46, 47, 77, 78-81
Koczalski, Raoul von 211
Kohn Brothers 158
Kohn, Erich 220
Kolisch Quartet 99
Königstein 197
Kopecký, Václav 254, 282
Krása, Hans 134, 136, 146-7, 158, 203
Kraus, Edith 97-9, 247-8, 254, 256-7
    Alice's 100th birthday 326
    Israel 289
    returns to Prague 243-4
    Theresienstadt 140, 143, 169, 171-2,
        201, 203-4, 205, 206, 208,
        209, 234, 240
    transport 116
Kraus, Rudolf 68-9, 70-1, 73, 76, 95
Kraus, Trude 68
Kurz, Wilhelm 60

Laber, Louis 72
Landowska, Wanda 185
The Last 218
Lauscherová, Irma 222-3, 230, 250,
    253, 269
Leydensdorff, Herman 234, 240
Liszt, Franz 61-2, 74
The Little Glow-worm 233, 234, 236-8,
    240
Long, Marguérite 43
Lössl, Margarete 69
Löw, Rabbi 123

Mahler, Bernhard 23-4
Mahler, Gustav 24-5, 119
    Eighth Symphony 71-2
Mahler, Marie 24
Mahler-Werfel, Alma 72
Mahler, Willy 169-71
Mandl, Thomas 166, 169, 179
Mareš, Michael 267-8, 275, 282-3
Marianne (Alice's maid) 110

Maria Theresa, Empress 4-5, 128
Mark, Fredy 158
Marteau, Henry 57
Martin, Maud 309
Martinu, Bohuslav 276
    Three Dances 95-6, 98, 171
Masaryk, Charlotte Garrigue 59
Masaryk, President Jan 59, 281-2
Masaryk, President Tomás[v] Garrigue
    52, 53-4, 58-9, 275
Mautner, Edith (Leopold's sister) 249,
    270, 277
Mautner, Felix (Edith's husband)
    99-100, 249, 270, 277-8
Mautner, Ilse (Edith's daughter) 249,
    270, 277-8
Mautner, Thomas (Edith's son) 249, 270,
    277-8
Meier, Eduard 242
Meissner, Alfred 242
Mendelssohn's Octet 44-5
Mengele, 176
Meyer, Kurt 177-8
mica-processing 206, 208-9, 234
Mikuli, Carl 74, 211
Möhs, SS-Hauptsturmführer Ernst 197
Mozarteum 90
Mühlstein, Maria 136
Mühlstein, Pinta 136
Munich International Cello Competition
    315
Murmelstein, Benjamin 197, 206, 219,
    220

Nettl, Bruno 111
Nettl, Paul 111, 265
Niemann, Walter 74
Novák, Vítezslav 60, 84, 230-1
    Eroica Sonata 89-90

Orenstein, Zdenek 136
Orlik, Emil 87-9
Ostrcil, Otakar 84
Ott, Sylvia see Sommer, Sylvia

Patent of Tolerance 5
Pathfinder Movement 281
Pau, Maria de la 309
Pehlken, Thomas 219
Piatigorsky Competition 315

Piatigorsky, Gregor 315
Pick, Herr 45
Pick, Rudolf 172
Pimentel, Beatrice 234
Podelier, Marion 206, 240
Polack, Maria 300
Polak, Josef 207
Prague Circle 35, 42
Pravazniková, Marie 185–6
Priessnitz Sanatorium 85–9, 106

Radio Jerusalem 308
Rahm, SS-Obersturmführer Karl 197,
    201, 206, 212–13, 219, 220,
    232–3, 239
Reichssicherheitshauptamt (RHSA) 117,
    155, 232
Reinhold, Joseph 86–7, 88, 270–1
Rellstab, 185
Ribbentrop, Joachim von 103–4
Rilke, Rainer Maria 87
Rosenbaum, Kamilla 158, 233
Rosenthal, Moriz 73–4, 76, 95
Roubicková, Eva 195
Rubinstein, Arthur 118, 211
Rudolfinum 284
Růžičková, Zuzana 185–7

Sachsel, Robert 82–3, 271, 272–3, 318
Sádlo, Pravoslav 279–80
Santiago de Compostela competition 315
Sattler, Otto 177–8
Sauer, Emil 95
Schächter, Rafael 134, 135, 136, 148,
    175, 183, 203, 226
Scheitmayer Room 89–90
Schliesser, 199
Schnabel, Arthur 96–7, 98
Schoenová, Vlasta 233, 238
Schönberg, Arnold 53, 84, 88, 119
Schorsch, Gustav 203
Schreker, Franz 98
Schubert, Franz 88
    Sonata in D major 275
Schulz, Dr 311
Schulz, Fanny (Alice's grandmother) 2, 7,
    10–11, 14, 20–5, 33, 56
Schulz, Ignatz (Alice's grandfather) 2, 21
Schulz, Otto (Alice's uncle) 96
Schumann, Clara 66, 67, 69

Schumann, Robert 37–8, 66, 67, 212
    Abegg Variations 64, 259–60
    Fantasy in C Major 69, 70, 88, 161,
        166
    Symphonic Studies 95, 96, 275
    Träumerei 37–8
Schwarz-Klein, Ada 206, 234
Seder 32–4
Selbstwehr 76–7, 104, 108
Serkin, Rudolf 315
Short, Tony 322
Singer, Dr Kurt 182–4
Six Day War 316–17
Smetana, Bedrich
    Bartered Bride 135, 158, 186, 226
    Czech Dances 60, 86, 161, 167, 239,
        276, 299
Solomon Trio 324
Sommer, Ariel (Alice's grandson) 318,
    321, 322, 323, 324
Sommer, David (Alice's grandson) 317,
    318, 321, 322, 323
Sommer, Eva (Hans' daughter) 249,
    270
Sommer, Genevieve (Stephan's 2nd wife)
    321
Sommer, Hans (Leopold's brother) 242,
    249, 258, 270
Sommer, Helena (Leopold's mother) 83,
    111, 116, 249, 270
Sommer, Leopold (Alice's husband) 91,
    93–5, 112–13
    Belgium 113–14, 115
    Brundibár 135–6, 139–40
    children 99–100
    Dachau 261–3
    death 263, 265
    deportation 120–2, 123–4, 125–7
    first meeting 82–3
    Friedrich's death 92
    German occupation 103–4
    hundreds 134, 138
    letter 79–81, 82
    loses job 109–10
    marriage to Alice 94
    propaganda film 194–5
    Sofie's deportation 117
    Stephan's accident 163–4
    Stephan's birthday 138–40
    Theresienstadt 129–200

Sommer, Leopold (*cont.*)
  transport 196–7, 198–200
  violin 221
Sommer, Otto (Hans' son) 249, 270
Sommer, Stephan 'Raphael' (Alice's son)
    101, 104, 273
  6th birthday 138–9
  accident 162–4
  acting 308
  bar mitzvah 305–7
  birth 100
  Brundibár 135–40, 157–9, 190–1,
      193, 232
  cello 278–80, 288–9, 301, 309, 310,
      313, 314–15, 323–4
  Christmas 210
  competitions 314–15
  death 323
  deportation 120–2, 124, 125–7
  divorce 318
  father's transport 200
  holiday 250–1, 253–4
  hopes for father 241–2
  illness 242–3
  journey to Israel 288–93
  The Little Glow-worm 236–8
  London 316, 318, 322
  and Mareš 268
  name change 297
  page turning 193, 195, 235
  Paris 313, 315
  piano 103, 111–13, 119, 259,
      269–70, 299–300
  return to Prague 243–9
  school 268–9, 299–300, 310
  Theresienstadt 129–243
  trams 263–5
  wedding 315–16
Sommer, Sylvia (née Ott; Stephan's 1st
    wife) 315–16, 318
Sommer, Zdenka (Hans' wife) 249, 270
Spiess, Gerty 210
Starke, Käthe 184
Stein, Eva 136
Štepán, Václav 28, 43–4, 54, 59–61, 74,
      76, 83–4, 100, 118, 161, 231, 270
Štepánova, Ilonka 60, 74, 270, 286–7
Steuermann, Eduard 84–5
Stifter, Adalbert 28
Stravinsky, Igor 72

Suez Canal Company 311–12
Suk, Josef 60, 84
Süssmann, Romuald 158
Švenk, Karel 217–19
swimming 35, 109, 323
Switzerland 212–13

Taube, Carlo 181–2, 202
Taube, Erika 181–2
Taussig, Elsa 107
Theatre D 34 95
Thein, Hanuš 233
Theresienstadt (Terezín) 121–243
  Baeck visit 257–8
  journey to 121–9
  liberation 243
  propaganda film 190–4
  Sofie's deportation 115–17, 140
Theresienstadt Symphony 181–2
Thieberger, Friedrich 306, 307
Tortelier, Paul 309, 313, 315
Tortelier, Yan Pascal 309
Toulouse-Lautrec painting 268, 285, 302
Treblinka 117, 249, 250, 270
Treichlinger, Honza 136

Ullmann, Viktor 119, 144, 165–7, 203,
      223–4
Ungar, Otto 225
Utitz, Emil 166

Verdi's *Requiem* 183, 226
Vienna International Piano Competition
    95–6

Wachtel, Erich 221
Wedekind, Frank 240
Weingartner, Felix 95
Weinmann, Rudolf 238–9
Weis, Dr Felix 132–3
Weiskopf, Franz Carl 39, 104
Weiskopf, Helene 39, 47–8, 111, 276–7
Weiss, Arnošt 221–2, 229–30, 239
Weissenstein, Franta 175–6
Weiss, Fritzek 158
Weizmann, Chaim 294
Weltsch, Felix (Irma's husband) 30–2,
      34, 35, 75, 104, 106, 266, 286
  Alice in Israel 294
  emigration 105, 107–8

Georg's letter 49
holiday 54–5
Israel 307
Jewish religion 306
Klanovice 36
marriage 41–2, 50–2
radio programme 267
refugees 49–50
Selbstwehr 76–7, 104, 108
Weltsch, Heinrich (Felix's father) 30, 31
Weltsch, Irma (née Herz; Alice's sister) 7,
    9, 27–31, 34, 39, 57–8, 74–5, 266,
    307
Alice in Israel 294
and Brod 36
emigration 104–5
holiday 54–5
and Kafka 35, 43, 51–2
marriage 41–2, 50–2
and Paul 236
radio programme 267
school 45
temper 28–9, 50, 307

war 48–9
Weltsch, Luise (Felix's mother) 31
Weltsch, Ruth (Alice's niece) 283, 284–5,
    293, 301–2, 307, 316
Alice in Israel 294
birth 55
emigration 105
radio programme 267
Weltsch, Willi (Felix's brother) 293
Werfel, Franz 72
Wieck, Clara *see* Schumann, Clara
Witztum, Amoz 319
Wurzel, Gisa 206, 240

Zelenka, František 134, 158, 203
Zemlinsky, Alexander von 53, 57–8,
    71–2, 75
Zionism 32, 76–7, 281, 288
Ziv, Dr 292
Zucker, Otto 123, 145, 154, 197, 198,
    199, 201
Zuzumi, Sujoschi 315
Zweig, Stefan 275, 321

The Raphael Sommer Music Scholarship

This scholarship has been established by Raphael Sommer's mother, Alice Herz-Sommer and his widow Genevieve Sommer to remember Raphael Sommer's name and work by providing bursaries for talented young string players to further their studies. The focus is in the field of chamber music performance which can be of such critical importance to developing musicians and where opportunities for advanced performance coaching and experience are generally rather limited after students leave the teaching institutions.

The scholarships are awarded during the annual 'Festival Estival de Musique de Chambre en Pays de Gex' founded by Raphael and Genevieve Sommer in 1988. The festival takes place each August/September in Ferney-Voltaire in France.

For further information, as well as donations and grants, please contact:

Genevieve Sommer
55 Quickswood
London NW3 3SA

e-mail: sraphi2137@aol.com

ALICE HERZ-SOMMER spielt
Bach, Beethoven, Schubert, Chopin, Smetana, Debussy

*An extraordinary testament to the talent and
versatility of the pianist Alice Herz-Sommer*

Contents (running time 78 min)

JOHANN SEBASTIAN BACH (1685–1750):
Partita in B-Flat Major BWV 825

LUDWIG VAN BEETHOVEN (1770–1827):
Largo from D-Major Sonata Op. 10, No. 3

FRANZ SCHUBERT (1797–1828):
Molto moderato from B-Flat Major Sonata

FRÉDÉRIC CHOPIN (1810–49):
Étude Op.10, Nos 2, 4 and 9 and Op. 25 Nos 2 and 9

BEDRICH SMETANA (1824–84):
Czech Dances vol. 2, nr 1–3

CLAUDE DEBUSSY (1862–1918): Préludes Bk 1, Nos. 10, 12;
Images Bk 1, No. 1 and Bk 2, No. 5, 6; L'isle joyeuse

The recordings were taken at private performances, some in
Israel in the 1960s, some in London between 1986 and 1995.
The CD also has a short introduction from Alice Herz-Sommer,
recorded in her hundredth year.

£10.00 *plus postage and packing*

Orders should be sent to:
Reinhard Piechocki, Dorfstrasse 37a, D-18581 Kasnevitz, Germany
fax: +49 3830162238 e-mail: reinhard.piechocki@t-online.de